The Developmental Psychology of Reasoning and Decision-Making

Logical thinking is a critically important cognitive skill. It is not just essential for mathematical and scientific understanding, it is also of prime importance when trying to navigate our complex and increasingly sophisticated world. Written by world class researchers in the field, *The Developmental Psychology of Reasoning and Decision-Making* describes the ways that children learn to reason, and how reasoning can be used to overcome the influence of beliefs and intuitions.

The chapters in this edited collection focus on new, revolutionary paradigms in reasoning and cover the recent research on the development of reasoning in two important areas:

- Cognitive abilities required to reason well and how these abilities develop in children and adolescents
- Recent empirical data showing the effect intuition and prior belief have on reasoning, even when the outcome is inappropriate.

Different theoretical and empirical perspectives from recent Piagetian theory, mental models and gist processing are examined, along with empirical results looking at specific aspects of reasoning in children. The key theme of the book is to better understand how reasoning develops not only through examining 'logical' reasoning, but also the nature of the interactions between people's intuitions and their reasoning abilities.

The Developmental Psychology of Reasoning and Decision-Making provides an overview of the main theories and key empirical results related to the development of reasoning and should be of particular interest to students and researchers in developmental psychology and education, along with those in cognitive psychology.

Henry Markovits is Professor of Developmental Psychology at the Université du Quebec à Montréal, Canada. He has been studying children's reasoning for many years and has published over 90 articles and chapters on various facets of reasoning. He has been associate editor of the *European Journal of Cognitive Psychology*, and is currently associate editor of the journal *Thinking & Reasoning*.

Current Issues in Thinking and Reasoning
Series Editor: Linden Ball

Current Issues in Thinking and Reasoning is a series of edited books that reflects the state of the art in areas of current and emerging interest in the psychological study of thinking processes.

Each volume is tightly focussed on a specific topic and consists of from seven to ten chapters contributed by international experts. The editors of these volumes are leading figures in their field and all provide an introductory overview.

Example topics include thinking and working memory, visual imagery in problem solving, evolutionary approaches to thinking, cognitive processes in planning, creative thinking, decision making processes, pathologies of thinking, individual differences, neuropsychological approaches and applications of thinking research.

Emotion and Reasoning
Edited by Isabelle Blanchette

New Approaches in Reasoning Research
Edited by Wim De Neys, Magda Osman

The Developmental Psychology of
Reasoning and Decision-Making
Edited by Henry Markovits

The Developmental Psychology of Reasoning and Decision-Making

Edited by
Henry Markovits

Psychology Press
Taylor & Francis Group
LONDON AND NEW YORK

First published 2014
by Psychology Press
27 Church Road, Hove, East Sussex BN3 2FA

and by Psychology Press
711 Third Avenue, New York, NY 10017

Psychology Press is an imprint of the Taylor & Francis Group, an informa business

© 2014 Henry Markovits

British Library Cataloguing in Publication Data
A catalogue record for this book is available from the British Library

Library of Congress Cataloging in Publication Data
    The developmental psychology of reasoning and decision-making /
    edited by Henry Markovits.
    pages cm
    Includes bibliographical references and index.
    1. Reasoning in children. 2. Reasoning (Psychology)
    3. Decision making. 4. Child development. I. Markovits, Henry.
    BF723.R4D48 2014
    155.4'134—dc23
    2013024968

ISBN: 978-1-84872-145-6 (hbk)
ISBN: 978-1-84872-146-3 (pbk)
ISBN: 978-1-31585-656-8 (ebk)

Typeset in Times New Roman
by Swales & Willis Ltd, Exeter, Devon

Contents

Contributors

Pierre Barrouillet, Université de Genève, Switzerland

Sarah R. Beck, University of Birmingham, UK

Jonathan C. Corbin, Cornell University, USA

Wim De Neys, Paris-Descartes University, France

Wejdan S. Felmban, University of Northern Colorado, USA

Caroline Gauffroy, Université de Genève, Switzerland

Paul A. Klaczynski, University of Northern Colorado, USA

Henry Markovits, Université du Québec à Montréal, Canada

David Moshman, University of Nebraska-Lincoln

Valerie F. Reyna, Cornell University, USA

Kevin J. Riggs, University of Hull, UK

Keith E. Stanovich, University of Toronto, Canada

Maggie E. Toplak, York University, Canada

Rebecca B. Weldon, Cornell University, USA

Richard F. West, James Madison University, USA

1 Introduction

Henry Markovits

Reasoning and decision-making are at the core of advanced thinking. Determining how these develop over time is thus critical for both educational purposes and for our theoretical understanding. In the following chapters, we have a state-of-the-art overview of the latest developmental approaches. Although there is no current consensus as to the exact nature of the underlying processes used for advanced thinking, there has been a striking change in the way that these processes have been articulated that illuminates the complexity of human reasoning. Initial developmental studies of reasoning were motivated by Piaget's theory. The stage of formal reasoning was characterized by the ability to reason logically, and was considered to be the end-point of development. In this perspective, development could be considered to be a long but consistent march towards better and more logical thinking. This in turn was considered to involve the gradual independence of reasoning from "empirical knowledge and beliefs", leading to the ability to use essentially abstract rules and structures.

Many, although not all studies during this period did find increases in the ability to reason logically with age. Developmental research thus often contrasted the Piagetian position with the idea that younger children were more "logical" than anticipated and that advanced thinking was really accessible at a much earlier age. These studies were done with the underlying assumption that adults were indeed logical thinkers, just as Piagetian theory would predict. At the same time, studies of adult reasoning and decision-making were showing that even well-educated people have great difficulty in making logical decisions. From the influential heuristic and biases program of Kahneman and Tversky to reasoning studies deriving from Wason's seminal observation that even doctoral students are not able to analyze a seemingly simple selection task in a logical way, it has been convincingly shown that people very often reason in what appears to be completely illogical ways. Thus, even adults who should be in the formal stage of reasoning are strongly influenced by empirical knowledge and belief when reasoning.

The tension between these two sets of results is clear; they highlight the necessity of understanding the interactions between processes that can lead to logical thinking and those that lead to use of heuristic, belief-based reasoning. Dual-process theories have attempted to codify these effects by distinguishing between System 1 intuitive, rapid forms of reasoning and System 2, abstract rule-governed processes. The most straightforward reading of this approach would suggest that children should be more prone to intuitive reasoning leading to logical mistakes and that, with age, the impact of System 2 processes should increase. However, as pointed out in several chapters in this book, this simply does not correspond to what can be observed; the developmental pattern of interactions between heuristic factors and logic is in fact quite complex.

Given the strong tendency of adults to make intuitive judgments that are not logically, or rationally appropriate, it is clear that a simple replacement model whereby irrational, intuitive processes are gradually superseded by more complex forms of logical reasoning must be wrong. This raises some interesting questions which in one way or another underlie much of current developmental approaches to reasoning. The first of these is the epistemological status of intuition. There is a natural tendency to presume that any kind of rapid heuristic reasoning must be inherently illogical. However, there are sensible biological grounds to suppose that intuition, while possibly more variable than more explicit forms of analytic processing, must be reasonably rational in some sense. If this is the case, then the trade-off between heuristic and analytic processing must be more complicated at any age, since both forms of reasoning can be considered to have both benefits and costs. Thus, it becomes possible to argue, as we see in Chapter 3 by Weldon, Corbin and Reyna and Chapter 7 by De Neys, that intuitive processes allow access to some form of logical reasoning. In contrast, logic and rationality can also be conceived as the domain of explicit higher-level forms of processing, as witnessed by Moshman's metacognitive analysis or Gauffroy and Barrouillet's mental model approach.

A second, related question has to do with the degree of independence of intuitive and analytic processes. Once again, a simple version of the intuitive versus analytic dichotomy would claim that the two systems do not overlap in the way that they use information. This would suggest that intuitive processing relies on surface characteristics and heuristic shortcuts, while analytic processing requires a deeper semantic analysis. However, the sheer variability of logical reasoning and the fact that some research suggests that younger children are not susceptible to the same degree of heuristic biases as adults suggests that both processes might share some common sources. The interaction between emotion (which can be seen as a form of heuristic) and reasoning is clearly seen in Beck and Riggs' analysis of counterfactual reasoning.

Thus, it has become increasingly clear that understanding the nature and development of reasoning and decision-making requires looking at the specific processes that can explain how both familiar and abstract forms of knowledge can be derived from what might be a common base, which includes both learned information and biologically based tendencies, and importantly how these processes can interact in a complex developmental progression. This has necessarily led away from the logical or not dichotomy that has often characterized developmental studies towards more process-oriented analyses that have the potential to explain how the interactions between empirical knowledge, belief and logic develop. The following chapters represent an invaluable synthesis of the different ways that these interactions can be currently understood.

These chapters can be divided into two categories. Part 1 provides large scale syntheses and theory. Chapter 2 by Toplak, West and Stanovich distinguishes between intelligence and rationality. These authors make the critical point that reasoning and judgment require understanding how these relate to some criteria of rationality, which involves using intelligence in a much more complex way than is usually imagined. They provide an analysis of rationality based on the fluid versus crystalized dichotomy and give an exhaustive and original survey of the judgment and decision-making field that makes an excellent starting point for any analysis of the developmental literature. Their approach suggests that while rationality cannot be equated to intelligence, the two do co-vary in some basic sense. Weldon, Corbin and Reyna in Chapter 3 provide a very different analysis of the interaction between intelligence and rationality. Gist theory claims that intuition underlies rationality; more specifically, that intuitive processes allow extraction of logical rules from complex information leading to what can be called an intuitive logic. In this perspective, conscious processing of information often leads to misleading analysis of surface characteristics, missing the underlying rationality. An opposing theory is provided in Chapter 4 by Gauffroy and Barrouillet's adaptation of mental model theory to development. While allowing a clear role for heuristic processes, this theory considers that the chief component of development is the increase in working-memory capacity. Reasoning is seen as a conscious and effortful attempt to process the underlying semantics of propositions by the construction of explicit models. Finally, Klaczynski and Felmban in Chapter 5 provide a detailed analysis of developmental patterns of heuristic responding, with emphasis on the role of developmental inversions. While not tied to a specific theory, this analysis provides a useful methodological overview of just what heuristic responding might mean, and how to reasonably measure it.

Part 2 provides more detailed analyses of the specific cognitive functions that must underlie development. Moshman in Chapter 6 highlights the importance of understanding both the general progression from specific inferential processes, which often remain unconscious, to a more reflective metacognitive form of reasoning that can explicitly consider truth as an explicit construct. However, he also points out the domain specificity of such reasoning, implying that while there might be some underlying general processes involved, it is impossible to understand how more complex forms of reasoning develop without understanding the specific constraints of each domain. De Neys in Chapter 7 reports the results of a recent, innovative research program that shows that people have an intuitive form of logic detection. More specifically, when making heuristic judgments that are not "logical", both children and adults who are on the surface very comfortable with these responses, show unconscious signs of discomfort. Such a process is, of course, an important mechanism that could potentially provide a proximal mechanism by which intuition might lead to logical reasoning, even in very young children. This idea suggests that logic must be somewhat primitive, if it can be intuitively processed. In contrast, in Chapter 8 Markovits suggests that reasoning can be seen as motivated by the coordination of divergent thinking across multiple levels of abstraction. Reasoning is not considered as logic per se, but involves the ability to conceive of possibilities, with necessity requiring elimination of possibility. This model places emphasis not on logic as a rule-driven process, but as an increasingly abstract way of analyzing real-world knowledge. Finally, in Chapter 9, Beck and Riggs give a synthesis of their research program on the development of counterfactual reasoning. Such reasoning is not only a logical milestone, but represents a link with social and emotional worlds that clearly show the complexity of the relations between rationality and these other perspectives. They convincingly demonstrate that a dichotomous model does not correspond well to what is known about counterfactual reasoning, and that a more nuanced model that can account for a variety of different forms of competencies is required.

What these approaches share is an increasingly nuanced perspective about the way that different forms of information processing, rational and intuitive, concrete and abstract, interact in order to produce an adult who is sometimes capable of amazing feats of formal logic, and who at the same time makes judgments and reasons in curiously illogical ways. How children develop into such adults is critical for our understanding of what reasoning is and how to facilitate its acquisition. This book provides a synthesis of current understanding of the processes underlying this development.

Part I

Overview and theory

2 Assessing the development of rationality

Maggie E. Toplak, Richard F. West and Keith E. Stanovich

Variation in intelligence has been one of the most studied topics in psychology for many decades (Deary, 2001; Geary, 2005; Lubinski, 2004), and the development of the cognitive abilities related to intelligence is likewise a central topic in developmental science (Anderson, 2005; Bjorklund, 2004). Because assessments of intelligence (and similar tests of cognitive ability) are taken to be the sine qua non of good thinking, it might be thought that such measures would serve as proxies for the developmental trajectories for judgment and decision-making skills. It is important to understand why such an assumption would be misplaced.

Judgment and decision making are more properly regarded as components of rational thought, and it is often not recognized that rationality and intelligence (as traditionally defined) are two different things conceptually and empirically. Distinguishing between rationality and intelligence helps explain how adolescents can be, at the same time, intelligent *and* irrational (Reyna & Farley, 2006; Stanovich, 2006). Thus, the developmental trajectories of the cognitive skills that underlie intelligence and those that underlie rational thinking must both be studied in their own right because they are conceptually and empirically separable, as we will argue in the next section. Judgment and decision-making skills, as critical components of rational thought, have a developmental trajectory that cannot just be inferred from the development of general cognitive ability.

Distinguishing rationality and intelligence in modern cognitive science

Cognitive scientists recognize two types of rationality: instrumental and epistemic. The simplest definition of instrumental rationality is: behaving in the world so that you get exactly what you most want, given the resources (physical and mental) available to you. Somewhat more technically, we could characterize instrumental rationality as the optimization of the individual's goal fulfillment. Economists and cognitive scientists have refined the notion of optimization of goal fulfillment into the technical notion of expected utility. The model of rational judgment used by decision scientists is one in which a person chooses options based on which option has the largest expected utility (Baron, 2008; Dawes, 1998).

The other aspect of rationality studied by cognitive scientists is termed epistemic rationality. This aspect of rationality concerns how well beliefs map onto the actual structure of the world. Epistemic rationality is sometimes called theoretical rationality or evidential rationality (Manktelow, 2004; Over, 2004). Instrumental and epistemic rationality are related. The aspects of beliefs that enter into instrumental calculations (that is, tacit calculations) are the probabilities of states of affairs in the world.

One of the fundamental advances in the history of modern decision science was the demonstration that if people's preferences follow certain patterns (the so-called axioms of choice—things like transitivity and freedom from certain kinds of context effects), they are behaving as if they are maximizing utility. They are acting to get what they most want (Luce & Raiffa, 1957; Savage, 1954). This is what makes people's degrees of rationality measurable by the experimental methods of cognitive science. Although it is difficult to assess utility directly, it is much easier to assess whether one of the axioms of rational choice is being violated. This has been the logic of the seminal heuristics and biases research program inaugurated in the much-cited studies of Kahneman and Tversky (1973, 1979; Tversky & Kahneman, 1974; see Kahneman, 2011).

Researchers in the heuristics and biases tradition have demonstrated in a host of empirical studies that people violate many of the strictures of rationality and that the magnitude of these violations can be measured experimentally. For example, people display confirmation bias, they test hypotheses inefficiently, they display preference inconsistencies, they do not properly calibrate degrees of belief, they overproject their own opinions onto others, they combine probabilities incoherently, and they allow prior knowledge to become implicated in deductive reasoning (for summaries of the large literature, see Baron, 2008; Stanovich, 2009, 2011). These are caused by many well-known cognitive biases: base-rate neglect, framing effects, representativeness biases, anchoring biases, availability bias, outcome bias, vividness effects, and various types of attribute substitution (Kahneman & Frederick, 2002), to name just a few. Degrees of rationality can be assessed in terms of the number and severity of such cognitive biases that individuals display. The important point, however, is that none of these processes are assessed directly on intelligence tests.

Conceptually as well, intelligence (as actually measured) concerns cognitive components quite different from the judgment and decision-making components that define human rationality. Intelligence, as measured on many commonly used tests, is often separated into fluid and crystallized components, deriving from the Cattell/Horn/Carroll (CHC) theory of intelligence (Carroll, 1993; Horn & Cattell, 1967). Sometimes termed the theory of fluid and crystallized intelligence (symbolized Gf/Gc theory), this theory posits that tests of mental ability tap, in addition to a general factor (g), a small number of broad factors, of which two are dominant (Geary, 2005; Horn & Noll, 1997). Fluid intelligence (Gf) reflects reasoning abilities operating across of variety of domains—in particular, novel ones. It is measured by tasks of abstract reasoning such as figural analogies, Raven Matrices, and series completion. Crystallized intelligence (Gc) reflects declarative knowledge acquired from acculturated learning experiences. It is measured by vocabulary tasks, verbal comprehension, and general knowledge measures. Ackerman (1996) discusses how the two dominant factors in the CHC theory reflect a long history of considering two aspects of intelligence: intelligence-as-process (Gf) and intelligence-as-knowledge (Gc).

In our theoretical approach to intelligence, our stance has been the standard one in cognitive science—to tie the concept to the actual empirical operationalizations in the relevant literature. In the wider literature on intelligence in education, there is a contrary tradition. That contrary tradition leads to the distinction between broad and narrow theories of intelligence (Stanovich, 2009). Broad theories include aspects of functioning that are captured by the *vernacular* term intelligence (adaptation to the environment, showing wisdom, displaying creativity, etc.) *whether or not* these aspects are actually measured by existing tests of intelligence. Narrow theories of intelligence, like that adopted in our discussion, confine the concept to the set of mental abilities actually tested on extant IQ tests. Our position is that broad theories of intelligence have been the source of much confusion both within the field and among the general public. They have led to overvaluing what IQ tests can tell us about intellectual functioning.

To think rationally means adopting appropriate goals, holding beliefs that are commensurate with available evidence, and taking the appropriate action given one's goals and beliefs. None of the currently used tests of intelligence assess any of these functions. However, it could still be the case that measures of intelligence correlate with measures of rational thinking, despite the fact that the latter are not directly assessed on tests of the former. Empirically, however, research indicates that intelligence and rational thinking skills are so modestly related that the former cannot be reliably used as a proxy for the latter (see Stanovich, 2011, for a review). The developmental trajectories of judgment and decision-making skills—the skills of rational thought—must be assessed in their own right.

Assessment of the development of rational thinking

Rationality is a multifarious concept—not a single mental quality. Cognitive scientists have developed ways to test both epistemic rationality and instrumental rationality as they were defined above. For example, psychologists have studied aspects of epistemic rationality such as the ability to avoid: overconfidence in knowledge judgments; taking into account base-rates in judgments; seeking to falsify hypotheses; avoiding the tendency to try to offer causal explanations of chance events; evaluating evidence with myside bias in check; and consideration of alternative hypotheses.

Additionally, psychologists have studied aspects of instrumental rationality such as the ability to avoid: inconsistent preferences because of framing effects; avoidance of default biases; overriding the tendency to substitute affect for difficult evaluations; weighing long-term well-being over short-term rewards; recognizing when vivid stimuli and irrelevant context affect choices.

Figure 2.1 displays a framework for the assessment of the development of rational thought. The first partition in the figure indicates that rational thought

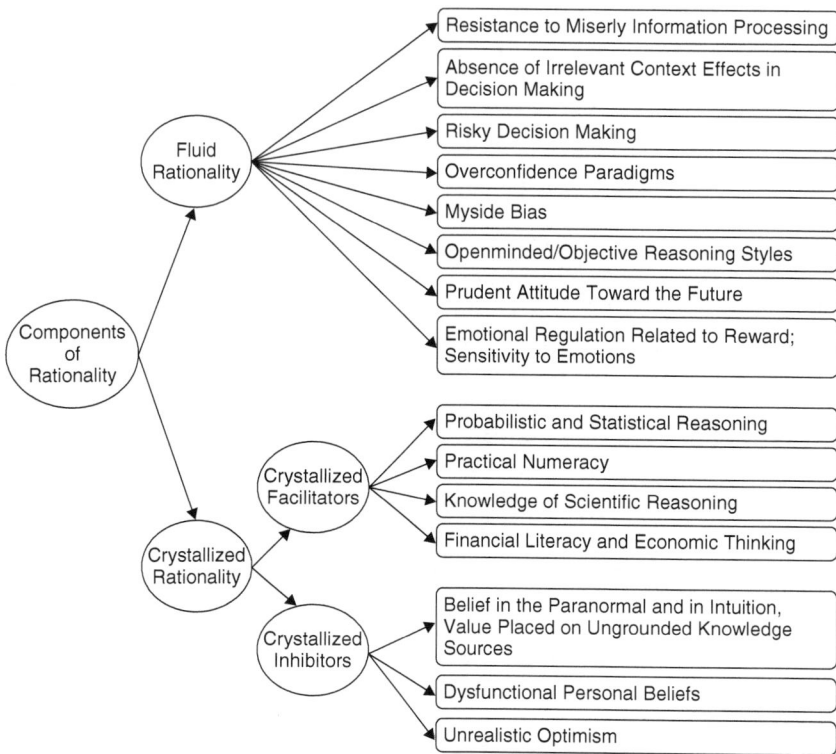

Figure 2.1 Framework for the assessment of the development of rational thought

can be partitioned into fluid and crystallized components by analogy to the Gf and Gc of the Cattell/Horn/Carroll fluid-crystallized theory of intelligence (Carroll, 1993; Cattell, 1963, 1998; Horn & Cattell, 1967). Fluid rationality encompasses the process part of rational thought—the thinking dispositions of the reflective mind (see Stanovich, 2009) that lead to rational thought and action. The top part of Figure 2.1 illustrates that unlike the case of fluid intelligence, fluid rationality is likely to be multifarious—composed of a variety of cognitive styles and disposi- tions. As a multifarious concept, fluid rationality cannot be assessed with a single type of item in the manner that the homogeneous Raven Progressive Matrices, for example, provides a measure of Gf.

Crystallized rationality is likewise multifarious. However, the bottom part of Figure 2.1 illustrates that the concept of crystallized rationality introduces another complication. Problems with rational thinking in the domain of mindware come in two types—mindware gaps and contaminated mindware (Stanovich, 2009). Mindware gaps occur because people lack declarative knowledge that can facili- tate rational thought—they lack crystallized facilitators as indicated in Figure 2.1. A different type of mindware problem arises because not all mindware is helpful—either to attaining our goals (instrumental rationality) or to having accurate beliefs (epistemic rationality). In fact, some acquired mindware can be the direct cause of irrational actions that thwart our goals. This type of problem has been termed contaminated mindware (Stanovich, 2009; Stanovich, Toplak, & West, 2008). It occurs when a person has acquired one (or more) of the crystallized inhibitors listed in Figure 2.1.

Figure 2.1 presents components of rationality that are of all three types—components of fluid rationality as well as some of the most common crystallized facilitators and crystallized inhibitors. Figure 2.1 should not be mistaken for the kind of list of "good thinking styles" that appears in textbooks on critical thinking. In terms of providing a basis for a system of rational thinking assessment, it goes considerably beyond such lists in a number of ways. First, unlike the many committee-like attempts to develop feature-lists of critical thinking skills (e.g., Facione, 1990), our conceptual components are grounded in paradigms that have been extensively researched within the literature of cognitive science. This will be illustrated more concretely when we discuss Table 2.1. Second, many textbook attempts at lists of "good thinking styles" deal only with aspects of fluid rationality and give short shrift to the crystallized knowledge bases that are necessary supports for rational thought and action. In contrast, our framework for rationality assessment emphasizes that crystallized knowledge underlies much rational responding (crystallized facilitators) and that crystallized knowledge can also be the direct cause of irrational behavior (crystallized inhibitors). Even more important than these points, however, is that unlike many such lists of thinking skills in textbooks, the fluid characteristics and crystallized knowledge bases listed in Figure 2.1 are each grounded in a task or paradigm (often more than one) in the literature of cognitive science.

Table 2.1 shows some of the paradigms that ground the component concepts and that could be used as the basis for constructing test items. The left column of the table lists the major dimensions of rational thought that were illustrated in Figure 2.1. The next column lists some of the paradigms that have been used to measure that major dimension. So, for example, we can see that the major dimension of fluid rationality of resistance to miserly processing has been measured using belief bias paradigms, attribute substitution paradigms, outcome bias tasks, and hindsight bias tasks. Finally, to the right of each paradigm are some exemplars of developmental studies that have looked at the age trend of that component. In some cases where cognitive ability associations with rational thinking were indicated, these findings are also reported to examine converging (or not converging) data patterns. The paradigms we have chosen serve as pointers to the operations that might be used to measure that domain of rational thinking. Indeed, the paradigms are the actual ones we are using to develop a comprehensive device to assess rational thinking (Stanovich, 2011; Stanovich, West, & Toplak, 2011).

We present Table 2.1 as a snapshot of where the field of developmental psychology presently stands regarding empirical knowledge of the growth of components of rational thought. Because rational thinking is multifarious and complex, it will come as no surprise that there is no easy way to summarize the state of the

Table 2.1 Potential measurement paradigms for the major dimensions of rational thought and samples of developmental findings

		Components of Rational Thought	
Fluid Rationality			
MAJOR DIMENSIONS	*MEASUREMENT PARADIGMS*	*DEVELOPMENTAL FINDINGS*	
Resistance to Miserly Information Processing	Belief Bias Paradigm	Kokis, Macpherson, Toplak, West, & Stanovich (2002): 13 year olds outperformed 11 year olds on conflict items (no-conflict items were ceiled). Higher cognitive ability (intelligence) was associated with lower belief bias.	
		De Neys & Van Gelder (2009): 20 year olds outperformed both 12 year olds and 65+ year olds on a belief bias syllogistic reasoning task. No age effect was found for the no-conflict problems.	
		Steegen & De Neys (2012): 12, 14, and 17 year olds performed a belief bias syllogistic reasoning task. The older adolescents outperformed middle adolescents, who outperformed young adolescents. No age effect was found for the no-conflict problems.	
		Evans & Perry (1995): 10–11 year olds displayed significantly more premise based reasoning and less belief bias than 7–8 year olds.	
		Markovits & Bouffard-Bouchard (1992): 25 year olds made fewer errors on belief-biased syllogisms than 17 year olds.	
		Handley, Capon, Beveridge, Dennis, & Evans (2004): 10 year olds' performance on relational conditional reasoning tasks with conflict was predicted by working memory and inhibitory control performance.	
		Toplak, West, & Stanovich (in press): 13 year olds outperformed 10 year olds on a belief bias syllogistic reasoning task. Higher cognitive ability (intelligence and executive functions) was associated with lower belief bias.	
	Attribute Substitution (Vividness)	Kokis et al. (2002): 13 year olds showed more reliance on noncausal baserates and less reliance on experience/case information than 11 year olds. Cognitive ability correlated positively with baserate usage.	
		Jacobs & Potenza (1991): 7, 9, 11, and 20 year olds did not differ in their use of baserate information in object condition, but differed in use of baserate information in social condition. Davidson (1995): Older children in a sample of 8, 10, and 12 year olds were more likely to make baserate consistent responses than younger children on stereotypic and nonstereotypic problems.	

	Attribute Substitution (Denominator Neglect)	Klaczynski (2001): 12 year olds showed more reliance on baserate information than 16 year olds. Toplak et al. (in press): 11 year olds showed more reliance on baserate information than 9 year olds. Higher cognitive ability (intelligence and executive functions) was associated with less reliance on vivid individuating information. Klaczynski (2001): 17 and 22 year olds showed less denominator neglect than 13 year olds. Kokis et al. (2002): 11 and 13 year olds did not differ in denominator neglect problem. Cognitive ability (intelligence) was correlated with the normative choice. Toplak et al. (in press): 11 year olds outperformed 9 year olds on a ratio bias/denominator neglect task. Higher cognitive ability (intelligence and executive functions) was associated with lower reliance on attribute substitution.
	Outcome Bias Paradigm	Klaczynski (2001): 16 year olds showed less Outcome Bias than 12 year olds.
	Hindsight Bias Paradigm	Klaczynski (2001): No significant differences between 16 year olds and 12 year olds on Hindsight Bias.
Absence of Irrelevant Context Effects in Decision Making	Framing Effects	Reyna & Ellis (1994): 4 year olds displayed no framing effects, 8 year olds displayed reverse framing effects, and 11 year olds displayed a mixture of framing effects. Schlottman & Tring (2005): 7 and 9 year olds preferred sure thing more in positive than negative frame in gambles with equal expected value. Toplak et al. (in press): 11 year olds were more resistant to framing than were 9 year olds in a within-subject design task. Higher cognitive ability (intelligence and executive functions) was associated with more resistance to framing.
	Avoidance of Irrelevant Anchoring	Smith (1999): 9, 10, and 19 year olds estimated the number of jelly beans in a container subsequent to indicating whether it held more or fewer than 50 (low anchor) or 250 (high anchor) jelly beans. An anchoring effect was found for each age group. The size of the effect did not differ between groups.
Risky Decision Making	Adherence to Basic Probability/Utility Tradeoffs in SEU Theory; Preferences in Line with SEU Axioms; Stable Preferences; Preference Reversals	Levin, Weller, Pederson, & Harshman (2007): Adults made more risky choices on risk-advantageous trials than 6 year olds on a risky decision-making task. Adults also made fewer risky choices on risk-disadvantageous trials than 6 and 9 year olds. Weller, Levin, & Denburg (2011): A lifespan sample of 5 to 85 year olds found that risk-taking decreased with age in the gain domain and was relatively uninfluenced by age in the loss domain. Expected value sensitivity increased from childhood to adulthood and then decreased for the elderly.

Table 2.1 Continued

Fluid Rationality		*Components of Rational Thought*
MAJOR DIMENSIONS	*MEASUREMENT PARADIGMS*	*DEVELOPMENTAL FINDINGS*
		Rakow & Rahim (2010): 21 year olds made choices more closely aligned with the expected value of observations than 9 year olds in a risky choice task that pitted risky choice against sure thing. Halpern-Felsher & Cauffman (2001): 11, 14, 15, 18, and 23 year olds were asked to help peers solve three hypothetical dilemmas. The 23 year olds were more likely to consider risks and benefits associated with decision and suggest seeking advice than were the adolescent and younger individuals.
Overconfidence Paradigms	Calibration Paradigms	Newman (1984): 16 year olds estimated the number of dots in a series of 55 to 203 dot arrays and rated their level of confidence in each estimation. Children with higher levels of basic numerical skills made more accurate estimations and were more sensitive to variations in the difficulty of making the estimations. Desoete & Roeyers (2006): Grades 2, 3, and 4 children overestimated their performance in mathematics tests. The size of the overestimation was especially large for the grade 2 children. Schneider, Visé, Lockl, & Nelson (2000): Although 9 and 11 year olds' immediate judgments-of-learning (JOLs) in a memory task were inaccurate, their delayed JOLs improved regardless of age. JOLs were typically more accurate for aggregate JOLs than for item-by-item JOLs.
Myside Bias	Unbiased Processing of Evidence in Argument Evaluation	Klacyznski & Lavallee (2005): 17 and 22 year olds showed myside bias in their evaluation of arguments and evidence (sample size an issue) that portrayed their vocational goals favorably or unfavorably. Age and cognitive ability did not predict additional bias beyond that associated with vocational identity and epistemic regulation. Klaczynski & Narasimham (1998): 11, 13, and 17 year olds showed myside bias in their ratings of flawed experiments that reached conclusions that cast their religious views in either positive or negative light. Although scientific reasoning increased in age, age did not consistently predict the magnitude of myside bias.

Openminded/Objective Reasoning Styles	Informal Reasoning Paradigms and Argument Generation	Toplak & Stanovich (2003): University students generated more reasons/arguments supporting positions they endorsed than opposed. The degree of this myside bias decreased systematically with year in university. No cognitive ability effects were found.
	Belief Flexibility: Actively Openminded Thinking	Kokis et al. (2002): Age and cognitive ability was positively correlated with an actively open minded thinking (AOT) scale in a sample of 11 and 13 year olds. Toplak et al. (in press): Age and cognitive ability positively correlated with AOT in a sample of 9, 10, and 13 year olds.
	Tendency to Fully Process Information: Need for Cognition and Typical Intellectual Engagement	Baron, Granato, Spranca, & Teubal (1993): No age effect was found between actively open minded thinking scale and the search for contrary evidence in a sample of 5–12 year olds. Kokis et al. (2002): Age and need for cognition were minimally related to each other in a sample of 11 and 13 year olds. Toplak et al. (in press): No relationship between age and need for cognition in a sample of 9, 10, and 13 year olds.
	Separating Fact from Opinion; Recognizing the Validity and Invalidity of Informal Arguments; Recognizing Contradiction and Consistency	Kuhn (1991): The older participants in a sample of 14 to 69 year olds were less successful in generating counterarguments on 2 or 3 important issues. Kuhn, Phelps, & Walters (1985): Age in 10–12, 13–14, 15–18, and 18–31 year olds was associated with improved ability to recognize when data were sufficient for making valid causal inferences. Older participants were better able to judge when independent variables were not associated. De Neys & Everaerts (2008): Counterexample generation increased with age in 11, 15, and 17 year olds. The acceptance of invalid affirmation of the consequent decreased across these age groups.
Prudent Attitude Toward the Future	Temporal Discounting of Reward	Steinberg et al. (2009): 10–11 and 12–13 year olds had higher discount rates than 14–15, 16–17, 18–21, 22–25, or 26–30 year olds. In addition, delay discounting and IQ significantly negatively correlated. Green, Fry, & Myerson (1994): 12, 20, and 68 year olds showed delay discounting. Discounting was highest for the youngest and lowest for the oldest group of participants. Prencipe et al. (2006): Younger children showed steeper temporal discount rates in a sample of 9, 11, 13, and 15 year olds. Temporal discounting also significantly correlated with Digit Span (positive) and Stroop test (negative, right direction).

Table 2.1 Continued

		Components of Rational Thought
Fluid Rationality		
MAJOR DIMENSIONS	*MEASUREMENT PARADIGMS*	*DEVELOPMENTAL FINDINGS*
	Future Orientation; Delay of Gratification Paradigms; Time Preference	Steinberg et al. (2009): 10–11, 12–13, 14–15, 16–17, 18–21, 22–25, and 26–30 year olds completed future orientation scale. Future orientation increased with age. Temporal orientation and anticipation of future consequences were associated with IQ. Mischel et al. (2011): Longitudinal follow-up studies of 4 year olds found that the duration that these preschoolers were able to resist the temptation of immediate rewards (e.g., a marshmallow) was significantly associated with their future cognitive abilities (e.g., SAT scores), educational achievements, and a variety of positive mental and physical health characteristics.
Emotional Regulation Related to Reward; Sensitivity to Emotions	Iowa Gambling Task	Steinberg (2010): Advantageous selection on the Iowa Gambling Task by 10–11, 12–13, 14–15, 16–17, 18–21, 22–25, and 26–30 year olds followed a curvilinear pattern, increasing between preadolescence and mid-adolescence, and then subsequently decreasing. Prencipe et al. (2006): Age was associated with improved performance on the Iowa Gambling, Digit Span, and Stroop tasks in a sample of 9, 11, 13, and 15 year olds. Lamm, Zelazo, & Lewis (2006): Advantageous selection on the Iowa Gambling Task by 7–16 year olds increased with age, and was correlated with GO RT and Go/No Go stimulus duration, but not with Digit Span. Crone & van der Molen (2004): Advantageous selection on an analogue of the Iowa Gambling Task by 13, 16, and 21 year olds increased with age. Hooper, Luciana, Conklin, & Yarger (2004): Advantageous selection on a modified Iowa Gambling Task by 10, 13, and 16 year olds increased with age.

Crystallized Rationality: Crystallized Facilitators

MAJOR DIMENSIONS	MEASUREMENT PARADIGMS	DEVELOPMENTAL FINDINGS
Probabilistic and Statistical Reasoning	Consistent Probability Judgments; Conjunction Effects; Appreciating Baserate; Importance of Sample Size; Resistance to Gambler's Fallacy	Chiesi, Primi, & Morsanyi (2011): 14 year olds outperformed 12 and 13 year olds on a variety of probabilistic reasoning tasks (e.g., conjunction, gambler's fallacy, marble, sample size). Probabilistic reasoning positively associated with cognitive ability. Klaczynski (2001): 16 year olds outperformed 12 year olds on the gambler's fallacy. No significant age differences were found in conjunction bias. Falk & Wilkening (1998): Older children in a 7-age group sample of 6–14 year olds performed better than younger children on a probability-adjustment task (competitive game) Kreitler & Kreitler (1986): Older children in a 3-age group sample of 5–12 year olds performed better than younger children on Piagetian probability tasks. Fishbein & Schnarch (1997): The conjunction effect was larger for 10–11, 12–13, and 14–15 year olds than for 16–17 year olds and college students.
Practical Numeracy	Decision and Risk-Based Numeracy Measures	Reyna & Brainerd (2007): Results from the National Assessment of Educational Progress (NAEP) measures of mathematics indicate that approximately two-thirds of US children in the grades 4 and 8 are unable to demonstrate grade-levels of proficiency with percentages, fractions, and probabilities. Adults who lack basic proficiency in these areas have been found to comprehend medically related information less accurately and make poorer health-related decisions.
Knowledge of Scientific Reasoning	Control Concepts; Variable Isolation; Control Groups; Placebo and Selection Effects; Converging Evidence; Diagnostic Hypothesis Testing; Diagnostic Covariation Judgment; Understanding Falsifiability	Tschirgi (1980): 7, 9, and 11 year olds and college students were given multivariate stories and asked to determine the cause of outcomes by testing hypotheses. Development was associated with a shift in strategy choice from "change all" to "vary one thing at a time." Klahr, Fay, & Dunbar (1993): 9 and 11 year olds and college students tested hypotheses by conducting experiments. The college students were more systematic and effective in their tests, and were more likely to discover correct rules. Koslowski, Okagaki, Lorenz, & Umbach (1989): 12, 14, and 21 year olds evaluated whether target factors were causally related to effects described in story problems. Age differences were marked when covariation was present, but slight when covariation was not present. Klaczynski (2001): 16 year olds made more normative responses than 12 year olds on Wason selection and covariation detection tasks.

Table 2.1 Continued

Components of Rational Thought

Crystallized Rationality: Crystallized Facilitators		
MAJOR DIMENSIONS	MEASUREMENT PARADIGMS	DEVELOPMENTAL FINDINGS
		Foltz, Overton, & Ricco (1995): Although 14 year olds outperformed 10 year olds on the selection task performance, the difference did not reach a level of significance
		Richardson (1992): In contrast to 6 year olds, 10 and 14 year olds demonstrated an understanding of covariation among three variables.
		Pillow (2002): In a sample of 5, 6, 8, and 21 year olds, age was associated with increasing differentiation in certainty associated with deductive inferences, inductive inferences, informed guesses, and pure guesses.
		Masnick & Morris (2008): Compared to 9 and 12 year olds, 20 year olds detected multiple data characteristics, used multiple data characteristics in combination, and provided explicit descriptions of data interpretations compared to younger participants.
		Li, Cao, Li, & Li (2009): 9 and 11 year olds made more inductive inferences than 6 and 7 year olds on a task assessing diverse examples.
		Tullos & Woolley (2009): The ability to infer the reality status of novel entities (e.g., a new animal) from evidence (supporting, irrelevant, and no evidence) develops incrementally between ages 4 and 6, and children perform better when their evaluation is free from bias.
Financial Literacy and Economic Thinking	Financial Literacy/ Illiteracy Scales	Chen & Volpe (1998): College students had low levels of basic knowledge about personal finance. Mandell (2009): College students demonstrated higher levels of financial literacy than high school students.
	Economic Understanding Avoiding Sunk Costs	Thompson & Siegler (2000): 7 and 9 year olds, but not 5 year olds, understood the goals of seeking profits, acquiring goods inexpensively, or competing successfully with sellers. Klaczynski (2001): 17 and 22 year olds outperformed 13 year olds on sunk cost problem. Strough et al. (2008): 74 year olds adults were less likely to show sunk cost effect than 19 year olds.
	Understanding Commons Dilemmas, Zero-sum, and Nonzero-sum Games	Brady, Newcomb, & Hartup (1983): 1st, 3rd, and 5th graders played a board game with many complex variations but there was a mild trend to increase cooperation with age.

Crystallized Rationality: Crystallized Inhibitors

MAJOR DIMENSIONS	MEASUREMENT PARADIGMS	DEVELOPMENTAL FINDINGS
Belief in the Par- anormal and in Intuition; Value Placed on Ungrounded Knowl- edge Sources	Paranormal, Superstitious Thinking, Luck scales, Intuition	Kokis et al. (2002): Age and cognitive ability were negatively associated with superstitious thinking in a sample of 10–11 and 13 year olds. Toplak et al. (in press): Age and cognitive ability were negatively associated with superstitious thinking in a sample of 9, 10, and 13 year olds. Preece & Baxter (2000). Skepticism about superstitious and pseudoscientific beliefs was increased with age in a sample of 14–16 and 17–18 year olds. Bolton, Dearsley, Madronal-Luque, & Baron-Cohen (2002): Scores on the Magical Thinking Questionnaire (MTQ) were not systematically associated with age in a sample of 5–17 year olds. Magical thinking and obsessive compulsion were correlated.
Dysfunctional Personal Beliefs	Measures of Irrational Personal Beliefs	Bernard & Cronan (1999): Child and Adolescent Scale of Irrationality (CASI) was given to grades 4–11 children. Total irrationality and the four irrational subscales with trait anxiety, anger, as well as with teacher ratings of students were correlated. Hooper & Layne (1983): No significant differences between 5th, 6th, and 7th graders on Common Belief Inventory for students (CBIS), a measure of irrational personal beliefs.
Unrealistic Optimism	Unrealistic Optimism Measures	Cohn, Macfarlane, Yanez, & Imai (1995): Compared with their parents, 13–18 year olds minimized the harm associated with periodic involvement in health-threatening activities.

literature. This table is not exhaustive of developmental studies that have examined related paradigms, but rather provides pointers to paradigms from the cognitive science literature that have been examined in the developmental literature.

Empirical trends in the development of rational thinking

Predictably, some of the subcomponents of rational thought have received more attention than others. For example, the major dimension of resistance to miserly processing has been relatively heavily investigated with a variety of different paradigms. Within that dimension, the study of belief bias—that people have difficulty processing data pointing toward conclusions that conflict with what they think they know about the world—has produced a substantial literature of developmental studies. In contrast, another major dimension of fluid rationality—the avoidance of myside bias—has received much less attention.

The complexity of the entire framework makes *general* statements about developmental trends difficult. Sometimes there is convergence within the paradigms of a major dimension and sometimes not. Often, there is convergence within a *paradigm*, but sometimes there is a lack of convergence even there. We will nonexhaustively (due to the complexity and size of Table 2.1) give some examples of each of these situations of convergence and nonconvergence.

The assessment of rational thought in developmental studies

Table 2.1 provides a summary of developmental studies that have examined rational thinking in our taxonomy.

Fluid rationality

Fluid rationality is the largest domain encompassing the processing components of rational thinking; they are the "thinking dispositions of the reflective mind that lead to rational thought and action" (Stanovich, 2011, p. 193).

Resistance to miserly information processing

Belief bias, attribute substitution, and denominator neglect each involve a default to miserly information processing (Stanovich, 2009, 2011; Stanovich et al., 2008). The experimental paradigms used to operationalize them have been well-documented in the adult literature (Denes-Raj & Epstein, 1994; Evans, Barston, & Pollard, 1983; Kahneman & Frederick, 2002) and have been used in multiple studies in the developmental literature (Stanovich et al., 2008).

Belief bias syllogistic reasoning paradigms involve a conflict between the logical structure of a syllogism and the believability of its conclusion. In these tasks, participants are given explicit instructions to assume that the premises are true and to determine whether the conclusion follows logically from the premises. For example, given the following information: All living things need water (Premise 1), and roses need water (Premise 2), does it logically follow that roses are living things (Conclusion)? In this case, the conclusion does not logically follow from the premises, even though the conclusion is a believable statement. Studies that have examined belief bias reasoning in developmental samples have generally found that older children outperform younger children (De Neys & Van Gelder, 2009; Evans & Perry, 1995; Kokis et al., 2002; Markovits & Bouffard-Bouchard, 1992; Markovits & Thompson, 2008; Markovits et al., 1996; Moshman & Franks, 1986; Steegen & De Neys, 2012; Toplak et al., in press; but see Morsanyi & Handley, 2008). A converging pattern has also been reported with cognitive abilities. Better performance on intelligence and executive function measures has been associated with better performance on belief bias tasks in developmental samples (Handley et al., 2004; Kokis et al., 2002; Toplak et al., in press).

Vividness effects, which are indicators of attribute substitution (Fong, Krantz, & Nisbett, 1986; Stanovich et al., 2008), also reflect a default to miserly information processing (Stanovich, 2009; 2011; Stanovich et al., 2008). In these problems, participants are asked to make a choice informed by large-sample information versus salient personal testimony. Reliance on information from the large samples is normative and must override the cognitive miser's tendency to rely on the vivid and salient single-case testimony. Several studies have reported that increasing age is associated with more reliance on baserates and less reliance on salient vivid cases in older children and youth than in younger children (Kokis et al., 2002; Davidson, 1995; Klaczynski, 2001; Toplak et al., in press). Cognitive ability has also been reported to be significantly positively associated with baserate usage (Kokis et al., 2002; Toplak et al., in press). However, some studies have reported finding increased reliance on salient vivid cases in older participants when social stereotypes are involved (Davidson, 1995; De Neys & Vanderputte, 2011; Jacobs & Potenza, 1991). A plausible explanation of this finding is that it results from an increased knowledge of the stereotype that accompanies an increase in age (Stanovich et al., 2008).

Denominator neglect provides another example of the cognitive miser's failure to override a heuristic response (Denes-Raj & Epstein, 1994; Kirkpatrick & Epstein, 1992; Pacini & Epstein, 1999). Adults were presented with two bowls of jelly beans: one bowl had 9 white jelly beans and one red jelly bean, and the other bowl had 92 white jelly beans and 8 red jelly beans. The task was to randomly select a bean from whichever bowl offered the greatest chance of selecting a red bean for a one dollar prize. Although the majority picked the 10 percent bowl, a healthy minority (from 30 to 40 percent of the participants) picked the 8 percent bowl.

Using this paradigm, Kokis et al. (2002) found no significant trend for denominator neglect to decrease across groups of 10–11 year olds and 13–14 year olds. However, Klaczynski (2001) found that 17 and 22 year olds outperformed 13 year olds, and Toplak et al. (in press) found a developmental effect on a variant of this task with 9 and 11 year olds (see also Acredolo, O'Connor, Banks, & Horobin, 1989; Furlan, Agnoli, & Reyna, 2012; Stanovich et al., 2008).

Although less frequently used with developmental samples, outcome bias and hindsight bias paradigms provide additional indicators of the tendency toward myside processing.

Absence of irrelevant context effects in decision making

Framing effects represent an example from the classic heuristics and biases literature of defaulting to a cognitive miser with a focal bias (Stanovich, 2009, 2011). Framing effects reflect the passive acceptance of—and differential response to—what are in fact mere redescriptions of the same situation. For example, participants in Tversky and Kahneman's (1981) famous disease framing problem were risk averse when framing emphasized gains ("200 [of 600] people will be saved"), but risk seeking when framing emphasized loses ("400 [of 600] people will die").

Relative to the vast adult literature (Kahneman & Tversky, 1984, 2000; Kühberger, 1998; Levin, Gaeth, Schreiber, & Lauriola, 2002; Maule & Villejoubert, 2007), the literature on framing effects with children is relatively sparse. Some investigators have creatively adapted framing paradigms for children (Levin & Hart, 2003; Reyna & Ellis, 1994; Schlottman & Tring, 2005), but the results of these experiments have not converged (Stanovich et al., 2008). Toplak et al. (in press) presented 9 and 11 year olds with positively and negatively framed versions of the same problems using a within-subject design. For example, one framing of a question for participants read: "Imagine that Jimmy played 8 games at a carnival. He won 6 of the 8 games he played. Rate how happy Jimmy was after playing the carnival games." This question was identical in the second framing except that this time Jimmy "lost 2 of the 8 games." The 11 year olds were more resistant to the framing manipulation than the 9 year olds. In addition, higher cognitive abilities (intelligence and executive function performance) were associated with more resistance to framing. These findings are consistent with the adult literature, where framing effects have been found to be associated with cognitive abilities in within-subject designs, but not in between-subject designs (Stanovich & West, 2008b). Other developmental patterns are discussed by Reyna and Ellis (1994).

Avoidance of irrelevant anchoring is another paradigm that has been used widely to assess context effects in decision making in adults, but sparingly with children.

Risky decision making

Higher levels of education and cognitive ability are associated with increased preference for gambles with risky but higher expected values over certain but lower values in adults (Benjamin & Shapiro, 2005; Donkers, Melenberg, & van Soest, 2001; Frederick, 2005). The "cups" task has been used to examine risky decision making in developmental samples (Levin, Weller, Pederson, & Harshman, 2007; Weller, Levin, & Denburg, 2011). Three variables were manipulated: gain versus loss trials, different levels of probability for the risky choices (0.20, 0.33, 0.50), and different levels of outcomes. Each trial required a choice between a certain or risky option. For example, participants choose between a sure gain of 25 cents and a 20 percent chance of winning 50 cents. The risky option offered either a higher or lower expected value. Feedback was given following each choice, and the accumulated money earned was received at the conclusion of the experiment. Adults were more likely to select the options that offered higher expected values than children (Levin et al., 2007; Weller et al., 2011). This developmental finding has been replicated using somewhat different procedures (Rakow & Rahim, 2010, but see Schlottmann, 2000, 2001).

Overconfidence

Overconfidence is an important domain of fluid rationality. It has been assessed using knowledge calibration paradigms that compare a participant's estimation of the likelihood of an outcome with its actual statistical likelihood. For example, Fischhoff et al. (2000) asked adolescents to report how likely it was that they "will be a parent between now and when they turn 20 years of age," "will be the victim of a violent crime at least once in the next year," and "will die from any cause." Overall, the adolescents provided relatively reasonable estimates of the various outcomes happening to them, with the exception that they tended to over-estimate the likelihood of death in the near future. Older children have been found to provide more accurate estimations of their abilities and competence compared to younger children (Desoete & Roeyers, 2006; Lipko, Dunlosky, & Merriman, 2009; Newman, 1984; Schneider, Visé, Lockl, & Nelson, 2000).

Myside bias

Myside bias, another dimension of fluid rationality, refers to the tendency to test hypotheses in a manner that is biased toward one's own opinions (Baron, 1995; Perkins, Farady, & Bushey, 1991; Stanovich, 2011; Toplak & Stanovich, 2003). One factor that sets myside bias apart from some of the other rational thinking components is its typical lack of association with cognitive ability. Stanovich and West (2007, 2008a) examined natural myside bias in an adult sample, asking participants to evaluate a variety of controversial propositions with no implicit or explicit inducements to be objective. No association between natural myside bias and cognitive ability was found.

Toplak et al. (in press) used an argument generation task with a developmental sample to examine the myside bias effect. Participants first indicated their prior belief on whether children should have cell phones. Following this question, they were prompted to give reasons in favor of children having a cell phone, followed by reasons against children having a cell phone. The interviewer prompted participants for additional reasons until no additional reasons were given. As in studies with adults using this paradigm, no explicit cues or instructions were given to set aside one's own prior beliefs in answering the question. A myside bias effect was found, as participants generated more unique reasons in favor of their own position than unique reasons against their position. This finding is consistent with those obtained using other procedures that examined the unbiased processing of evidence in argument evaluation (Klaczynski & Fauth, 1997; Klaczynski & Gordon, 1996; Klaczynski & Lavallee, 2005; Klaczynski & Narasimham, 1998). Myside bias does not seem to differ much across different developmental levels and has not been associated with cognitive abilities in developmental samples. There is evidence, however, that increased years of university-level education may have a moderating effect on myside bias (Toplak & Stanovich, 2003).

Open-minded and objective reasoning styles

Several studies have examined developmental differences with paradigms that necessitate open-minded or objective reasoning in order to evaluate evidence. Examples include paradigms in which participants must differentiate fact from opinion, recognize the validity or invalidity of informal arguments, and recognize contradictions. Overall, several studies suggest that older participants outperform younger participants: older participants were better able to recognize when data were sufficient for making valid causal inferences, or when independent variables were not associated (Kuhn, Phelps, & Walters, 1985); they were more skilled in considering the risks and benefits in hypothetical dilemmas (Halpern-Felsher & Cauffman, 2001), and generating counterexamples (De Neys & Everaerts, 2008, but see Kuhn, 1991). Although extensively studied with adults, there has been considerably less research examining belief flexibility, actively open-minded thinking, and the tendency to fully process information (such as Need for Cognition and Typical Intellectual Engagement) in children.

Prudent attitude toward the future

A prudent attitude toward the future shifts the focus from "here and now" to consideration of future outcomes. Several procedures have been used to measure attitudes toward the future, including temporal discounting, future orientation scales, and delay of gratification tasks. These tasks typically ask participants to choose between smaller immediate rewards or substantially larger delayed rewards. Selection of the larger delayed rewards is typically scored as more optimal (Ainslie, 1975; Kirby, 1997).

A number of developmental studies have found that increasing age is associated with less extreme temporal discounting (Green et al., 1994; Prencipe et al., 2006; Steinberg et al., 2009) and a more future orientation (Steinberg et al., 2009). Cognitive ability tends to be positively associated with a reduction in temporal discounting (Shamosh & Gray, 2008; Shamosh et al., 2008), and longitudinal studies have reported that positive long-term cognitive, educational, and career outcomes can be predicted from an early willingness to delay rewards (Mischel et al., 2011; Prencipe et al., 2006; Rodriguez, Mischel, & Shoda, 1989; Steinberg et al., 2009).

Emotion regulation related to reward; sensitivity to emotions

The Iowa Gambling Task (IGT; Bechara, Damasio, Damasio, & Anderson, 1994) has been widely used to assess this last dimension listed under fluid rationality in Table 2.1. A participant taking the IGT selects 100 cards, one at a time, from four 50-card decks. Each card is associated with various rewards and penalties that are revealed once the card is selected. Each deck is either advantageous or disadvantageous in terms of the eventual net rewards and penalties that will accrue over the course of several card selections. Poor performance on the IGT has been attributed to a dysregulation of somatic markers that hinders the learning of a deck's relative advantageous or disadvantageous nature as the decks are initially haphazardly sampled (Damasio, 1994, 1996, 1999). Namely, individuals who perform poorly on this task purportedly have weaker somatic or physiological cues to guide risky choices (Damasio, 1994, 1996, 1999).

Older participants generally outperform younger participants on the IGT (Crone & van der Molen, 2004; Garon & Moore, 2004; Hooper, Luciana, Conklin, & Yarger, 2004; Hongwanishkul, Happaney, Lee, & Zelazo, 2005; Lamm et al., 2006; Overman et al., 2004; Prencipe et al., 2006; Steinberg, 2010). Positive associations have also been reported between IGT performance and cognitive ability measures, but these associations tend to be small to modest, indicating that considerable variability in performance on the IGT is not captured by current measures of executive function and intelligence (Toplak, Sorge, Benoit, West, & Stanovich, 2010).

Crystallized rationality: crystallized facilitators

Crystallized rationality is the second major component of rational thinking. It is composed of mindware (Perkins, 1995), a term that refers to rules, knowledge, procedures, and strategies that can be used in decision making. As discussed previously, crystallized rationality is separated into crystallized facilitators and crystallized inhibitors. The former category refers to declarative knowledge that can assist rational thinking: understanding probability and statistics, practical numeracy, knowledge of scientific reasoning, and financial and economic thinking.

Probabilistic and statistical reasoning

Older participants typically do better than younger participants on a broad set of measures that assess probabilistic and statistical reasoning. For example, older participants typically do better on gambler's fallacy and sample-size problems (Chiesi, Primi, & Morsanyi, 2011), probability adjustment tasks (Falk & Wilkening, 1998), and class inclusion and Piagetian probability tasks (Agnoli, 1991; Kreitler & Kreitler, 1986).

Tversky and Kahneman's (1983) classic conjunction problem presented adult participants with a stereotypical description of a student named Linda who would have seemed to be much more likely to become an active feminist than a bank teller. A majority of adults given this problem make an error by judging the likelihood of the conjunction of two possibilities ("Linda is a bank teller and is active in the feminist movement") as being more likely than the individual possibilities ("Linda is a bank teller"). The findings for conjunction problems with developmental samples have been mixed: the conjunction effect has sometimes been smaller for older children (Chiesi et al., 2011), sometimes been smaller for younger children (Davidson, 1995; Fishbein & Schnarch, 1997; Morsanyi & Handley, 2008), and sometimes not differed with age (Klaczynski, 2001). Possibly relevant to the latter finding, the conjunction effect has been shown to be relatively independent of individual differences in intelligence when studied using between-subject designs (Stanovich & West, 2008b). All conjunction-effect problems depend on participants having well-instantiated knowledge of particular stereotypes, and the extent to which the mixed developmental finding may reflect differential knowledge of the relevant stereotypes is unknown (Stanovich et al., 2011).

Practical numeracy is another domain of helpful mindware, and refers to competence in using and applying mathematical knowledge to real-world situations. Adults who lack basic proficiency in this type of knowledge have been shown to be less accurate in comprehending medically related information and to make poorer health-related decisions (Reyna & Brainerd, 2007).

Knowledge of scientific reasoning

The development of knowledge of scientific reasoning has been extensively studied (see Table 2.1). Scientific thinking involves knowledge about how to test and revise theories, design proper controls for extraneous variables, and objectively evaluate evidence (Zimmerman, 2007). Understanding the need for experimental controls, such as isolating variables and inclusion of control conditions, increases with age in children (Klahr, Fay, & Dunbar, 1993; Klahr & Nigam, 2004; Masnick & Morris, 2008; Tschirgi, 1980). Older children are also more likely to take covariation among variables into account and resist inappropriate causal inferences (Klaczynski, 2001; Koslowski, Condry, Sprague, & Hutt, 1996; Koslowski, Okagaki, Lorenz, & Umbach, 1989; Richardson, 1992).

Financial literacy and economic thinking

The rational thinking domain of financial literacy and economic thinking is increasingly important in our modern society. This domain of crystallized facilitators involves declarative knowledge of basic facts about how financial institutions operate (such as, stocks versus savings accounts), knowledge of economics concepts (such as, supply and demand), recognizing sunk costs, and understanding zero-sum games. The pitfall of honoring sunk costs involves persisting in an activity with negative expected value because a significant investment has already been made (Arkes & Ayton, 1999; Arkes & Blumer, 1985).

Commons dilemmas are well known and are often studied using variations of the Prisoner's Dilemma paradigm, where a choice to cooperate is pitted against a choice to compete.

In the limited work that has been done using these paradigms with developmental samples, older participants have demonstrated higher levels of financial literacy and more economic thinking than younger participants (Mandell, 2009; Thompson & Siegler, 2000). Empirical findings on sunk cost effects with developmental samples have been more mixed. Sometimes older participants have been found to honor sunk costs more often than younger participants (Klaczynski, 2001; Strough, Mehta, McFall, & Schuller, 2008) and sometimes no developmental effects have been found (Baron, Granato, Spranca, & Teubal, 1993; Morsanyi & Handley, 2008). Older children have been found to be somewhat more likely to cooperate in multiple sessions of Prisoner's Dilemma games than younger children (Brady et al., 1983; Matsumoto, Haan, Yabrove, Theodorou, & Carney, 1986).

Crystallized rationality: crystallized inhibitors

Mindware can also involve crystallized inhibitors that hinder rationality by subverting our goals or by being composed of dysfunctional beliefs (Stanovich, 2011). For example, adults who have fewer superstitious beliefs are better able to evaluate arguments in an unbiased manner (Stanovich & West, 1997). Superstitious thinking is also associated with such maladaptive real-world behaviors as pathological gambling (Stanovich, 2011; Toplak, Liu, MacPherson, Toneatto, & Stanovich, 2007). Overall, relevant developmental research in the domain of crystallized inhibitors has been sparse. Developmental research has found negative associations between superstitious thinking and both age and cognitive abilities (Kokis et al., 2002; Preece & Baxter, 2000; Toplak et al., in press). These beliefs often have adverse consequences (Stanovich, 2009). The belief that one possesses "good luck" may inhibit rational goal pursuit and the development of necessary talents. It might displace more efficacious behavioral strategies.

Developmental of rational thinking: conclusions

To summarize, Figure 2.1 provides an overview of our taxonomy for assessing the development of rational thinking. Table 2.1 provides examples showing how all the major dimensions of rational thinking have been operationalized in the developmental literature. Given the complexity of the framework and characteristics of the developmental studies themselves, no overly broad generalizations about the development of rational thinking should be made. Currently, some developmental patterns are more clear than others. For example, research with belief bias syllogisms have consistently shown that children's performance improves with age, which is consistent with the positive correlations that are found between belief bias syllogisms performance and cognitive ability in adults (Stanovich &

West, 2008b). The picture with respect to many other developmental differences in the table (framing effects, for example) is much less clear.

Understanding the developmental trajectories of all of the components of rational thinking will require enormous scientific effort, much of which is still ahead of us. Because the operational measures that are used are often borrowed from adult studies, it is crucial that great care be taken to ensure that the adapted measures are age-appropriate for younger participants (Stanovich et al., 2011). As illustrated by the sampling of studies described in Table 2.1, there has been some initial progress in understanding the development of each rational thinking component. The listing of measurement paradigms and the corresponding sampling of findings in Table 2.1 highlight the fact that rational thinking in children is both measurable and, importantly, separable from cognitive ability as it is currently measured.

Author note

Preparation of this chapter was supported by grants from the Social Sciences and Humanities Research Council of Canada to Maggie Toplak and from the John Templeton Foundation to Keith Stanovich and Richard West. The opinions expressed in this publication are those of the authors and do not necessarily reflect the views of the John Templeton Foundation.

References

Ackerman, P. L. (1996). A theory of adult development: Process, personality, interests, and knowledge. *Intelligence, 22*, 227–257.

Acredolo, C., O'Connor, J., Banks, L., & Horobin, K. (1989). Children's ability to make probability estimates: Skills revealed through application of Anderson's functional measurement methodology. *Child Development, 60*, 933–945.

Agnoli, F. (1991). Development of judgmental heuristics and logical reasoning: Training counteracts the representativeness heuristic. *Cognitive Development, 6*, 195–217.

Ainslie, G. (1975). Specious reward: A behavioral theory of impulsiveness and impulse control. *Psychological Bulletin, 82*(4), 463–496.

Anderson, M. (2005). Marrying intelligence and cognition: A developmental view. In R. J. Sternberg & J. E. Pretz (Eds.), *Cognition and intelligence* (pp. 268–287). New York: Cambridge University Press.

Arkes, H. R., & Ayton, P. (1999). The sunk cost and Concorde effects: Are humans less rational than lower animals? *Psychological Bulletin, 125*, 591–600.

Arkes, H. R., & Blumer, C. (1985). The psychology of sunk cost. *Organizational Behavior and Human Decision Processes, 35*, 124–140.

Baron, J. (1995). Myside bias in thinking about abortion. *Thinking & Reasoning, 1*, 221–235.

Baron, J. (2008). *Thinking and deciding (Fourth Edition)*. Cambridge, MA: Cambridge University Press.

Baron, J., Granato, L., Spranca, M., & Teubal, E. (1993). Decision making biases in children and early adolescents: Exploratory studies. *Merrill-Palmer Quarterly, 39*, 22–46.

Bechara, A., Damasio, A. R., Damasio, H., & Anderson, S. (1994). Insensitivity to future consequences following damage to human prefrontal cortex. *Cognition, 50*, 7–15.

Benjamin, D., & Shapiro, J. (2005, February 25). Does cognitive ability reduce psychological bias? *Journal of Economic Literature, J24, D14, C91.*

Bernard, M. E., & Cronan, F. (1999). The child and adolescent scale of irrationality: Validation data and mental health correlates. *Journal of Cognitive Psychotherapy: An International Quarterly, 13*, 121–132.

Bjorklund, D. F. (2004). *Children's thinking: Cognitive development and individual differences*. Stamford, CT: Wadsworth.

Bolton, D., Dearsley, P., Madronal-Luque, R., & Baron-Cohen, S. (2002). Magical thinking in childhood and adolescence: Development and relation to obsessive compulsion. *British Journal of Developmental Psychology, 20*, 479–494.

Brady, J. E., Newcomb, A. F., & Hartup, W. W. (1983). Context and companion's behavior as determinants of cooperation and competition in school age children. *Journal of Experimental Child Psychology, 36*, 396–412.

Carroll, J. B. (1993). *Human cognitive abilities: A survey of factor-analytic studies*. Cambridge: Cambridge University Press.

Cattell, R. B. (1963). Theory for fluid and crystallized intelligence: A critical experiment. *Journal of Educational Psychology, 54*, 1–22.

Cattell, R. B. (1998). Where is intelligence? Some answers from the triadic theory. In J. J. McArdle & R. W. Woodcock (Eds.), *Human cognitive abilities in theory and practice* (pp. 29–38). Mahwah, NJ: Erlbaum.

Chen, H., & Volpe, R. P. (1998). An analysis of personal financial literacy among college students. *Financial Services Review, 7*(2), 107–128.

Chiesi, F., Primi, C., & Morsanyi, K. (2011). Developmental changes in probabilistic reasoning: The role of cognitive capacity, instructions, thinking styles, and relevant knowledge. *Thinking & Reasoning, 17*(3), 315–350.

Cohn, L. D., Macfarlane, S., Yanez, C., & Imai, W. K. (1995). Risk-perception: differences between adolescents and adults. *Health Psychology, 14*, 217–222.

Crone, E. A., & van der Molen, M. W. (2004). Developmental changes in real life decision making: Performance on a gambling task previously shown to depend on the ventromedial prefrontal cortex. *Developmental Neuropsychology, 25*, 251–279.

Damasio, A. R. (1994). *Descartes' error*. New York: Putnam.

Damasio, A. R. (1996). The somatic marker hypothesis and the possible functions of the prefrontal cortex. *Philosophical Transactions of the Royal Society (London), 351*, 1413–1420.

Damasio, A. R. (1999). *The feeling of what happens*. New York: Harcourt Brace.

Davidson, D. (1995). The representativeness heuristic and the conjunction fallacy effect in children's decision making. *Merrill-Palmer Quarterly, 41*, 328–346.

Dawes, R. M. (1998). Behavioral decision making and judgment. In D. T. Gilbert, S. T. Fiske & G. Lindzey (Eds.), *The handbook of social psychology (Vol. 1)* (pp. 497–548). Boston: McGraw-Hill.

De Neys, W., & Everaerts, D. (2008). Developmental trends in everyday conditional reasoning: The retrieval and inhibition interplay. *Journal of Experimental Child Psychology, 100*, 252–263.

De Neys, W., & Van Gelder, E. (2009). Logic and belief across the lifespan: The rise and fall of belief inhibition during syllogistic reasoning. *Developmental Science, 12*(1), 123–130.

De Neys, W., & Vanderputte, K. (2011). When less is not always more: Stereotype knowledge and reasoning development. *Developmental Psychology, 47*, 432–441.

Deary, I. J. (2001). *Intelligence: A very short introduction*. Oxford: Oxford University Press.

Denes-Raj, V., & Epstein, S. (1994). Conflict between intuitive and rational processing: When people behave against their better judgment. *Journal of Personality and Social Psychology, 66*, 819–829.

Desoete, A., & Roeyers, H. (2006). Metacognitive macroevaluations in mathematical problem solving. *Learning and Instruction, 16*, 12–25.

Donkers, B., Melenberg, B., & van Soest, A. (2001). Estimating risk attitudes using lotteries: A large sample approach. *Journal of Risk and Uncertainty, 22*, 165–195.

Evans, J. St. B. T., & Perry, T. (1995). Belief bias in children's reasoning. *Cahiers de Psychologie Cognitive, 14*, 103–115.

Evans, J. St. B. T., Barston, J., & Pollard, P. (1983). On the conflict between logic and belief in syllogistic reasoning. *Memory & Cognition, 11*, 295–306.

Facione, P. (1990). *Critical thinking: A statement of expert consensus for purposes of educational assessment and instruction (Executive Summary of the Delphi Report)*. La Cruz, CA: California Academic Press.

Falk, R., & Wilkening, F. (1998). Children's construction of fair chances: Adjusting probabilities. *Developmental Psychology, 34*, 1340–1357.

Fischhoff, B., Parker, A. M., de Bruin, W., Downs, J., Palmgren, C., Dawes, R., & Manksi, C. F. (2000). Teen expectations for significant life events. *Public Opinion Quarterly, 64*, 189–205.

Fishbein, E., & Schnarch, D. (1997). The evolution with age of probabilistic, intuitively-based misconceptions. *Journal for Research in Mathematics Education, 28*, 96–105.

Foltz, C., Overton, W. F., & Ricco, R. (1995). Proof construction: Adolescent development from inductive to deductive problem-solving strategies. *Journal of Experimental Child Psychology, 59*, 179–195.

Fong, G. T., Krantz, D. H., & Nisbett, R. E. (1986). The effects of statistical training on thinking about everyday problems. *Cognitive Psychology, 18*, 253–292.

Frederick, S. (2005). Cognitive reflection and decision making. *Journal of Economic Perspectives, 19*, 25–42.

Furlan, S., Agnoli, F., & Reyna, V. F. (2012). Children's competence or adults' incompetence: Different developmental trajectories in different tasks. *Developmental Psychology*. Advance online publication.

Garon, N., & Moore, C. (2004). Complex decision-making in early childhood. *Brain and Cognition, 55*, 158–170.

Geary, D. C. (2005). *The origin of the mind: Evolution of brain, cognition, and general intelligence*. Washington, DC: American Psychological Association.

Green, L., Fry, A. F., & Myerson, J. (1994). Discounting of delayed rewards: A life-span comparison. *Psychological Science, 5*(1), 33–36.

Halpern-Felsher, B. L., & Cauffman, E. (2001). Costs and benefits of a decision: Decision-making competence in adolescents and adults. *Applied Developmental Psychology, 22*, 257–273.

Handley, S. J., Capon, A., Beveridge, M., Dennis, I., & Evans, J. St. B. T. (2004). Working memory, inhibitory control and the development of children's reasoning. *Thinking & Reasoning, 10*, 175–195.

Hongwanishkul, D., Happaney, K. R., Lee, W. S. C., & Zelazo, P. D. (2005). Assessment of hot and cool executive function in young children: Age-related changes and individual differences. *Developmental Neuropsychology, 28*, 617–644.

Hooper, C. J., Luciana, M., Conklin, H. M., & Yarger, R. S. (2004). Adolescents' perfor-mance on the Iowa Gambling Task: Implications for the development of decision mak-ing and ventromedial prefrontal cortex. *Developmental Psychology, 40*, 1148–1158.

Hooper, S. R., & Layne, C. C. (1983). The common belief inventory for students: A mea-sure of rationality in children. *Journal of Personality Assessment, 47*, 85–90.

Horn, J. L., & Cattell, R. B. (1967). Age differences in fluid and crystallized intelligence. *Acta Psychologica, 26*, 1–23.

Horn, J. L., & Noll, J. (1997). Human cognitive capabilities: Gf-Gc theory. In D. Flanagan, J. Genshaft & P. Harrison (Eds.), *Contemporary intellectual assessment: Theories, tests, and issues* (pp. 53–91). New York: Guilford Press.

Jacobs, E., & Potenza, M. (1991). The use of judgment heuristics to make social and object decisions: A developmental perspective. *Child Development, 62*, 166–178.

Kahneman, D. (2011). *Thinking, fast and slow*. New York: Farrar, Straus & Giroux.

Kahneman, D., & Frederick, S. (2002). Representativeness revisited: Attribute substitu-tion in intuitive judgment. In T. Gilovich, D. Griffin & D. Kahneman (Eds.), *Heuristics and biases: The psychology of intuitive judgment* (pp. 49–81). New York: Cambridge University Press.

Kahneman, D., & Tversky, A. (1973). On the psychology of prediction. *Psychological Review, 80*, 237–251.

Kahneman, D., & Tversky, A. (1979). Prospect theory: An analysis of decision under risk. *Econometrica, 47*, 263–291.

Kahneman, D., & Tversky, A. (1984). Choices, values, and frames. *American Psychologist, 39*, 341–350.

Kahneman, D., & Tversky, A. (Eds.). (2000). *Choices, values, and frames*. Cambridge: Cambridge University Press.

Kirby, K. (1997). Bidding on the future: Evidence against normative discounting of delayed rewards. *Journal of Experimental Psychology: General, 126*(1), 54–70.

Kirkpatrick, L., & Epstein, S. (1992). Cognitive-experiential self-theory and subjective probability: Evidence for two conceptual systems. *Journal of Personality and Social Psychology, 63*, 534–544.

Klaczynski, P. A. (2001). Analytic and heuristic processing influences on adolescent rea-soning and decision making. *Child Development, 72*, 844–861.

Klaczynski, P. A., & Fauth, J. (1997). Developmental differences in memory-based intrusions and self-serving statistical reasoning biases. *Merrill-Palmer Quarterly, 43*, 539–566.

Klaczynski, P. A., & Gordon, D. H. (1996). Self-serving influences on adolescents' evalu-ations of belief-relevant evidence. *Journal of Experimental Child Psychology, 62*, 317–339.

Klaczynski, P. A., & Lavallee, K. L. (2005). Domain-specific identity, epistemic regu-lation, and intellectual ability as predictors of belief-based reasoning: A dual-process perspective. *Journal of Experimental Child Psychology, 92*, 1–24.

Klaczynski, P. A., & Narasimham, G. (1998). Development of scientific reasoning biases: Cognitive versus ego-protective explanations. *Developmental Psychology, 34*, 175–187.

Klahr, D., & Nigam, M. (2004). The equivalence of learning paths in early science instruc-tion: Effects of direct instruction and discovery learning. *Psychological Science, 15*(10), 661–667.

Klahr, D., Fay, A. L., & Dunbar, K. (1993). Heuristics for scientific experimentation: A developmental study. *Cognitive Psychology, 25*, 111–146.

Kokis, J., Macpherson, R., Toplak, M., West, R. F., & Stanovich, K. E. (2002). Heuristic and analytic processing: Age trends and associations with cognitive ability and cognitive styles. *Journal of Experimental Child Psychology, 83*, 26–52.

Koslowski, B., Condry, K., Sprague, K., & Hutt, M. (1996). Beliefs about covariation and causal mechanisms – Implausible as well as plausible. Experiment 4. In B. Koslowski, *Theory and evidence: The development of scientific reasoning.* MIT Press: Cambridge, MA.

Koslowski, B., Okagaki, L., Lorenz, C., & Umbach, D. (1989). When covariation is not enough: The role of causal mechanism, sampling method, and sample size in causal reasoning. *Child Development, 60,* 1316–1327.

Kreitler, S., & Kreitler, H. (1986). Development of probability thinking in children 5 to 12 years old. *Cognitive Development, 1,* 365–390.

Kühberger, A. (1998). The influence of framing on risky decisions: A meta-analysis. *Organizational Behavior and Human Decision Processes, 75,* 23–55.

Kuhn, D. (1991). *The skills of argument.* Cambridge: Cambridge University Press.

Kuhn, D., Phelps, E., & Walters, J. (1985). Correlational reasoning in an everyday context. *Journal of Applied Developmental Psychology, 6,* 85–97.

Lamm, C., Zelazo, P. D., & Lewis, M. D. (2006). Neural correlates of cognitive control in childhood and adolescence: Disentangling the contributions of age and executive function. *Neuropsychologia, 44*(11), 2139–2148.

Levin, I. P., & Hart, S. S. (2003). Risk preferences in young children: Early evidence of individual differences in reaction to potential gains and losses. *Journal of Behavioral Decision Making, 16,* 397–413.

Levin, I. P., Gaeth, G. J., Schreiber, J., & Lauriola, M. (2002). A new look at framing effects: Distribution of effect sizes, individual differences, and independence of types of effects. *Organizational Behavior and Human Decision Processes, 88,* 411–429.

Levin, I. P., Weller, J. A., Pederson, A. A., & Harshman, L. A. (2007). Age-related differences in adaptive decision making: Sensitivity to expected value in risky choice. *Judgment and Decision Making, 2*(4), 225–233.

Li, F., Cao, B., Li, Y., & Li, H. (2009). The law of large numbers in children's diversity-based reasoning. *Thinking & Reasoning, 15*(4), 388–404.

Lipko, A. R., Dunlosky, J., & Merriman, W. E. (2009). Persistent overconfidence despite practice: The role of task experience in preschoolers' recall predictions. *Journal of Experimental Child Psychology, 103,* 152–166.

Lubinski, D. (2004). Introduction to the special section on cognitive abilities: 100 years after Spearman's (1904) "General Intelligence, Objectively Determined and Measured". *Journal of Personality and Social Psychology, 86,* 96–111.

Luce, R. D., & Raiffa, H. (1957). *Games and decisions.* New York: Wiley.

Mandell, L. (2009). *The financial literacy of young American adults.* Washington, DC: JumpStart Coalition for Personal Financial Literacy.

Manktelow, K. I. (2004). Reasoning and rationality: The pure and the practical. In K. I. Manktelow & M. C. Chung (Eds.), *Psychology of reasoning: Theoretical and historical perspectives* (pp. 157–177). Hove, England: Psychology Press.

Markovits, H., & Bouffard-Bouchard, T. (1992). The belief-bias effect in reasoning: The development and activation of competence. *British Journal of Developmental Psychology, 10,* 269–284.

Markovits, H., & Thompson, V. (2008). Different developmental patterns of simple deductive and probabilistic inferential reasoning. *Memory & Cognition, 36*(6), 1066–1078.

Markovits, H., Venet, M., Janveau-Brennan, G., Malfait, N., Pion, N., & Vadeboncoeur, I. (1996). Reasoning in young children: Fantasy and information retrieval. *Child Development, 67,* 2857–2872.

Masnick, A. M., & Morris, B. J. (2008). Investigating the development of data evaluation: The role of data characteristics. *Child Development, 79*(4), 1032–1048.

Matsumoto, D., Haan, N., Yabrove, G., Theodorou, P., & Carney, C. C. (1986). Preschoolers' moral actions and emotions in prisoner's dilemma. *Developmental Psychology, 22,* 663–670.

Maule, J., & Villejoubert, G. (2007). What lies beneath: Reframing framing effects. *Thinking & Reasoning, 13,* 25–44.

Mischel, W., Ayduk, O., Berman, M. G., Casey, B. J., Gotlib, I. H., Jonides, J., et al. (2011). 'Willpower' over the life span: Decomposing self-regulation. *SCAN, 6,* 252–256.

Morsanyi, K., & Handley, S. J. (2008). How smart do you need to be to get it wrong? The role of cognitive capacity in the development of heuristic-based judgment. *Journal of Experimental Child Psychology, 99,* 18–36.

Moshman, D., & Franks, B. (1986). Development of the concept of inferential validity. *Child Development, 57,* 153–165.

Newman, R. S. (1984). Children's numerical skill and judgments of confidence in estimation. *Journal of Experimental Child Psychology, 37,* 107–123.

Over, D. E. (2004). Rationality and the normative/descriptive distinction. In D. J. Koehler & N. Harvey (Eds.), *Blackwell handbook of judgment and decision making* (pp. 3–18). Malden, MA: Blackwell Publishing.

Overman, W. H., Frassrand, K., Ansel, S., Trawalter, S., Bies, B., & Redmond, A. (2004). Performance on the Iowa card task by adolescents and adults. *Neuropsychologia, 42,* 1838–1851.

Pacini, R., & Epstein, S. (1999). The relation of rational and experiential information processing styles to personality, basic beliefs, and the ratio-bias phenomenon. *Journal of Personality and Social Psychology, 76,* 972–987.

Perkins, D. N. (1995). *Outsmarting IQ: The emerging science of learnable intelligence.* New York: Free Press.

Perkins, D. N., Farady, M., & Bushey, B. (1991). Everyday reasoning and the roots of intelligence. In J. Voss, D. Perkins & J. Segal (Eds.), *Informal reasoning and education* (pp. 83–105). Hillsdale, NJ: Erlbaum.

Pillow, B. H. (2002). Children's and adults' evaluation of the certainty of deductive inferences, inductive inferences, and guesses. *Child Development, 73,* 779–792.

Preece, P. F. W., & Baxter, J. H. (2000). Scepticism and gullibility: The superstitious and pseudo-scientific beliefs of secondary school students. *International Journal of Science Education, 22*(11), 1147–1156.

Prencipe, A., Kesek, A., Cohen, J., Lamm, C., Lewis, M. D., & Zelazo, P. D. (2006). Development of hot and cool executive function during the transition to adolescence. *Journal of Experimental Child Psychology, 108,* 621–637.

Rakow, T., & Rahim, S. B. (2010). Developmental insights into experience-based decision making. *Journal of Behavioral Decision Making, 23*(1), 69–82.

Reyna, V. F., & Brainerd, C. J. (2007). The importance of mathematics in health and human judgment: Numeracy, risk communication, and medical decision making. *Learning and Individual Differences, 17,* 147–159.

Reyna, V. F., & Ellis, S. (1994). Fuzzy-trace theory and framing effects in children's risky decision making. *Psychological Science, 5,* 275–279.

Reyna, V. F., & Farley, F. (2006). Risk and rationality in adolescent decision making. *Psychological Science in the Public Interest, 7*, 1–44.

Richardson, K. (1992). Covariation analysis of knowledge representation: Some developmental studies. *Journal of Experimental Child Psychology, 53*, 129–150.

Rodriguez, M. L., Mischel, W., & Shoda, Y. (1989). Cognitive person variables in delay of gratification of older children at risk. *Journal of Personality and Social Psychology, 57*, 358–367.

Savage, L. J. (1954). *The foundations of statistics.* New York: Wiley.

Schlottmann, A. (2000). Children's judgments of gambles: A disordinal violation of utility. *Journal of Behavioral Decision Making, 13*, 77–89.

Schlottmann, A. (2001). Children's probability intuitions: Understanding the expected value of complex gambles. *Child Development, 72*, 103–122.

Schlottmann, A., & Tring, J. (2005). How children reason about gains and losses: Framing effects in judgement and choice. *Swiss Journal of Psychology, 64*(3), 153.

Schneider, W., Visé, M., Lockl, K., & Nelson, R. O. (2000). Developmental trends in children's memory monitoring: Evidence from a judgment-of-learning task. *Cognitive Development, 15*, 115–134.

Shamosh, N. A., & Gray, J. R. (2008). Delay discounting and intelligence: A meta-analysis. *Intelligence, 36*, 289–305.

Shamosh, N. A., DeYoung, C. G., Green, A. E., Reis, D. L., Johnson, M. R., Conway, A. R. A., et al. (2008). Individual differences in delay discounting relation to intelligence, working memory, and anterior prefrontal cortex. *Psychological Science, 19*(9), 904–911.

Smith, L. (1999). Necessary knowledge in number conservation. *Developmental Science, 2*, 23–27.

Stanovich, K. E. (2006). Rationality and the adolescent mind. Editorial. *Psychological Science in the Public Interest, 7*, i–ii.

Stanovich, K. E. (2009). *What intelligence tests miss: The psychology of rational thought.* New Haven, CT: Yale University Press.

Stanovich, K. E. (2011). *Rationality and the reflective mind.* New York: Oxford University Press.

Stanovich, K. E., & West, R. F. (1997). Reasoning independently of prior belief and individual differences in actively open-minded thinking. *Journal of Educational Psychology, 89*, 342–357.

Stanovich, K. E., & West, R. F. (2007). Natural myside bias is independent of cognitive ability. *Thinking & Reasoning, 13*(3), 225–247.

Stanovich, K. E., & West, R. F. (2008a). On the failure of intelligence to predict myside bias and one-sided bias. *Thinking & Reasoning, 14*, 129–167.

Stanovich, K. E., & West, R. F. (2008b). On the relative independence of thinking biases and cognitive ability. *Journal of Personality and Social Psychology, 94*, 672–695.

Stanovich, K. E., Toplak, M. E., & West, R. F. (2008). The development of rational thought: A taxonomy of heuristics and biases. *Advances in Child Development and Behavior, 36*, 251–285.

Stanovich, K. E., West, R. F., & Toplak, M. E. (2011). The complexity of developmental predictions from dual process models. *Developmental Review, 31*, 103–118.

Steegen, S., & De Neys, W. (2012). Belief inhibition in children's reasoning: Memory-based evidence. *Journal of Experimental Child Psychology, 112*, 231–242.

Steinberg, L. (2010). A dual systems model of adolescent risk-taking. *Developmental Psychobiology, 52*, 216–224.

Steinberg, L., Graham, S., O'Brien, L., Woolard, J., Cauffman, E., & Banich, M. (2009). Age differences in future orientation and delay discounting. *Child Development, 80,* 28–44.

Strough, J., Mehta, C. M., McFall, J. P., & Schuller, K. L. (2008). Are older adults less subject to the sunk-cost fallacy than younger adults? *Psychological Science, 19,* 650–652.

Thompson, D. R., & Siegler, R. S. (2000). Buy low, sell high: The development of an informal theory of economics. *Child Development, 71,* 660–677.

Toplak, M. E., & Stanovich, K. E. (2003). Associations between myside bias on an informal reasoning task and amount of post-secondary education. *Applied Cognitive Psychology, 17*(7), 851–860.

Toplak, M. E., Liu, E., MacPherson, R., Toneatto, T., & Stanovich, K. E. (2007). The reasoning skills and thinking dispositions of problem gamblers: A dual-process taxonomy. *Journal of Behavioral Decision Making, 20*(2), 103–124.

Toplak, M. E., Sorge, G. B., Benoit, A., West, R. F., & Stanovich, K. E. (2010). Decision-making and cognitive abilities: A review of associations between Iowa Gambling Task performance, executive functions, and intelligence. *Clinical Psychology Review, 30,* 562–581.

Toplak, M. E., West, R. F., & Stanovich, K. E. (in press). Rational thinking and cognitive sophistication: Development, cognitive ability, and thinking dispositions. *Developmental Psychology.*

Tschirgi, J. E. (1980). Sensible reasoning: A hypothesis about hypotheses. *Child Development, 51,* 1–10.

Tullos, A., & Woolley, J. D. (2009). The development of children's ability to use evidence to infer reality status. *Child Development, 80*(1), 101–114.

Tversky, A., & Kahneman, D. (1974). Judgment under uncertainty: Heuristics and biases. *Science, 185,* 1124–1131.

Tversky, A., & Kahneman, D. (1981). The framing of decisions and the psychology of choice. *Science, 211,* 453–458.

Tversky, A., & Kahneman, D. (1983). Extensional versus intuitive reasoning: The conjunction fallacy in probability judgment. *Psychological Review, 90,* 293–315.

Weller, J. A., Levin, I. P., & Denburg, N. L. (2011). Trajectory of risky decision making for potential gains and losses from ages 5 to 85. *Journal of Behavioral Decision Making, 24,* 331–344.

Zimmerman, C. (2007). The development of scientific thinking skills in elementary and middle school. *Developmental Review, 27,* 172–223.

3 Gist processing in judgment and decision making

Developmental reversals predicted by fuzzy-trace theory

Rebecca B. Weldon, Jonathan C. Corbin and Valerie F. Reyna

This chapter will examine the role of gist in reasoning throughout human development. Fuzzy-trace theory (FTT) encompasses many domains of reasoning and decision making, including memory, cognition, and emotion (e.g., Reyna, 2012). A central construct of FTT is gist, a memory representation of the bottom-line meaning of an experience. Unlike information-processing theories that put intuition in the realm of mindless associationism (Reyna, 2012), a large corpus of data has demonstrated that gist-based intuition is an advanced form of reasoning that is largely unconscious and develops with experience (Reyna et al., 2011; Reyna & Farley, 2006).

We will begin by covering the research that has defined and validated gist as a psychological construct. We will review research that demonstrates independence between verbatim and gist memory traces (Reyna & Brainerd, 1995) as well as work that demonstrates independence between verbatim memory (memory for exact surface detail) and reasoning, and positive dependency between gist memory and reasoning (Reyna et al., 2011). Next, we will go over research that has uncovered the developmental trends pertaining to gist. Specifically, we will describe how gist memory development is reliant on experience, and therefore relationships between gist memory and reasoning grow with age (Brainerd, Reyna, & Ceci, 2008).

Given that gist reliance increases with age, we are then able to predict certain kinds of reasoning and decision-making errors that should also increase with age. These types of errors are called developmental reversals, because they contradict both conventional wisdom and traditional theories of reasoning that predict improvements in memory and reasoning with age (Reyna & Brainerd, 2011). Finally, we will demonstrate instances in which reliance on gist can improve decision making in the context of reasoning, expert decision making, and risky decision making.

Gist-verbatim distinction resolves reasoning/remembering paradoxes

Originally, the concepts of gist and verbatim memory were linked in psycholinguistics. It was believed that people initially encoded verbatim (surface form) traces, and then extracted the gist (essential meaning) from the verbatim trace (Clark & Clark, 1977). Once the gist was extracted, the verbatim traces were discarded, leaving an individual with long-term memory representations that only captured their overall gist of an experience. This contructivist notion that long-term memory is constructed from one's understanding was supported by evidence showing that when adults were given sentences like "The ants ate the sweet jelly" and "The sweet jelly was on the table," after a delay, they often would misreport seeing "The ants ate the sweet jelly that was on the table" (Bransford & Franks, 1971). However, these results conflicted with studies on the misinformation effect (Loftus, 1979), showing that as people age, their memory for detail improves, allowing them to better reject information that they had not actually experienced. The conclusions from constructivism and the misinformation paradigms appeared to be at odds.

The contradictory findings that suggest that both constructive and source-memory improve with age has been settled by work on predictions of FTT. This research suggests that both verbatim and gist traces improve with age, and that these memory traces operate independently and in opposition to one another (Reyna, 2012). In recognition memory experiments, when subjects are instructed to focus on matching the surface form of the initially-presented stimulus, they are more likely to rely on verbatim memory to reject meaning-consistent distractors (Brainerd, Reyna, Wright, & Mojardin, 2003). When prompted to focus on the items' meaning for recognition, people will rely on gist memory, and will therefore accept meaning-consistent distractors (Reyna & Kiernan, 1994; Garcia-Marques, Ferreira, Nunes, Garrido, & Garcia-Marques, 2010). These types of experiments have been run using word lists as well as brief narratives, linear syllogisms, and metaphorical language (Reyna & Kiernan, 1994, 1995).

In contrast to traditional dual-process models of reasoning, which consider intuition to be a lower-level process largely guided by associationist ideas, in FTT, gist is considered an advanced form of reasoning that relies on understanding and meaningful connections. Rather than consisting of rote associations formed by stimulus-response (or stimulus-stimulus) connections (delegated to verbatim memory in FTT), gist memory relies on context to get at the underlying structure of an experience. For example, Doherty, Campbell, Tsuji, and Phillips (2010) found that in a size discrimination task (e.g., judging the size of a circle), adults were more biased by contextual factors (the sizes of circles surrounding the target circle) when making their judgments (i.e., demonstrated the Ebbinghaus illusion) than children.

Reasoning and decision making as gist

Gist processes in reasoning and decision making

Many scholars have argued that logical reasoning consists of abstracting information like Suzie is taller than Nate, who is taller than Amanda, into A > B > C which allows one to deduce that A > C, regardless of contextual factors (that these are humans and we are comparing height; Khemlani & Johnson-Laird, 2012). The ability to deduce that if A > B and B > C, then A > C, is often referred to as "transitive reasoning." Some authors (Johnson-Laird, 2010) have pointed out that transitive reasoning is not completely content-free. Recent work suggests that transitive reasoning is comprised of abstract and associative processes, similar to the concepts of analytic and intuitive thinking that constitute the traditional dual-process model (Wright, 2012). Findings from tests of FTT predictions have shown that rather than relying on meaningless abstraction, people show a preference for gist-based reasoning. Reliance on gist is even more marked with respect to prag-matic inference (Reyna, 2012). For instance, making inferences about whether something is inside or outside depends on one's interpretation of context (e.g., I can be inside a tent while camping outside).

Fuzzy-trace theory has extended this work on gist reliance for transitive reason-ing to other areas of reasoning and decision making. A number of decision biases have been shown to be attributable to gist representation, memory retrieval errors as well as processing errors including class-inclusion illusions (i.e., ratio bias, conjunction and disjunction biases; Adam & Reyna, 2005; Reyna & Adam, 2003; Wolfe & Reyna, 2010) and framing effects (Kühberger & Tanner, 2010; Reyna & Brainerd, 1991; Reyna et al., 2011). Class-inclusion illusions such as the conjunc-tion bias are due to an individual's difficulty with keeping track of overlapping classes (i.e., processing errors), failures to retrieve relevant reasoning principles as well as a propensity to rely on a simplified gist representation set up by the particular problem (Reyna, 1991; Reyna & Brainerd, 2008). For instance, in the classic "Linda Problem," information pertaining to Linda's past and personality are given to subjects, which is meant to convey a strong gist that Linda cares about women's rights and is politically active. The majority of subjects respond that it is more likely for the following statement to be true: "Linda is a bank teller *and* Linda is active in the feminist movement" than for this statement to be true: "Linda is a bank teller." This effect is considered an "illusion," because subjects are fully aware of the fact that there are more bank tellers than feminist bank tellers, but they fail to retrieve the cardinality principle (e.g., if class B includes class A, then class B is larger (or equal to) class A and B). Given this problem, subjects tend to accept the overall gist of Linda while simultaneously neglecting the denominators for each class (feminist bank tellers and bank tellers; see Table 3.1 for examples of the conjunction task and other reasoning and decision-making tasks that typically result in fallacies).

As for risky-choice framing effects, research has shown that the preference for a sure option in the gain frame ($200 for sure) and the preference for a risky option in the loss frame (of equal expected value; e.g., 1/3 probability of gaining $600 and 2/3 probability of gaining $0) are due to reliance on the bottom-line gist of the problem. Prospect theory (Kühberger & Tanner, 2010) predicts that the fram-ing effect occurs due to the distortions in perceptions of the magnitudes of gains versus losses on a value function (e.g., 2/3 probability 600 people die), whereas FTT predicts that framing is due to a some–none comparison between the two options. Specifically, FTT predicts that the gist of the framing problem lies in the

Table 3.1 Reasoning and decision-making tasks used in recent developmental studies

Study	Task	Task example	Fallacy demonstrated
De Neys & Vanderputte (2010)	Base-rate	<<The experimenter puts 10 cards in front of the child>> "On these cards you can see nine girls and one boy. On the back side of each card there is a picture of each kid's favorite toy." "OK. As you can see, I'm shuffling the cards really well now, and then I put them in this bag. OK. Now, I'm going to draw one card from the bag without looking." "See, this is the back side of the card that I drew." (A truck appears.) "Now what do you think is most likely; will there be a boy or a girl on the front?"	Base-rate neglect: Because of the stereotype knowledge that boys like trucks more than girls, subjects will choose a boy. They will neglect the information that there are 90 percent girls in the group, and therefore the toy most likely belongs to a girl.
Morsanyi & Handley (2008)	Conjunction fallacy	Sarah is 12. She is very talkative and sociable. She goes to drama classes and she learns to play the guitar. She wants to be a pop singer or an actress. Read the following statements. Your task is to mark the statement that is the most likely to be true with number 1, the next one with number 2, and so on. Mark the statement which is the least likely to be true with number 4. (a) Sarah has lots of CDs and DVDs. (b) Sarah likes to cook. (c) Sarah has many friends at school. (d) Sarah likes to cook and she collects pop magazines.	The conjunction fallacy is committed by indicating that (d) is more likely than (b). It is more likely that Sarah likes to cook than that she likes to cook *and* collects pop magazines, since class A (those who like to cook) includes class B (those who like to cook and collect pop magazines). Therefore, distracted by the "pop music" theme, subjects fail to recognize that class A is larger (or equal to) class A and B.
Morsanyi & Handley (2008)	If-only fallacy	Tom went camping with his family and he put his bike inside the caravan. His mother told him to put his bike on the roof rack like his sister did, but he didn't listen to her. As luck would have it, Tom's bike got broken. Now listen to the next story. Robert went camping with his family and he put his bike inside the caravan. He had to put it in there because there was a kayak on the roof rack. As luck would have it, Robert's bike got broken. What do you think about the two stories?	The heuristic response here is to choose (a), indicating that the first boy (Tom) made a worse decision than the second boy (Robert). The third response is the normatively correct response.

Table 3.1 Continued

Study	Task	Task example	Fallacy demonstrated
		(a) Tom made a worse decision than Robert. (b) Robert made a worse decision than Tom. (c) It wasn't their fault, it was just bad luck.	
Morsanyi & Handley (2008)	Sunk cost fallacy	You bought a cinema ticket from your pocket money. You paid $5. You start to watch the movie, but after 5 minutes you are bored and the film seems pretty bad. How much longer would you continue to watch it? (a) 10 more minutes (b) 30 more minutes (c) Watch until the end Now listen to the next story. You've got a free cinema ticket voucher and you go to the cinema and get a ticket for it. You start to watch the movie, but after 5 minutes you are bored and the film seems pretty bad. How much longer would you continue to watch it? (a) 10 more minutes (b) 30 more minutes (c) Watch until the end	The sunk cost fallacy is committed when an individual chooses to sit through the movie after paying $5, simply because there was already money invested in the movie. However, sunk costs should be ignored, since they are not retrievable anymore. Therefore, decisions in the two situations should be the same whether one paid for the ticket or not. This is considered to be the normative answer.
Morsanyi & Handley (2008)	Syllogistic reasoning	Children were given instructions emphasizing that they needed to accept the premises as true even if they sounded strange or funny, and then they needed to think about whether the conclusion followed from the premises or not. They had three response options from which to choose: "yes," "no," and "not certain." The instructions stated that children needed to circle "yes" if they thought that the conclusion definitely followed from the premises, they needed to	The belief bias may lead subjects to circle "no," since one might neglect what was read in the premise of the story and go with what seems like a plausible explanation. The normative answer is "yes."

circle "no" if they thought that the conclusion did not follow from the premises, and they needed to circle "not certain" if they thought that it was likely the conclusion followed from the premises but that there was still a possibility it did not. Then the following script was read out loud:

Scientists have discovered a planet in our galaxy which has animals and plants living on it. This planet is similar to Earth in many respects, but there are some differences as well. I give you some questions.
Please choose the answer which describes the animals and plants living on this planet the best.
Here is an example for an unbelievable valid syllogism:
On this planet flowers have thorns on them.
Daffodils are flowers.

Does it follow that on this planet daffodils have thorns on them?
Yes/No/Not certain

zero-complement in the problem (e.g., 1/3 probability 0 people die)—information that is useless in terms of prospect theory's value function (as anything multiplied by zero is zero). Prospect theory predicts that standard framing effects should occur regardless of the presence of the zero-complement, whereas FTT predicts indifference if the zero-complement is not given. This prediction was initially borne out by demonstrating non-numerical framing effects. When the numbers were deleted from framing problems and replaced with the vague words, "some" and "none" framing effects actually increased (Reyna & Brainerd, 1991, 1995). These predictions have been tested by giving subjects framing problems and leaving out the zero-complement, leaving out the non-zero complement, or giving them full information. Evidence from multiple experiments has confirmed the FTT prediction of indifference when the zero-complement is removed from the problem, as well as strong framing effects when only the zero-complement is given (Kühberger & Tanner, 2010; Mandel, 2001; Reyna & Brainerd, 1991).

It is important to note that FTT predicts that the effects of adding or removing the zero-complement are not a result of increased or decreased ambiguity in the problem. Even with clear instructions that explain the nature of the problem (e.g., that a 1/3 probability of 600 saved implies a 2/3 probability of 0 saved), subjects still show the predicted effects (Chick, Reyna, Corbin, & Hsia, under review). Similar to the conjunction problem, the framing effect can be considered a cognitive illusion, or a selective attention effect. Despite having perfect information, emphasizing certain aspects of the problem (200 saved for sure vs. 1/3 probability nobody saved) will guide the subject's formation of an overall gist (some saved vs. none saved). Provided that subjects hold specific values (in this case that saving lives is important), they will end up basing their decisions on principles guided by their gist of the problem (saving some is better than saving none). Interestingly, FTT predicts that encoding and retrieval of the bottom-line gist will increase with age, which leads to the prediction that in very specific instances (like framing), bias will increase with age.

Developmental reversals in reasoning and decision making

Gist leads to developmental reversals

Up to this point, we have described how adults' tendency to rely on gist for reasoning and decision making can lead to biases like conjunction fallacies and framing effects. This section will focus on the development of these biases—namely, how gist processes develop with age and experience, and how this can actually lead to more bias in adults as compared to children in specific instances. It is important to note that information-processing (computational) approaches assume that reasoning becomes more complex and abstract with age, and therefore that people should become less biased overall with age (Reyna & Farley, 2006). The previously demonstrated biases fly in the face of such a picture of human rationality.

Human cognitive development: What develops?

Regarding age-related changes in cognitive ability, Jacobs and Klaczynski (2002) posed the simple question—"What develops?" Children exhibit competence in certain domains from a very young age. For example, children as young as 5 years old demonstrate an understanding of base rates (De Neys & Vanderputte, 2010) and the ability to derive accurate estimates of probability (Jacobs & Potenza, 1991; Reyna & Brainerd, 1994). However, different types of reasoning develop with age (see Table 3.2). Vosniadou and Ortony (1983) conducted a study to investigate whether children could differentiate between three different types of statements: literal (e.g, "A river is like a lake"), metaphorical (e.g., "A river is like a snake"), and anomalous (e.g., "A river is like a cat"). Children were randomly assigned to one of two tasks. In the comparison task, the researchers asked the children to say whether "A is like B or C." In the categorization task, they were asked to say whether "A is the same kind of thing as B or C." They found that children as young as 3 years old were able to distinguish the meaningful statements (literal and metaphorical) from the anomalous statements. The 4-year-old children were able to distinguish between literal and metaphorical statements (Vosniadou & Ortony, 1983).

Understanding that there is a "middle concept" continues to develop through elementary school. Rabinowitz and Howe (1994) investigated this ability in children who ranged in age from kindergarten to fifth grade. The researchers presented stimuli that was either perceptual (e.g., number of dots on a card, color, gap size in a circle) or conceptual (e.g., letters in the alphabet, age, body parts) in category. Stimuli were presented in varying orders from left to right, and subjects were instructed to "point to the middle thing." The experimental group was given more specific instructions regarding the stimulus (e.g., "point to the middle age"). The researchers observed an age-related improvement in the ability to identify the middle concept in the group of stimuli. Subjects in kindergarten and first grade performed near chance level. Performance was enhanced in the first and second grade group with the more specific cue.

Scalar implicature reasoning ability, understanding the implicit meaning that goes beyond a single utterance, also improves with age. Scalar implicature involves interpreting given information (e.g., "Some students did well on the exam") in a different way (one could interpret this example as "Not all students did well on the exam"). Barner, Brooks, and Bale (2011) examined this ability in 4-year-olds by manipulating specificity of information ("some" versus "dog and cat") and grammatical strengthening (whether the test question contained the word "only"). They found that 4-year-old children are unable to correctly answer questions about general "some" or "none" questions related to pictures (e.g., "Are only some of the animals sleeping?"), but they are accurate when specifics are given (e.g., "Are only the cat and the cow sleeping?"). These findings, along with the Rabinowitz and Howe (1994) findings described above, demonstrate that performance in these different tasks often depends on the cue provided. This suggests that reasoning ability may be guided by the retrieval of logical rules or principles learned over time (as discussed in Reyna & Brainerd, 2011).

Table 3.2 Developmental studies showing an increase in reasoning ability with age

Study	Reasoning ability	Age/grade range	Results
Barner, Brooks, & Bale (2011)	Scalar implicature (e.g., understanding that "Some of the toys are on the table" means that not all of the toys are on the table).	60 4-year-olds (27 girls, mean age = 4 years, 6 months).	4-year-old children are unable to correctly answer questions about general "some" or "none" questions related to pictures (e.g., "Are only some of the animals sleeping?"), but they are accurate in answering when specifics are given (e.g., "Are only the cat and the cow sleeping?").
Klaczynski & Cottrell (2004)	Sunk cost fallacy: the tendency to invest effort, time, or money into a decision because an investment has already been made.	Study 1: 30 7–8-year-olds, 34 10–11-year-olds, 30 13–14-year-olds. Study 2: 107 9-year-olds, 110 12-year-olds, 110 15-year-olds.	Analytic decision-making abilities improve from childhood to adolescence, especially for sunk cost decisions. Further, the tendency to commit the sunk cost fallacy decreases with age.
Rabinowitz & Howe (1994)	Development of a middle concept (the idea that given three stimuli, one can be identified as the "middle" stimulus).	Experiment 1: 20 boys and 20 girls from each grade: kindergarten (mean age = 65.5 months), first grade (76.8), second grade (91.3), third grade (102.2), fourth grade (113.9), fifth grade (130.9). Experiment 2: 36 boys and 36 girls from each grade: second grade (mean age = 96.1 months), third grade (106.4), fourth grade (118.9), fifth grade (131.9).	Children demonstrated an age-related improvement in ability to identify the middle concept in the group of stimuli (e.g., different sized squares, number of dots, letters, ages).
Vosniadou & Ortony (1983)	Metaphorical reasoning.	20 3-year-olds, 20 4-year-olds, 20 6-year-olds, 20 adults (undergraduate students).	Even children as young as 3 years old could distinguish literal and metaphorical statements (meaningful statements) from anomalous statements. 4-year-olds could distinguish between literal and metaphorical statements, while 3-year-olds could not.

In addition to reasoning ability, many cognitive processes related to reasoning and decision making improve across the lifespan, such as inhibitory control (Bunge & Wright, 2007; Reyna & Farley, 2006), working-memory capacity (Camos & Barouillet, 2011), and long-term memory (Crone, Wendelken, Donohue, Van Leijenhorst, & Bunge, 2006). Monitoring ability, involved in monitoring previous behavior and subsequent adjustment of future behavior, also develops with age. For example, age differences in decision making suggest that adolescents have difficulty anticipating the consequences of their actions, but that this continues to improve from ages 12 to 18 (Crone & Van der Molen, 2007).

Summary of developmental reversals in reasoning and decision making

Therefore, memory, inhibitory control, and various other cognitive abilities improve throughout the course of development into young adulthood (e.g., Bunge & Wright, 2007; Crone et al., 2006), but there is evidence for a simultaneous increase in certain cognitive biases that often interfere with reasoning ability and decision making (De Neys & Vanderputte, 2010; Furlan, Agnoli, & Reyna, 2012). Thus, improvements in the development of gist lead to developmental reversals in specific contexts (Reyna & Farley, 2006), as depicted in Table 3.3. For example, framing effects (the tendency to take risks when a problem is framed as a loss and avoid risks when the problem is framed as a gain) develop later in life (Reyna & Ellis, 1994). Children treat gains and losses the same, while adults do not. Take the classic Asian disease problem that involves saving or losing lives. The subject must choose between a safe option (e.g., losing 200 lives for sure) and a risky option of equal expected value (e.g., 1/3 chance of losing 600 lives, 2/3 chance of losing 0 lives). Adults process the gist of the sure versus risky option (lose some versus lose none), opting for losing none (thus, the risky option is selected in the *loss* frame). On the other hand, when the problem is framed as a gain and the subject must choose between saving some and saving none, saving some sounds preferable. Therefore this leads one to choose the safe option in the *gain* frame.

Other phenomena that increase with age include the conjunction fallacy and transitivity error. As previously mentioned, the conjunction fallacy refers to judging the probability of two events in conjunction as more likely to occur than either one of the individual events alone (e.g., given the information that John is a boring person, one has to rate the probability that John is in a rock band versus the probability that John is in a rock band *and* is an accountant. In this example, the stereotype of a rock band does not usually equate to "boring"). Transitivity error, committed when it is wrongly assumed that Jen is a friend of Barb if given information that Jen is a friend of Sarah and Sarah is a friend of Barb, increases with age (Markovits & Dumas, 1999).

In the same vein, biconditional reasoning error (assuming that "if A then B" means "if B then A") also increases with age (Reyna & Farley, 2006). Sunk cost fallacy, investing in something solely because of a previous investment of time, money, or energy, is more prevalent in adults than in younger children (for a review, see Arkes & Ayton, 1999; but see also Klaczynski & Cottrell, 2004).

Table 3.3 Developmental studies showing an increase in cognitive illusions with age

Study	Cognitive illusion(s)	Age/grade range	Results
Davidson (1991)	Noncompensatory decision making: failing to trade off, not taking all information (pro and con) into account.	40 2nd-grade, 40 5th-grade, and 40 8th-grade children and adolescents.	In searching for predecisional information, 2nd graders were exhaustive in their search for information, whereas older subjects' decision making involved the use of less demanding, noncompensatory strategies.
Davidson (1995)	Conjunction fallacy and the representativeness heuristic (see below): probability judgments about conjunctive descriptions (elderly person *and* playing soccer) are biased by perceptions of representativeness.	20 2nd-grade, 20 4th-grade, and 20 6th-grade children and adolescents.	Older subjects were more likely to use information consistent with stereotypes about the story characters. Conjunction problems, concerning how likely elderly or young adults would be to engage in certain occupations or activities, showed subjects to be susceptible to the conjunction fallacy and the representativeness heuristic.
De Neys (2007)	Monty Hall dilemma: choosing to remain with initial choice because of the false belief that probability of winning game is equal.	42 8th grade students (mean age = 12.9), 25 9th grade students (mean age = 14.6), 20 10th grade students (mean age = 15.75), 16 11th grade students (mean age = 16.56), 29 12th grade students (mean age = 17.7).	In playing the Monty Hall game in which switching options is advantageous, students in grades 9–12 selected the correct switching option less frequently than the 8th graders. Furthermore, the erroneous "chances are equal" belief increases with age.
De Neys & Vanderputte (2010)	Reliance on heuristics and stereotypes for judgments of probability rather than actual base rates.	54 preschoolers (mean age = 5.64), 46 third grade students (mean age = 8.75).	Older subjects were more likely to use stereotypes to make probability judgments rather than use numerical information about base rates. When there was no conflict between base rate and stereotype, the third graders outperformed the preschoolers. When there was a conflict, the preschoolers outperformed the third graders, indicating less of a reliance on heuristics.

Study	Bias/concept	Sample	Findings
Jacobs & Potenza (1991)	Representativeness heuristic: judgments of probability are based on stereotypes (biased beliefs applied to individuals seen as fitting the stereotype) rather than actual base rates or frequencies.	66 1st-grade, 86 3rd-grade, and 82 6th-grade children and adolescents, and a comparison sample of 95 college students.	Older subjects were more likely than younger ones to use stereotypes to make probability judgments rather than numerical information about base rates. When both stereotypical individuating and base-rate information was given, in the social domain, base-rate responses were chosen significantly less often with increasing age. Explanations based on perceived representativeness also increased in the social domain (but not in the object domain).
Klaczynski & Narasimham (1998)	Biconditional reasoning error: assuming "if A then B" implies "if B then A".	Study 1: 40 preadolescents (mean age = 10 years, 11 months), 40 middle adolescents (mean age = 14 years, 1 month), and 40 older adolescents (mean age = 17 years, 1 month). Study 2A: 56 college students (mean age = 22 years, 10 months). Study 2B: 64 college students (mean age = 19 years, 2 months).	Reasoning fallacies increased with age on problems containing causal conditional relations; the generation of plausible alternative antecedents is more difficult on causal than on permission conditional rules. Conditional (if-then) reasoning was used to solve permission problems, and biconditional reasoning was more typically used on causal problems. If the truth rules of conditional reasoning are imposed to evaluate performance, deductive-reasoning competence simultaneously increases (on permission problems) and declines (on causal problems) with age.
Markovits & Dumas (1999)	Transitivity error: treating relations such as "is a friend of" as though they were transitive like length.	Study 1: 360 6–9-year-old children. Study 2: 114 7-, 9-, and 11-year-old children and adolescents.	Transitive interferences using both a linear dimension (A is longer than B) and a nonlinear dimension (A and B are friends) were examined. Older subjects wrongly inferred that if A is a friend of B and B is a friend of C, then A is a friend of C. Younger children did not make that error.
Mata, Von Helversen, & Rieskamp (2011)	Adaptive strategy selection: employing an information-intensive strategy, in which all available information is incorporated versus an information-frugal strategy, in which only important information is used.	50 9–10-year-olds, 50 11–12-year-olds, 50 adults (mean age = 22.7 years).	Youngest subjects (9–10-year-olds) tended to adopt an information-intensive strategy that incorporates all available information in the environment while older children tend to narrow their selection of information.

Table 3.3 Continued

Study	Cognitive illusion(s)	Age/grade range	Results
Morsanyi & Handley (2008)	Belief bias (acceptance of a believable conclusion irrespective of logical validity), if-only fallacy (the belief that a negative outcome could have been prevented), conjunction fallacy (the belief that the likelihood of two events occurring in conjunction is greater than the likelihood of either event occurring alone).	42 girls and 42 boys between the ages of 5 years 2 months and 11 years 7 months (mean age = 8 years 6 months).	Increase in heuristic responding with age for all three types of tasks (in other words, susceptibility to the if-only fallacy, conjunction fallacy, and belief bias increased with age).
Reyna & Ellis (1994)	Framing effect: choosing a sure option when outcomes are described as gains and a gamble option when the objectively identical outcomes are described as losses.	28 preschoolers (mean age = 4 years, 8 months), 40 2nd grade (mean age = 8 years, 0 months), and 43 5th grade (mean age = 11 years, 1 month) children and adolescents.	Older subjects were more likely to assimilate quantitative differences and show framing effects. Younger subjects responded to quantitative differences (i.e., in objective probabilities and magnitudes of outcomes), and did not exhibit framing effects (risk avoidance for gains, risk seeking for losses).
Weller, Levin, & Denburg (2011)	Preference effect: showing preference for risk avoidance in gain frame and risk taking in loss frame.	743 subjects, ages 5 to 85 years old. Subjects were divided into six age groups: 37 5–7-year-olds, 111 8–11-year-olds, 358 18–22-year-olds, 106 24–44-year-olds, 61 44–64-year-olds, 61 65–85-year-olds.	Older subjects (ages 18 and older) were more likely to show standard framing preference effects. Younger subjects (age groups 5–7 years old and 8–10 years old) were more likely to treat the gain and loss problems similarly, demonstrating more rational decision making.

Kahneman and Tversky (1973) conducted a simple base rate task in which subjects' responses can be influenced by stereotype knowledge. For example, a subject is presented with a base rate of 80 football players and 20 golfers. That is, the subject is told that there is a sample of 100 people, 80 of whom are football players and 20 of whom are golfers. Therefore, the subject receives the probabilities and understands that there are more football players than golfers in the sample. The subject is then given a description of a person. This person enjoys classical music, fine wine, and is often dressed in white shorts and a polo shirt. The subject is then asked, is it more likely that this person is a football player or a golfer?

Based on probability, it is more likely that this person is a football player. However, Kahneman and Tversky (1973) conducted a simple base rate task and found that adults tend to neglect base rate information in favor of stereotypes. That is, adults will opt for the "golfer" answer based on societal stereotypes that a golfer may be more likely to embody certain characteristics such as an appreciation of wine and classical music.

Interestingly, Jacobs and Potenza (1991) showed that adults and children differ in their performance in this task. A study that they conducted with children showed that 7-year-olds actually tend to rely on base rates over stereotypes, therefore resulting in higher accuracy than the adults (e.g., if a 7-year-old doesn't know what a stereotypical football player does or dresses like, but knows that there are four times as many football players as golfers in the sample, he or she will rely on the base rate to make the decision). The absence of stereotype knowledge actually benefits children for reasoning ability, because they are not biased by experience in the way that adults are. Their research was important in demonstrating that stereotype knowledge is probably an important determinant of children's reasoning ability.

In the study conducted by Jacobs and Potenza (1991), the authors concluded that children tended to favor the base rate response, therefore outperforming adults and older children who tended to rely on stereotype knowledge. Actual stereotype knowledge, however, was only inferred. Thus, De Neys and Vanderputte (2010) set out to test the hypothesis that younger children do not have knowledge of stereotypes that older children or adults have, and that this can, in turn, influence reasoning ability, sometimes in their favor. The researchers followed up on the Jacobs and Potenza (1991) investigation of the effects of stereotype knowledge in base rate tasks. They took a sample of 5-year-old preschoolers and a sample of 8-year-old third graders. De Neys and Vanderputte varied stereotype familiarity in the youngest group of 5-year-old preschoolers, so that some of the stereotypes presented were familiar to this age group, and some were unfamiliar (but were familiar to the 8-year-old third grade age group). They also manipulated conflict, so that the cued heuristic and base rate triggered the same response (no-conflict condition) or different responses (conflict condition).

An interesting pattern of performance differences was observed. For the unfamiliar no-conflict problems, 8-year-olds had greater accuracy than 5-year-olds. The logic here is that the 8-year-olds probably relied on heuristic knowledge, and this worked in their favor in the no-conflict condition. Since heuristic processing is less taxing than analytic processing, the 8-year-olds have the advantage in this condition. However, the conflict condition presented a very interesting result. On unfamiliar conflict problems (unfamiliar stereotype for 5-year-olds but familiar stereotype for 8-year-olds), they found that the 5-year-olds outperformed the 8-year-olds. However, when the stereotype was familiar to both groups (5- and 8-year-olds), the age-related differences were not as robust, suggesting that heuristics started to have an effect on the 5-year-olds as well. De Neys and Vanderputte conclude that perhaps it is the case that *less* of a reliance on heuristics in the younger group actually results in *more* logical reasoning. These findings converge nicely with FTT predictions that gist processes develop with age, supporting the idea that the development of gist processes can actually lead to more bias (and decreased reasoning performance) in certain situations (Reyna, 2012).

An assessment of decision making across development prompts us to again revisit Jacobs and Klaczynski's (2002) question as to what exactly develops as we age. So many cognitive processes contribute to decision making: attention, inhibitory control, and memory are only a few examples. Thus, it is critically important to dissociate these contributing factors when we talk about the development of decision making. Disentangling memory and decision making was the aim of a study conducted by Van Duijvenvoorde, Jansen, Bredman, and Huizenga (2012). The researchers used a modified version of the classic Iowa Gambling Task (IGT) to investigate the role of memory in age-related changes in decision making. The typical finding in the IGT is that one's performance improves with age. However, what is it about the IGT that is difficult for children? The authors aimed to investigate the role of memory by presenting two different versions of a gambling task: an informed version and a non-informed version. The non-informed version was conducted in the way the IGT is normally conducted: subjects are presented with zero information about probabilities. They must use working-memory processes to figure out what decks (A, B, C, or D) are most advantageous to draw from (i.e., result in the lowest gains and lowest losses) versus a deck that will be less advantageous to draw from (because it results in high gains and high losses). The informed version gave subjects access to information about the gains, losses, and frequency of losses.

This study demonstrated that the simple inclusion of a memory aid resulted in the reduction in age-related differences on the IGT. The authors showed that advantageous decision making *could* take place in children younger than 12 years old. This study demonstrates the importance of measuring the contributions of both verbatim and gist memory processes in decision making; if these processes are not yet fully developed (as in children and adolescents), decision making can suffer. However, by giving access to the information, the age-related differences in advantageous decision making were significantly reduced. Further research will have to examine what this means about decision making in children and adults, and whether actual decision-making processes are more similar across ages than we may have initially thought.

In addition to memory, there are other cognitive processes that contribute to decision making. Deriving the meaning of an option (e.g., whether it is a gain or loss) and calculating the expected value (EV) are two important components of decision making. Individuals must compute expected values when calculating the risk of a sure versus a risky option, and the ability to understand EV has been observed in children as young as 4 years old (Schlottmann & Tring, 2005). Weller et al. (2011) used a task called the "Cups" task (Levin & Hart, 2003) to investigate risk taking for gains versus losses, and EV sensitivity as a function of age. The Cups task involves two different types of framing (gain, loss), three levels of probability (0.20, 0.33, 0.50), and three levels of outcome magnitude for the risky option (2, 3, 5 quarters). The sure option was always the same reward: 1 quarter. The expected value for sure and risky options was either equal, risk-advantageous (advantageous for the risky option), or risk-disadvantageous (advantageous for the sure option). The researchers varied the outcome magnitudes and expected values. Subjects had to select the risky or riskless option on each trial. The gain and loss trials were grouped into blocks, and gain and loss block orders were counterbalanced across subjects. The Cups task was used in this experiment because it allows for the separation of response to risky gains and response to risky losses. The researchers examined decision-making tendencies across the entire lifespan, ages 5 to 85, aiming to understand at what age it is that we make the most rational choices.

Weller et al. (2011) found that risk taking differed depending on whether the subject was taking a risk to achieve a gain or avoid a loss. They found that risk taking in the gain frame decreased over the lifespan. Risk taking in the loss domain, however, was relatively stable across age. Expected value sensitivity showed an inverted-U-shaped function, suggesting that EV sensitivity increases from childhood to adulthood, and then decreases again in the older adult years.

Importantly, the Weller et al. (2011) study revealed that children treat gains and losses equally. So, even if children tended to be more risky, they treated both conditions similarly, making a consistent decision to take a risk when the problem was phrased as either a gain *or* a loss, therefore demonstrating a more rational decision-making approach than that of the adults (who showed a typical "preference shift" effect, demonstrating significantly greater risk taking for losses than for gains). Therefore, the Weller et al. (2011) results convey that again, the developmental reversal of cognitive ability is observed, this time in the rational decision-making domain. Furthermore, these findings are consistent with observations of increased framing effects with age and with other FTT predictions (Reyna, 2012), as discussed at more length in the next section.

Reasoning and decision making across the lifespan: inconsistencies with traditional dual-process models of cognitive development

The observation of developmental reversals suggests that predictions pertaining to cognitive development are not straightforward. They are, in fact, relatively complex (Stanovich, West, & Toplak, 2011). Dual-process models cannot perfectly account for the complexity of human cognitive development. The classic dual-process model depicts two types of processing: System 1 and System 2. System 1 processing is automatic and emotional, an evolutionarily primitive process. System 2 (labeled according to its recency in evolution) processing is analytic, working-memory dependent, and less biased by emotion. System 2 also includes inhibitory functions, allowing it to override System 1 responses (whereas FTT models inhibition as a third, independent process). However, cognitive development does not necessarily follow a linear trajectory: It has been repeatedly demonstrated that developmental reversals occur in decision making (Reyna & Farley, 2006). Dual-process models assume that System 2 reasoning is more sophisticated and rational, and thus "better." Therefore, an important distinction between dual-process models and FTT is the interpretation of the more advantageous "system" of processing. While dual-process models assume that advanced thinking is rational and analytic, FTT predicts that advanced reasoning is gist-based and intuitive (Reyna, 2012).

Fuzzy-trace theory distinguishes between two types of processing: verbatim and gist. Similar to other dual-process theories, verbatim processing is more precise, relying on abstract quantitative analysis. Unlike dual-process theories, gist is not simply intuition, but is a meaningful bottom-line representation. Individuals can encode multiple gists at varying levels of specificity. They tend to rely on the simplest gist that task demands permit. If a problem can be solved with the most basic type of gist, then that is the type of reasoning selected. As the task requires more precision, one must apply more complex representations (up to the exact verbatim representation).

Fuzzy-trace theory can tell us something about the susceptibility to heuristics and biases as we age, given that there seems to be this increase in gist processing with age. This naturally prompts further questions about the development of reasoning and decision making. Does relying on gist processing diminish our reasoning ability? In light of the initial question as to what develops with age, does reasoning get better or worse across development? How does gist fit into this picture? The following section describes how gist processing actually protects against risk in real-world decision making.

Fuzzy-trace theory: gist processing can lead to better outcomes in risky decision making

According to FTT, people encode multiple mental representations of information in parallel, and these mental representations can range from verbatim (the literal stimulus) to gist (the basic meaning of the stimulus). Gist processing often results in better outcomes than verbatim processing, and this has been demonstrated in a number of domains (Mills, Reyna, & Estrada, 2008; Reyna et al., 2011). In the following section, we will focus on the role of gist processing in real-life risky decision making.

It is remarkable that even slight changes in the wording of a stimulus can elicit different types of information processing, and furthermore, that this effect on information processing has subsequent effects on behavior. This phenomenon has been demonstrated using the classic framing task (Tversky & Kahneman, 1986), in which individuals tend to make choices differently depending on how a set of outcomes is framed (as a gain versus a loss), violating principles of human rationality. As mentioned earlier, the difference in preference for risky versus safe options based on how the question is framed is often referred to as the framing effect. Fuzzy-trace theory predicts that framing occurs when individuals rely on bottom-line categorical distinctions between options rather than exact numerical outcomes (Kühberger & Tanner, 2010; Reyna & Brainerd, 1991). Thus, although framing effects are considered irrational in a traditional expected value approach, FTT research has found evidence that supports a protective role of qualitative gist in real-life risky decision making (Mills et al., 2008; Reyna et al., 2011), as we proceed to discuss in further detail.

Notably, it has been discovered that type of information processing (precise detail versus fuzzy gist) actually affects the likelihood of taking a risk. Previous research has examined questions of this nature, that is, how it is that eliciting different types of information processing affects risk-taking behavior. Mills et al. (2008) examined the relationship between risk perception and risk taking. The main theoretical rationale for their study derived from previous studies that presented contradictory findings regarding the relationship between risk perception and risk taking. Some literature supports a negative correlation between risk perception and risk taking (the greater the perceived risk, the *less* likely one is to take a risk; for a review, see Reyna & Farley, 2006) while there is also evidence for a positive correlation between risk perception and risk taking (the greater the perceived risk, the *more* likely one is to take a risk; Johnson, McCaul, & Klein, 2002). Mills et al. (2008) set out to examine this contradiction by aiming to understand what types of information processing (qualitative, gist-based versus quantitative, verbatim-based) may result in a negative versus positive correlation. They employed behavioral measures that varied by cue type (specific or global) and response precision (verbatim or gist). The rationale here is based on previous research that suggests that these two factors influence type of retrieval (verbatim versus gist; Reyna & Brainerd, 1995). For example, subjects would either be asked a specific question about previous sexual activity (e.g., "I am likely to have an STD by age 25") or a more general, gist-based question (e.g., "If you keep having unprotected sex, risk adds up and you will get an STD"). The purpose of varying cue and response precision was to elicit different types of processing (verbatim versus gist) and then examine subsequent effects on risk-taking behavior, specifically, behavioral intentions to have sex.

Interestingly, Mills et al. (2008) did find differences in the correlation between risk perception and risk taking depending upon the *type of information processing* elicited by the cue. They found that the measures that cued qualitative, gist-based processing resulted in a negative correlation between risk perception and risk taking. The notion here is that decision makers take the bottom-line gist of the information presented (e.g., rating agreement with "Better to not have sex than risk getting HIV-AIDS"; the bottom-line gist here is that HIV-AIDS is categorically "bad" and should therefore be avoided). This qualitative sort of processing will thus lead to decreased risk taking and increased risk perception. On the other hand, quantitative, verbatim-based processing of risk triggered by more specific cues (e.g., rating the probability of the statement "I am likely to have an STD in the next 6 months") results in the retrieval of specific memories of past behavior. Therefore, low-risk individuals will retrieve memories of their low-risk behavior (e.g., watching a movie alone on a Saturday night), and thus rate lower on both risk perception *and* risk-taking behavior. High-risk individuals will retrieve specific memories based on the cue (e.g., unprotected sex the week before), and therefore will rate higher on both perception of the risk and risk-taking behavior. Therefore, Mills et al. (2008) concluded that individuals are more risk-averse (less likely to take a risk) while engaging in gist (versus verbatim) processing, as evidenced by the negative correlation between risk perception and risk taking when gist processing was elicited.

The idea that gist-based, qualitative processing has a protective effect on risk taking is interesting, yet somewhat counterintuitive. One may reason that "more information is better," and thus assume that a comprehensive, verbatim-based approach would lead to optimal decision making and behavior. However, verbatim processing is actually maladaptive in the long run, despite appearances. Verbatim processing actually promotes risk taking through a focus on the quantitative differences between reward in the sure versus gamble option when the net consequences are equal. That is, subjects may focus on the risk of a single act versus a cumulative risk, suggesting that risk is very low and that the reward in the gamble option actually outweighs any small risk incurred by one act (e.g., having unprotected sex). Therefore, the observations that suggest that gist processing is correlated with lower risk taking argue for a bottom-line meaning approach when it comes to information processing and decision making.

The observed age difference in type of information processing certainly forms a convincing argument for gist-based information processing. The developmental literature and FTT both suggest that adults tend to engage in gist processing more than adolescents (Reyna et al., 2011). It is suggested that there is a reliance on verbatim processing early on in development (Reyna & Ellis, 1994). Then, verbatim and gist processing both improve throughout development, but there is an increased reliance on gist processing with age (Brainerd et al., 2008). It has been repeatedly demonstrated that mature decision makers (e.g., adults) process risk as categorical and tend to avoid risk. That is, adults who tend to rate high on questions like "It only takes once" and "Even low risk adds up to 100 percent if you keep doing it" have better health outcomes (Mills et al., 2008; Reyna et al., 2011). Therefore, the benefit of a risky decision (e.g., unprotected sex) does not outweigh the cost (e.g., possible exposure to HIV-AIDS). Once an individual gains expert knowledge about something, there is an increase in the likelihood of gist-based processing. However, it is important to note that one does not necessarily need knowledge to show increases in gist-based intuition with development (Reyna, 2012).

In contrast to adults, young children and adolescents rely on processing risk and reward in a *quantitative* manner, calculating the costs and benefits of choices. Younger children (of preschool age) have demonstrated the disappearance of the framing effect (Reyna & Ellis, 1994). This finding has been explained by suggesting that children tend to engage in verbatim, quantitative processing. Reyna and Ellis (1994) used a spinner task with brightly colored superballs as the prizes. Children could opt to pick a sure option or spin the wheel to determine whether they would win a prize or not. By calculating the equal net consequences across frames, the preschoolers did not differ in the number of risky options that they select in the gain frame versus the loss frame. Older children (second graders) show a reverse framing effect, selecting the risky option in the *gain* frame more often than in the loss frame. This can be partially explained by a greater reward sensitivity in this age group. The primary focus is on the reward. Therefore, when options are presented as gains, children and adolescents will be more likely to select a risky option. Fifth graders showed a similar reverse framing effect that varied as a function of reward size difference (e.g., winning 1 superball prize versus 2 superball prizes yielded smaller reverse framing effects than winning 30 superball prizes versus 60 superball prizes), suggesting that there is reliance on quantitative processing in children that is different from the gist-based processing reliance observed in adults (Reyna & Ellis, 1994). This was replicated using different types of stimuli. Further, there are two additional studies replicating this reverse framing effect (Reyna & Farley, 2006).

Thus, the intuition, meaning-based approach suggests that acquiring the bottom-line gist may equate to less information but actually results in better outcomes, as FTT suggests (Mills et al., 2008). Reyna et al. (2011) presented the first study of risk taking in adults versus adolescents using the classic framing task. Reward and risk were manipulated factorially, so that the effects of risk and reward could be dissociated. Therefore, all combinations of risk and reward were possible (e.g., low risk–high reward, high risk–low reward, etc.). Options were presented as gains or losses. Behavioral measures included the Behavioral Activation Scale and Behavioral Inhibition Scale, which measure approach behavior and inhibitory behavior, respectively, and the Sensation Seeking Scale. Measures from the framing task and the other behavioral measures were then related to measures of real-life sexual behavior (using a sexual history and intentions scale and self-reported risky behavior). Adolescents exhibited reverse framing effects, in that they tended to opt for the risky option in the *gain* frame, rather than the loss frame, providing further support for quantitative, verbatim-based processing in younger individuals. Furthermore, the researchers investigated real-life risk taking through self-reported risky behaviors and behavioral intentions to engage in sex. They found that framing responses correlated with measures of real-life risky sexual behavior (Reyna et al., 2011). Importantly, evidence for real-life implications of this nature is extremely valuable for further understanding the causal link between information processing and decision making.

Brain changes throughout development

The empirical findings that illustrate the advantages of gist processing, as well as the idea that reliance on gist processing increases with age, forms a story that aligns nicely with the major brain changes that occur throughout development (Chick & Reyna, 2012). Two major brain changes that occur during adolescence correlate with the behavioral findings related to gist-based processing: the pruning of synapses and grey matter and the increase in fiber tracts in the brain. Synaptic pruning refers to the reduction in the overall number of synapses, which in turn results in more efficient synaptic connectivity. Myelinated axons are those wrapped with a fatty white matter substance (myelin) that results in a faster speed of information transfer down axons. Therefore, the process of myelination results in increased overall speed of neural processing. Thus, there is a correlation between behavioral and brain evidence for changes in information processing throughout development (see also Reyna, 2011). That is, the observation that adults tend to rely on gist processing while adolescents tend to rely on quantitative, verbatim-based thinking (Brainerd et al., 2008), and that processing becomes increasingly "gistified" with age, aligns with what we know about changes in the brain during adolescence and young adulthood.

Adults engage in less risk-taking behavior

Given the link between gist processing and protection against risk, and the findings that gist processing increases throughout development (Brainerd et al., 2008), the relationship between age and risk taking is not surprising. Adults get to the bottom line (gist) of risk and thus exhibit less risky decision making. Adolescents, on the other hand, tend to calculate risk in a quantitative manner, and end up engaging in more risky decision making. Intuitively, it does not make sense that quantitative processing would result in less rational decision making and more risk taking. However, imagine the example of an adolescent determining whether to have unprotected sex. One major risk of unprotected sex is contracting HIV. With HIV, there is a low probability of transmission. Therefore, if one is to quantitatively compute the benefits versus the risks of unprotected sex, the benefits of sex outweigh the risk of contracting HIV. So quantitatively calculating this would result in greater expected utility for the risky option (and therefore, adolescent will opt for unprotected sex). Adults, who tend to rely on gist-based categorical thinking, would simply determine "HIV = bad risk" and would therefore opt for *not* engaging in unprotected sex (Reyna & Farley, 2006; Reyna et al., 2011).

Thus, type of information processing (gist-based versus verbatim-based) has a significant effect on decision making and risk taking behavior. This research has extensive implications for various health behaviors and health outcomes. Gist processing may be considered in future educational domains, eliciting a type of mental representation of information that has proven to be protective against risk taking. This knowledge is especially valuable in relation to a particularly vulnerable period of development, that of adolescence.

Conclusion

In this chapter, we have reviewed evidence for the important role that intuition (i.e., gist) plays in advanced reasoning and decision making. This evidence is in discordance with more traditional notions of reasoning that assume that rational, analytic processing produces optimal responses. We have included reasoning and decision-making findings that highlight the central role that intuition plays in advanced reasoning.

Type of information processing (qualitative, gist-based versus quantitative, verbatim-based) largely affects reasoning and decision making. We have explained the transformation from traditional concepts of gist and verbatim processing to current empirical findings, and how these findings can be explained by FTT. In contrast to traditional dual-process models of reasoning that associate gist and intuition with a lower-level process, FTT takes a different stance on intuition. According to FTT, gist is considered a higher form of reasoning that relies on understanding and meaning. Thus, FTT predicts that gist-based processing can constitute advanced reasoning, a notion contrary to standard dual-process model beliefs.

We have also highlighted findings of developmental reversal that can be attributed to the increase in specific biases in reasoning over the course of development. De Neys and Vanderputte (2010) demonstrated a developmental reversal in base rate tasks due to an increase in stereotype biases with age, as adults have to deal with managing conflict between actual base rates and stereotypes. Other studies investigate decision making across development. In some ways, decision making becomes "better"—adults may tend to make decisions that are not as risky as adolescents (Weller et al., 2011). However, in other ways, children and adolescents exhibit more rational behavior, outperforming adults on tasks that may elicit biases and heuristics that children are not as susceptible to (De Neys & Vanderputte, 2010; Reyna & Farley, 2006). Other examples of developmental reversal, such as increases in the conjunction fallacy (Reyna & Farley, 2006), availability heuristic, and biconditional reasoning error (Davidson, 1995) with age suggest that the classic dual-process model is not sufficient to explain some of the counterintuitive findings of cognitive development. The classic dual-process model argument suggests that System 1 reasoning, characterized by more automatic, evolutionarily primitive processing, develops early in life. System 2 reasoning, analytic and more controlled processing, develops later in life with the development of prefrontal circuitries, along with working-memory capacity and cognitive control. The developmental reversals that have been repeatedly observed clash with these theories. Enter FTT, a theory that outlines how gist can explain increases in bias with development (Reyna, 2012), but also how the development of gist can be advantageous (e.g., resulting in less unhealthy risk taking; e.g., Mills et al., 2008; Reyna et al., 2011).

As we have discussed, FTT accounts for both the appearance of reasoning biases and the improvements in reasoning observed across development (Reyna & Brainerd, 2011). According to FTT, people encode multiple mental representations of information in parallel, and these mental representations can range from verbatim (the literal stimulus) to gist (the basic meaning of the stimulus). Gist processing actually results in less risk taking, and is therefore the superior form of processing. Verbatim processing may give the appearance of advanced reasoning and decision making under certain conditions, but is actually sub-optimal and maladaptive (Reyna et al., 2011).

Decision making is also heavily influenced by verbatim versus gist processing. Interestingly, eliciting different types of processing through gist or verbatim types of cues can result in varied propensities for risk taking. Mills et al. (2008) cued quantitative processing and qualitative processing in subjects, and found that subjects were more likely to engage in risky sexual behavior when given specific verbatim cues that would be more likely to engage specific memories of specific events in one's life. Meanwhile, subjects rated lower on risk-taking measures when qualitative processing was cued.

Decision making research has focused on framing tasks, in which sure and risky options are framed as a loss or a gain. Reyna et al. (2011) found that risk-taking on a framing task correlated with real life risk-taking behavior. Although framing effects are normatively irrational, standard framing effects (due to reliance on gist) were predictive of superior decision making in real-life situations, whereas reverse framing (due to verbatim reliance) was related to more risky decision-making in these situations.

Meanwhile, although it has been found that both verbatim and gist processing improve with age, the tendency to rely on gist processing increases across development (Brainerd et al., 2008), findings that correspond to brain changes that take place during the adolescent years, such as synaptic pruning and an increase in myelination (Chick & Reyna, 2012). Children are more likely to engage in analytic, quantitative processing, while adults are more likely to engage in gist-based, qualitative processing. It should be noted that this does not mean that children have superior analytic capabilities, but rather that children tend to rely on this type of processing rather than a gist-based, bottom-line meaning type of processing. Hence, given these findings, it is not surprising that adults tend to engage in less risk taking than adolescents. These findings regarding the effects of cuing type of processing have interesting implications for methods of educating adolescents about smart decision making versus risky decision making.

In sum, we have included examples from a growing body of literature that emphasize the importance of gist processing in reasoning and decision making. We have demonstrated how certain findings of cognitive development that suggest that gist is superior to verbatim processing cannot necessarily be explained by standard dual-process accounts but can be reconciled by FTT. Future research into reasoning and decision making should consider type of information processing, since this has been shown to have profound implications for predicting human behavior.

References

Adam, M. B., & Reyna, V. F. (2005). Coherence and correspondence criteria for rationality: Experts' estimation of risks of sexually transmitted infections. *Journal of Behavioral Decision Making, 18*, 169–186. doi:10.1002/bdm.493

Arkes, H. R., & Ayton, P. (1999). The sunk cost and Concorde effects: Are humans less rational than lower animals? *Psychological Bulletin, 125*(5), 591–600.

Barner, D., Brooks, N., & Bale, A. (2011). Accessing the unsaid: The role of scalar alternatives in children's pragmatic inference. *Cognition, 118*, 84–93. doi:10.1016/j.cognition.2010.10.010

Brainerd, C. J., Reyna, V. F., & Ceci, S. J. (2008). Developmental reversals in false memory: A review of data and theory. *Psychological Bulletin, 134*(3), 343–382. doi:10.1037/0033-2909.134.3.343

Brainerd, C. J., Reyna, V. F., Wright, R., & Mojardin, A. H. (2003). Recollection rejection: False-memory editing in children and adults. *Psychological Review, 110*, 762–784. doi:10.1037/0033-295X.110.4.762

Bransford, J. D., & Franks, J. J. (1971). The abstraction of linguistic ideas. *Cognitive Psychology, 2*(4), 331–350.

Bunge, S. A., & Wright, S. B. (2007). Neurodevelopmental changes in working memory and cognitive control. *Current Opinion in Neurobiology, 17*, 243–250.

Camos, V., & Barrouillet, P. (2011). Developmental change in working memory strategies: From passive maintenance to active refreshing. *Developmental Psychology, 47*(3), 898.

Chick, C. F., & Reyna, V. F. (2012). A fuzzy-trace theory of adolescent risk-taking: Beyond self-control and sensation seeking. In V. F. Reyna, S. Chapman, M. Dougherty, & J. Confrey (Eds.), *The adolescent brain: Learning, reasoning, and decision making* (pp. 379–428). Washington DC: American Psychological Association.

Chick, C. F., Reyna, V. F., Corbin, J., & Hsia, A. (under review). Framing effects are robust to linguistic disambiguation.

Clark, H. H., & Clark, E. V. (1977). *Psychology and language: An introduction to psycholinguistics*. New York: Harcourt Brace Jovanovich.

Crone, E. A., & Van der Molen, M. W. (2007). Development of decision making in school-aged children and adolescents: Evidence from heart rate and skin conductance analysis. *Child Development, 78*(4), 1288–301.

Crone, E., Wendelken, C., Donohue, S., Van Leijenhorst, L., & Bunge, S. (2006). Neurocognitive development of the ability to manipulate information in working memory. *Proceedings of the National Academy of Sciences, 103*, 9315–9320. doi:10.1073/pnas.0510088103

Davidson, D. (1991). Children's decision-making examined with an information-board procedure. *Cognitive Development, 6*, 77–90.

Davidson, D. (1995). The representativeness heuristic and the conjunction fallacy effect in children's decision making. *Merrill-Palmer Quarterly: Journal of Developmental Psychology, 41*, 328–346.

De Neys, W. (2007). Developmental trends in decision making: The case of the Monty Hall Dilemma. In J. A. Elsworth (Ed.), *Psychology of decision making in education, behavior, and high risk situations* (pp. 271–281). Hauppauge, NY: Nova Science.

De Neys, W., & Vanderputte, K. (2010). When less is not always more: Stereotype knowledge and reasoning development. *Developmental Psychology, 47*(2), 432–441. doi:10.1037/a0021313

Doherty, M. J., Campbell, N. M., Tsuji, H., & Phillips, W. A. (2010). The Ebbinghaus illusion deceives adults but not young children. *Developmental Science, 13*, 714–721. doi:10.1111/j.1467-7687.2009.00931.x

Furlan, S., Agnoli, F., & Reyna, V. F. (2012). Children's competence or adults' incompetence? Different developmental trajectories in different tasks. *Developmental Psychology*. Advance online publication. doi:10.1037/a0030509

Garcia-Marques, L., Ferreira, M. B., Nunes, L. D., Garrido, M. V., & Garcia-Marques, T. (2010). False memories and impressions of personality. *Social Cognition, 28*(4), 556–568. doi:10.1521/soco.2010.28.4.556

Jacobs, J. E., & Klaczynski, P. A. (2002). The development of judgment and decision-making during childhood and adolescence. *Current Directions in Psychological Science, 11*, 145–149.

Jacobs, J. E., & Potenza, M. (1991). The use of judgment heuristics to make social and object decisions: A developmental perspective. *Child Development, 62*, 166–178.

Johnson, R. J., McCaul, K. D., & Klein, W. M. P. (2002). Risk involvement and risk perception among adolescents and young adults. *Journal of Behavioral Medicine, 25*, 67–82.

Johnson-Laird, P. N. (2010). Mental models and human reasoning. *Proceedings of the National Academy of Sciences, 107*(43), 18243–18250.

Kahneman, D. & Tversky, A. (1973). On the psychology of prediction. *Psychological Review, 80*, 237–251. doi:10.1037/h0034747

Khemlani, S., & Johnson-Laird, P. N. (2012). Theories of the syllogism: A meta-analysis. *Psychological Bulletin, 138*(3), 427–457. doi:10.1037/a0026841

Klaczynski, P. A., & Cottrell, J. M. (2004). A dual-process approach to cognitive development: The case of children's understanding of sunk cost decisions. *Thinking & Reasoning, 10*(2), 147–174.

Klaczynski, P. A., & Narasimham, G. (1998) Problem representations as mediators of adolescent deductive reasoning. *Developmental Psychology, 34*, 865–881.

Kühberger, A., & Tanner, C. (2010). Risky choice framing: Task versions and a comparison of prospect theory and fuzzy-trace theory. *Journal of Behavioral Decision Making, 23*(3), 314–329. doi:10.1002/bdm.656

Levin, I. P., & Hart, S. S. (2003). Risk preferences in young children: Early evidence of individual differences in reaction to potential gains and losses. *Journal of Behavioral Decision Making, 16*, 397–413.

Loftus, E. F. (1979). *Eyewitness testimony*. Cambridge, MA: Harvard University Press.

Mandel, D. R. (2001). Gain-loss framing and choice: Separating outcome formulations from descriptor formulations. *Organizational Behavior and Human Decision Processes, 85*(1), 56–76.

Markovits, H., & Dumas, C. (1999). Developmental patterns in the understanding of social and physical transitivity. *Journal of Experimental Child Psychology, 73*(2), 95–114.

Mata, R., Von Helversen, B., & Rieskamp, J. (2011). When easy comes hard: The development of adaptive strategy selection. *Child Development, 82*(2), 687–700.

Mills, B., Reyna, V. F., & Estrada, S. (2008). Explaining contradictory relations between risk perception and risk taking. *Psychological Science, 19*, 429–433. doi:10.1111/j1467-280.2008.02104.x

Morsanyi, K., & Handley, S. J. (2008). How smart do you need to be to get it wrong? The role of cognitive capacity in the development of heuristic-based judgment. *Journal of Experimental Child Psychology, 99*, 18–36.

Rabinowitz, F. M., & Howe, M. L. (1994). Development of the middle concept. *Journal of Experimental Child Psychology, 57*, 418–448. doi:10.1006/jecp.1994.1020

Reyna, V. F. (1991). Class inclusion, the conjunction fallacy, and other cognitive illusions. *Developmental Review, 11*, 317–336. doi:10.1016/0273-2297(91)90017-I

Reyna, V. F. (2011). Across the lifespan. In Fischhoff, B., Brewer, N. T., Downs, J. S. (Eds.), *Communicating risks and benefits: An evidence-based user's guide* (pp. 111–119). U. S. Department of Health and Human Services, Food and Drug Administration. Retrieved from http://www.fda.gov/ScienceResearch/SpecialTopics/RiskCommunication/default.htm

Reyna, V. F. (2012). A new intuitionism: Meaning, memory, and development in fuzzy-trace theory. *Judgment and Decision Making, 7*(3), 332–359.

Reyna, V. F., & Adam, M. B. (2003). Fuzzy-trace theory, risk communication, and product labeling in sexually transmitted diseases. *Risk Analysis, 23*(2), 325–342. doi:10.1111/1539-6924.00332

Reyna, V. F., & Brainerd, C. J. (1991). Fuzzy-trace theory and framing effects in choice. Gist extraction, truncation, and conversion. *Journal of Behavioral Decision Making, 4*, 249–262. doi:10.1002/bdm.3960040403

Reyna, V. F., & Brainerd, C. J. (1994). The origins of probability judgment: A review of data and theories. In G. Wright & P. Ayton (Eds.), *Subjective probability* (pp. 239–272). New York: Wiley.

Reyna, V. F., & Brainerd, C. J. (1995). Fuzzy-trace theory: An interim synthesis. *Learning and Individual Differences, 7*, 1–75. doi:10.1016/1041-6080(95)90031-4

Reyna, V. F., & Brainerd, C. J. (2008). Numeracy, ratio bias, and denominator neglect in judgments of risk and probability. *Learning and Individual Differences, 18*(1), 89–107. doi:10.1016/j.lindif.2007.03.011

Reyna, V. F., & Brainerd, C. J. (2011). Dual processes in decision making and developmental neuroscience: A fuzzy-trace model. *Developmental Review, 31*, 180–206. doi:10.1016/j.dr.2011.07.004

Reyna, V. F., & Ellis, S. C. (1994). Fuzzy-trace theory and framing effects in children's risky decision making. *Psychological Science, 5*, 275–279. doi:10.1111/j.1467-9280.1994.tb00625.x

Reyna, V. F., Estrada, S. M., DeMarinis, J. A., Myers, R. M., Stanisz, J. M., & Mills, B. A. (2011). Neurobiological and memory models of risky decision making in adolescents versus young adults. *Journal of Experimental Psychology: Learning, Memory, and Cognition, 37*(5), 1125–1142. doi:10.1037/a0023943

Reyna, V. F., & Farley, F. (2006). Risk and rationality in adolescent decision-making: Implications for theory, practice, and public policy. *Psychological Science in the Public Interest, 7*(1), 1–44. doi:10.1111/j.1529-1006.2006.00026.x

Reyna, V. F., & Kiernan, B. (1994). The development of gist versus verbatim memory in sentence recognition: Effects of lexical familiarity, semantic content, encoding instruction, and retention interval. *Developmental Psychology, 30*, 178–191. doi:10.1037/0012-1649.30.2.178

Reyna, V. F., & Kiernan, B. (1995). Children's memory and metaphorical interpretation. *Metaphor and Symbolic Activity, 10*, 309–331.

Schlottmann, A., & Tring, J. (2005). How children reason about gains and losses: Framing effects in judgment and choice. *Swiss Journal of Psychology, 64*(3), 153–171.

Stanowich, K. E., West, R. F., & Toplak, M. E. (2011). The complexity of developmental predictions from dual process models. *Developmental Review, 31*, 103–118.

Tversky, A., & Kahneman, D. (1986). Rational choice and the framing of decisions. *Journal of Business, 59*, S251–S278. doi:10.1086/296365

Van Duijvenvoorde, A. C. K., Jansen, B. R. J., Bredman, J. C., & Huizenga, H. M. (2012).

Age-related changes in decision making: Comparing informed and noninformed situations. *Developmental Psychology, 48*(1), 192–203.

Vosniadou, S., & Ortony, A. (1983). The emergence of the literal-metaphorical-anomalous distinction in young children. *Child Development, 54*, 154–161.

Weller, J. A., Levin, I. P., & Denburg, N. L. (2011). Trajectory of risky decision making for potential gains and losses from ages 5 to 85. *Journal of Behavioral Decision Making, 24*, 331–344.

Wolfe, C. R., & Reyna, V. F. (2010). Semantic coherence and fallacies in estimating joint probabilities. *Journal of Behavioral Decision Making, 23*(2), 203–223. doi:10.1002/bdm.650

Wright, B. C. (2012). The case for a dual-process theory of transitive reasoning. *Developmental Review, 32*, 89–124. doi:10.1016/j.dr.2012.04.001

4 A developmental mental model theory of conditional reasoning

Caroline Gauffroy and Pierre Barrouillet

Among the different varieties of human reasoning, conditional reasoning is of particular importance. Permitted by propositions containing the connector "*If*" such as "*If . . . then . . .*", "*. . . only if . . .*", or "*If and only if . . . then . . .*", conditional reasoning underpins the key processes of suppositional thinking and hypothesis testing involved in social (Harris & Nunez, 1996; Light, Blaye, Gilly, & Girotto, 1989), causal (Kushnir & Gopnik, 2007), or scientific (Kuhn, Amsel, & O'Loughlin, 1988) reasoning. Accordingly, how children and adolescents reason from "*If*" sentences and how this kind of reasoning develops with age are questions that have always attracted the interest of psychologists and received diverse answers.

Piaget considered conditional reasoning as a late achievement that depends on the construction of formal operations isomorphic in structure to formal logic during adolescence (Inhelder & Piaget, 1958). It is often overlooked, as far as propositional reasoning is concerned, that Piaget did not conceive these operations as inferential mechanisms for deriving conclusions from premises. Instead, when reasoning about a system of two propositions p and q, these operations would be the set of all the possible combinations of the products $p.\ q$, $p.\ \neg q$, $\neg p.\ q$, and $\neg p.\ \neg q$ (e.g., $p \supset q$, "*if p then q*", is an operation combining $p.\ q$, $\neg p.\ q$, and $\neg p.\ \neg q$). Transformations could be executed on these operations in such way that, for example, it can be understood that the operation $p.\ \neg q$ is the inverse of the operation $p \supset q$. When fully developed and properly coordinated, these transformations would constitute a structured whole known as the INRC group occurring only in late adolescence and enabling propositional reasoning.

Other authors proposed that human beings are endowed with a mental logic (Braine & O'Brien 1991; Rips, 1994). Individuals would have syntactic rules of inference that can be applied to the logical form of premises to produce conclusions. For example, according to Braine (1990), conditional reasoning is based on a Modus Ponens schema that derives the conclusion q from premises of the form *if p then q* and p, and on a schema for conditional proof that concludes *if p then q* when q can be derived from the supposition that p is true. Contrary to what Piaget assumed, these reasoning abilities would be either innate (Macnamara, 1986) or at least available early in development. For example, Braine (1990) suggested that toddlers acquire schemas for "*If*" by mapping the linguistic conditional connective onto a concept of contingency relation learned through mundane experience. Similarly, it has been proposed that conditional reasoning abilities would be based on the early acquisition of pragmatic reasoning schemas that are reasoning rules specific to socially relevant situations such as permissions (Cheng & Holyoak, 1985). Children as young as 3 years of age can reason correctly when problems are framed within these deontic contexts (Cummins, 1996; Harris & Nunez, 1996).

Is conditional reasoning a late developmental achievement or an early acquired, if not innate, ability? Studies that have examined the development of reasoning with "*If . . . then . . .*" premises have yielded mixed results, some of them reporting developmental patterns in line with the Piagetian hypothesis (Markovits & Vachon, 1990; Mueller, Overton, & Reene, 2001; O'Brien & Overton, 1980, 1982; Overton, Byrnes, & O'Brien, 1985; Overton, Ward, Noveck, Black, & O'Brien, 1987) while other have revealed surprising early deductive capacities (Richards & Sanderson, 1999; Dias & Harris, 1988, 1990; Kuhn, 1977). It should be noted that this apparent inconsistency in results, which are often obtained from tasks differing in nature and content, could be resolved if we abandon the hypothesis that any correct inference necessarily reveals a genuine deductive competence. The mental model theory proposed by Johnson-Laird (1983; Johnson-Laird & Byrne, 1991) constitutes an appropriate framework for understanding that a partial and even inaccurate understanding of the meaning of logical connectives can allow children to produce correct inferences in some circumstances. This theory assumes that people interpret sentences and reason from them without any recourse to logical structures or rules, but by simply constructing and manipulating mental models of the possibilities that can occur given the truth of the sentences. Concerning the understanding of "*If p then q*" conditional sentences (e.g., "if the piece is a square, then it is red"), the theory assumes that people would first construct a model representing the co-occurrence of the antecedent p and the consequent q (i.e., a red square). Because mental models are transient representations maintained in a limited-capacity working memory, cognitive economy would lead people to leave in an implicit format the other possibilities that they could imagine (i.e., those possibilities that can occur when the piece is not a square), resulting in an initial model represented in the following diagram:

$$p \qquad q$$
$$. \; . \; .$$

The first line explicitly represents the possibility that a square piece is red, while the three dots are a mental footnote or reminder that there are other possibilities that have been left implicit. This implicit information can be made explicit through a cognitive demanding and time-consuming process of fleshing out, by which other models can be added. First, people could think about the possibility of a piece that is not a square and not red (i.e., a $\neg p \; \neg q$ case), resulting in a biconditional interpretation in which square pieces are red and pieces which are not square are not red. The resulting set of mental models is represented in the following diagram:

$$
\begin{array}{cc}
p & q \\
\neg\, p & \neg\, q
\end{array}
$$

in which the sign $\neg$ refers to a mental tag for negation. However, people can also think about a third possibility in which pieces that are not square are, notwithstanding, red, resulting in a complete three-model conditional interpretation of the following form:

$$
\begin{array}{cc}
p & q \\
\neg\, p & \neg\, q \\
\neg\, p & q
\end{array}
$$

Though this theory has been elaborated by Johnson-Laird and his colleagues to account for interpretive and deductive processes in adults, it offers straightforward applications in the developmental domain. In this chapter, we present the successive versions of a developmental mental model theory for conditional reasoning that we have developed during the last 15 years.

The three hierarchical levels theory of conditional reasoning

According to Johnson-Laird's theory, mental models are ephemeral representations constructed and maintained in a limited-capacity working memory. Because it is known that working memory is strongly limited in children and develops with age (Case, Kurland, & Goldberg, 1982; Barrouillet, Gavens, Vergauwe, Gaillard, & Camos, 2009), we reasoned that this limited capacity should constrain the complexity of the representations of conditional sentences that children and adolescents can construct. First, there should exist a developmental level in which children are only able to construct a single-model representation, which would probably correspond to the explicit content of the initial model described by Johnson-Laird & Byrne (1991). This would result in the construction of the sole $p\ q$ model, which corresponds to a conjunctive interpretation of the conditional statements. Later in development, increases in cognitive capacity may allow children to evoke other possibilities. A second developmental level should be characterized by the addition to the $p\ q$ model of $\neg p\ \neg q$ model leading to a biconditional interpretation in which q results from p and *not q* from *not p*. Finally, probably in late adolescence, individuals should be able to construct the complete three-model representation by the addition of a $\neg p\ q$ model. Thus, the developmental trend would be from a conjunctive, to a biconditional, and finally to a conditional interpretation.

This developmental trend has been observed in several studies. Lecas and Barrouillet (1999) used a conditional falsification task in which third, sixth, and ninth graders were asked to identify the case(s) that violated an *if p then q* conditional rule among four possible combinations comprising $p\ q$, $\neg p\ q$, $p\ \neg q$, and $\neg p\ \neg q$. For example, the rule "If there is a rabbit in the cage, then there is a duck" was accompanied by drawings representing a rabbit and a duck ($p\ q$), a rabbit and a black bird ($p\ \neg q$), a guinea pig and a duck ($\neg p\ q$), and a guinea pig and a black bird ($\neg p\ \neg q$).

Third graders mostly showed a conjunctive interpretation, rejecting all the cases except *p q*. As expected, sixth graders mainly exhibited a biconditional interpretation, only rejecting ¬*p q* and *p* ¬*q* cases as falsifying the rule, whereas a majority of ninth graders tended to reject only *p* ¬*q* cases, thus adopting a conditional interpretation. This trend was also observed in a production task in which children had to produce those cases that were compatible with conditional rules by combining drawings: most of the third graders only constructed *p q* cases, whereas sixth graders mostly constructed *p q* and ¬*p* ¬*q* cases, while ninth graders constructed the three cases of the conditional interpretation. Barrouillet & Lecas (1999) also tested the hypothesis that this increase in the number of models that children and adolescents can construct results from an age-related increase in working memory capacity. Third, sixth, and ninth graders performed a counting span task to assess their working memory capacity along with the conditional production task. The results replicated the developmental trend going from conjunctive, biconditional, and then conditional interpretations but, more importantly, the number of cases that children and adolescents were able to produce was strongly correlated with their counting span, even when the effect of age was partialled out ($r = 0.648$). In each age group, children who exhibited a conjunctive response pattern had lower working memory spans than those who adopted a biconditional interpretation, who had in turn lower spans than conditional responders.

The same developmental pattern was also observed in a conditional syllogism task. In this task, a major premise of the form *If p then q* is paired with a minor premise that either affirms or denies the antecedent or the consequent. Participants are asked to formulate what follows from the premises. Four inferences can be drawn. The Modus Ponens (MP) consists in concluding *q* from *p*, the Modus Tollens (MT) in concluding ¬ *q* from ¬ *p*, the Affirmation of Consequent (AC) in concluding *p* from *q*, and the Denial of Antecedent (DA) in concluding ¬*q* from ¬*p*. In formal logic, only the affirmation of the antecedent (*p*, MP) and the negation of the consequent (*not q*, MT) lead to certain conclusions, which are *q* and *not p*, respectively. In contrast, neither affirming the consequent (*q*, AC) nor denying the antecedent (*not p*, DA) lead to certain conclusions, even though individuals often endorse or produce the putative conclusions *p* from AC and *not q* from DA. Note that, within the mental model theory, concluding *q* from *p* (MP) and *p* from *q* (AC) only requires the construction of the initial model *p q*. However, concluding *not p* from *not q* (MT) necessitates constructing a second ¬*p* ¬*q* model that also supports the conclusion *not q* from *not p* (DA). When the complete three-model representation is constructed, MP and MT are still valid inferences because *p* occurs in only one model in which it is associated with *q*, while *not q* occurs in only one model in which it is associated with *not p*. However, the third ¬*p q* model prevents the conclusion that *p* follows from *q*, because *q* occurs in two models, one in which it is associated with *p* and another in which it is associated with *not p*. In the same way, this third model also prevents concluding that *not q* follows from *not p* because it associates *q* with *not p*. This leads to straightforward developmental predictions. Children at the conjunctive level who construct only the *p q* model should produce the MP and AC inferences but would not reach certain conclusions from MP and

DA, because they have no model in their representation containing *not q* or *not p*. The biconditional level and its two models *p q* and ¬*p* ¬*q* would allow the production of certain conclusions for all the four inferences. At the conditional level, the addition of the ¬*p q* model would still permit certain conclusions to MP and MT, but would lead to responses of uncertainty for AC and DA (see Table 4.1).

Barrouillet, Grosset, and Lecas (2000) tested these predictions by presenting third, sixth, ninth graders and adults with the four conditional syllogisms. For each type of syllogism, participants were first asked to indicate whether the premises led to certain conclusion or not ("something follows" or "nothing follows" options) and, if so, to write down the conclusion they reached. The results confirmed the developmental mental model theory (Figure 4.1). As predicted, third graders

Table 4.1 Predictions about the type of inferences which should be produced (+) or not produced (−) as a function of the level of interpretation of the *if p then q* conditional premise

Minor premise	Putative conclusion	Inference	Levels of interpretation and mental models constructed		
			conjunctive	*biconditional*	*conditional*
			p q	*p q* ¬*p* ¬*q*	*p q* ¬*p* ¬*q* ¬*p q*
p	*q*	MP	+	+	+
q	*p**	AC	+	+	−
Not p	*Not q**	DA	−	+	−
Not q	*Not p*	MT	−	+	+

Note: * These conclusions are considered as fallacies according to formal logic, the logical conclusion being "nothing follows".

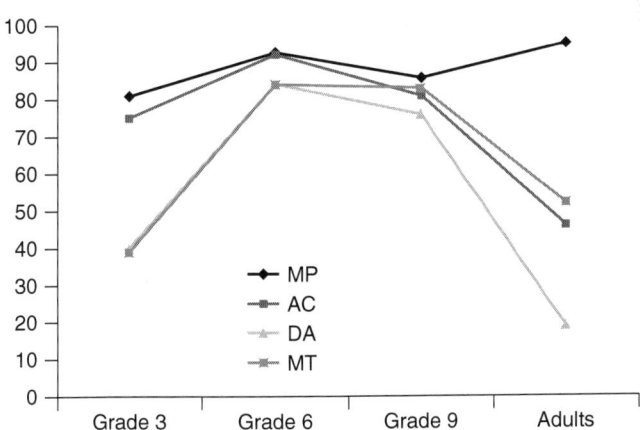

Figure 4.1 Production rates of the invited inference for the four inferences (*q*, *p*, *not q*, and *not p* for MP, AC, DA, and MT respectively) as a function of age groups

produced more conclusions for the MP and AC inferences than for DA and MT. These differences disappeared in adolescents who exhibited high production rates for all four inferences, revealing biconditional readings. Adults more often produced certain conclusions for MP and MT than for DA, reflecting the predominance of conditional interpretations, although the level of conclusion for AC remained high.

Content and context effects

Though the hypothesis issued from the mental model theory of a construction of models constrained by limited working memory capacities in children and adolescents received large empirical support, the developmental theory proposed by Barrouillet and Lecas (1998) went beyond the standard mental model theory by adding three key assumptions. First, they assumed that, at least in children and young adolescents, mental models should not involve formal operation such as negations. The alternative models to $p\,q$ should correspond to possibilities in which p is not verified, rather than to representations of a verified p indexed by a negation tag as it is the case in the standard theory. For example, if the proposition p is "the piece is a square", alternative cases would not represent the value "$\neg$ square" but instead states of affairs in which p is not verified (i.e., circle, triangle, etc.). Second, it was assumed that a conditional "*If p then q*" introduces a directional relation from a variable P, the value of which is specified by p, to another variable Q, the value of which is specified by q. For example, a statement like "If the piece is a square, then it is red" would inform people that the color of the pieces depends on their shape and specifies the value taken by Q (i.e., red) for one of the values of P (i.e., square). When children are able to exceed the initial model $p\,q$, they should attempt to flesh out their representation by inferring from their existing knowledge the nature of the variables P and Q involved in the conditional statement and the possible values that the variable Q could take for values of P that are not specified in this statement. These possible values should depend on the semantics of the terms, the context of enunciation, and the children's knowledge. Third, in producing alternative models to $p\,q$, individuals should attempt to increase the information conveyed by the conditional statement by constructing "complete" representations in which each value of P would be associated with a specific value of Q to establish, wherever possible, a one-to-one correspondence (the principle of *completeness*). This is why, when only two models are constructed, the second model corresponds to $\neg p\,\neg q$ and not to $\neg p\,q$.

This makes fleshing out an informal process because its results depend on the semantics involved in the conditional statement. Barrouillet and Lecas (1998) assumed that when the antecedent or the consequent have only one alternative value, fleshing out the initial representation should lead to explicitly representing this alternative value in the additional models. Thus, a conditional statement like "If the bird is a male, then it has dark plumage" would call for an alternative model containing the "female" and "light plumage" values instead of "$\neg$ male" or "$\neg$ dark". By contrast, when the antecedent or the consequent pertain to variables with numerous possibilities (e.g., "If the piece is a square, then it is red"), alternative values to *p* or *q* would remain indeterminate in the additional models constructed. Barrouillet and Lecas called *binary* the terms whose negation in a given context takes a determinate value (male/female for birds), and referred to as *BB* those conditionals with a binary term on both the antecedent and the consequent. These *BB* conditionals were contrasted with *NN* conditionals that contain no binary terms (i.e., numerous alternatives). The hypothesis that mental models do not involve formal operations of negation and the principle of completeness lead to a series of predictions concerning *BB* and *NN* conditionals. First, because *BB* conditionals allow for only one alternative value in both the antecedent and the consequent, the construction of a second model containing these alternative values should be facilitated, offering the possibility of a representation with explicit content (e.g., adding a *female–light* model to the first model *male–dark*). However, the construction of this additional model would lead to a complete representation (every value of the antecedent is associated with a value of the consequent) that would in turn block the fleshing out process, thereby impeding the construction of models of the form ¬*p q*. This should result in a frequent biconditional interpretation of *BB* conditionals with no strong evolution with age. By contrast, with *NN* conditionals, the first alternative model to *p q* should take the form of the co-occurrence of two indeterminate values that should not block the construction of a ¬*p q* representation in adolescents and adults who have sufficient working memory capacities to construct a three-model representation. Accordingly, Barrouillet and Lecas (1998) verified in a conditional production task that *BB* conditionals elicited a predominant biconditional interpretation in all of the age-groups studied (i.e., third, sixth, ninth graders and adults), while the conjunctive–biconditional–conditional developmental trend was observed with *NN* conditionals. Barrouillet and Lecas showed how their model also accounts for known effects like the matching bias (Evans, 1989), or the negative conclusion bias (Evans, 1977; Pollard & Evans, 1980; Wildman & Fletcher, 1977). They also anticipated Evans and Handley (1999) in predicting and demonstrating that conditional inferences are suppressed when based on implicit rather than explicit negative premises (e.g., *blue* instead of *not red*) for *NN* conditionals, but not for *BB* conditionals.

Interestingly, modulations in the interpretation of conditional statements are not restricted to the structure of the semantic spaces in which the antecedent and the consequent are involved. The same phenomena as those observed with *BB* conditionals can be observed with *NN* conditionals when they are embedded in restricting contexts that limit to only two the possible values on the antecedent and the consequent. For example, the statement "If the car is blue then it is a Peugeot" involves variables (i.e., makes and colors of car) with several possible values and corresponds to an *NN* conditional. However, restrictive contexts can limit the number of these values, turning *NN* into *BB* conditionals:

A company's vehicle pool consists of two makes of car: Peugeot and Citroën, present in the colors blue and green. After looking at all the cars, an observer claims to have found a rule linking the make of car and its color. The rule is: If the car is blue then it is a Peugeot.

Barrouillet and Lecas (2002) predicted and verified that these *NN* conditionals in restricted context (*NNR* conditionals) elicited the same biconditional interpretations as *BB* conditionals in adolescents aged 12 and 15, but not in adults who frequently endorsed the same conditional reading for *NN* and *NNR* conditionals. This suggests that adult reasoning is more knowledge-dependent than context-dependent.

Markovits and Barrouillet's (2002) theory

The three hierarchical levels theory was initially conceived by Barrouillet and Lecas (1998) to account for children's and adolescents' reasoning on conditionals involving artificial relations between the antecedent and the consequent, that are relations on which individuals do not have prior knowledge (e.g., "If the piece is a square, then it is red"). In focusing on these artificial relations, we aimed at examining reasoning capacities and their development when there is no available world-based knowledge. However, individuals most often reason on familiar relations. In order to account for this, Markovits and Barrouillet (2002) proposed a modified mental model theory in which retrieval of knowledge from long-term memory plays a crucial role in reasoning. In line with Barrouillet and Lecas (1998), it was assumed that children and adults have an understanding of "If . . . then . . ." statements that is inherently relational and that brings to bear a fairly rich linguistic and pragmatic experience. The models constructed from familiar relations were assumed to take the form of relational schemas as described by Halford, Bain, Maybery, and Andrews (1998). Specifically, the relational schemas are cognitive representations that include elements and their interrelations and represent the structure of a situation in the environment. However, when reasoning on familiar relations between objects or events, the process of searching alternative values of the antecedent and the consequent should be further executed by activating three classes of objects or events in long-term memory. The first class concerns objects or events that are complementary to those specified in the conditional. For example, a conditional like "if it rains then the street will be wet" would activate a complementary class of knowledge such as "if it is sunny, then the street will not be wet". Retrieving complementary items of knowledge should permit to construct $\neg p \ \neg q$ models. A second class, the *alternatives* class, is constituted of objects or events that share the same relation to the consequent as the antecedent does, thereby leading to the construction of $\neg p \ q$ model. For example, children can retrieve from memory that "if the street cleaner passes, then the street will be wet too". Finally, the *disabling* class concerns conditions that allow the relation between the antecedent and the consequent to be violated. For example, "if it rains, but the street is covered, then the street will not be wet". We predicted that these premises would automatically activate related knowledge from long-term memory, the strength of this activation depending on the accessibility of information (i.e., its base-level activation) and the efficiency of a given person's retrieval processes. Thus, those elements that are sufficiently activated should enter working memory and become available for further processing. Within this framework, limitations on reasoning are due to both the number of models that must be maintained and manipulated in a capacity-limited working memory, and on-line memory access.

Because working memory capacity is limited in children, Markovits and Barrouillet (2002) assumed, following Halford (Andrews & Halford, 1998; Halford, Wilson, & Phillips, 1998), that young children would be limited to processing two simultaneous relational schemata. Moreover, young children have less efficient retrieval processes than older children and adolescents and they have less available knowledge, rendering the retrieval of relevant information less likely. As a consequence, Markovits and Barrouillet predicted that, when reasoning with premises for which there is little knowledge easily activated, young children would be limited to the retrieval of items from the complementary class and consequently to a biconditional interpretation of "If . . . then . . ." sentences. For premises for which alternative cases can be easily retrieved (i.e., cases of the form $a\ q$ or $\neg p\ q$), children and adolescents should produce responses of uncertainty for AC and DA, depending on the strength of activation of these alternative cases. These predictions were illustrated in a study in which adolescents and adults were invited to reason from causal conditionals that introduced either a strong or a weak relation between the antecedent and the consequent (Barrouillet, Markovits, & Quinn, 2001). A strong causal relation is a relation in which the antecedent is a frequent cause for the occurrence of the effect described in the consequent (e.g., "if a dog has fleas, then it will scratch constantly"), whereas a weak relation refers to a cause that does not come so easily to mind, even if it is plausible (e.g., "if a dog has a skin disease, then it will scratch constantly"). Quinn and Markovits (1998) had already observed that causal conditionals with strong antecedents elicited fewer responses of uncertainty to AC and DA than with weak antecedents. When the antecedent corresponds to the cause that is most strongly associated with the consequent (fleas for dogs scratching), alternative antecedents whose retrieval is needed to block AC and DA fallacies must be recruited amongst weakly associated causes, making their retrieval less probable. By contrast, with a weak cause (e.g., a skin disease), the most strongly associated cause receives a strong activation from the consequent and it is easily retrieved. As a consequence, when presented with a conditional like "if a dog has fleas, then it will scratch constantly" and the minor premise "a dog scratches constantly" (AC), people often conclude that this dog has fleas, whereas they tend to produce a response of uncertainty from the conditional "if a dog has a skin disease, then it will scratch constantly" because they easily envision that it might have a skin disease but could also have fleas.

Barrouillet et al. (2001) presented 12- and 15-year-old adolescents and adults with conditional premises involving either a strong or a weak causal relation between the antecedent and the consequent. As expected, correct uncertainty responses from AC and DA were more frequent from weak than strong relations, and this effect was modulated by the age of the participants such that it was greater in adolescents than in adults. These findings confirmed the hypothesis that correct responses of uncertainty to AC and DA depend on the efficiency of the retrieval of alternative antecedents from long-term memory, and that this efficiency increases with age, rendering adults less sensitive to the relative difficulty of retrieving relevant information from memory.

A developmental dual-process theory of the construction of mental models

Despite its capacity in accounting for a variety of phenomena related with conditional reasoning and, as we have seen, for its development, the mental model theory has been the subject of strong criticisms (Evans, Over, & Handley, 2005; Oberauer & Wilhelm, 2003). These criticisms are based on findings which revealed that individuals make different judgments when they have to evaluate the truth-value of a conditional than when they have to think about what is possible from the same conditional. As we have seen, and in line with Johnson-Laird's theory, when asked to evaluate what is possible given the truth of "if the piece is a square, then it is red", adults usually list the three possibilities which correspond to the complete three-model representation (i.e., $p\ q$, $\neg p\ \neg q$, and $\neg p\ q$). However, when they are asked to evaluate the truth or the falsity of the same conditional, they give different responses to these three cases. As could be expected, adults deem the conditional true when they are presented with a red square (i.e., $p\ q$ case) and false for a blue square (i.e., $p\ \neg q$ case). But, when they are presented with a blue circle or a red circle (i.e., $\neg p\ \neg q$ and $\neg p\ q$ cases, respectively), most adults consider that these two cases are irrelevant to judge the truth-value of the conditional, even though they list them as possible when they are told that the conditional is true. This pattern of response wherein the $p\ q$ case is considered as making the conditional true, the $p\ \neg q$ case as making it false, and the $\neg p$ cases as irrelevant for judging the truth-value of the sentence is known as the defective truth table (i.e., De Finetti table).

Evans and colleagues argued that, according to the principle of truth of the standard mental model theory, mental models represent true possibilities. As a consequence, reasoners who are able to construct the $p\ q$, $\neg p\ \neg q$ and $\neg p\ q$ models should deem the conditional true for the corresponding cases. However, as we have seen, this is not what occurs. It is worth noting that these criticisms are receivable only if it is agreed that the meaning of a basic conditional for the mental model theory is the truth function of the material implication in which the conditional is true for the $p\ q$, the $\neg p\ \neg q$ and the $\neg p\ q$ cases, which is not what Johnson-Laird and Byrne assume themselves (for a discussion see Barrouillet & Gauffroy, 2011, p. 195). However, even if these criticisms are in our point of view based on a misinterpretation of the principle of truth, they revealed one of the main weaknesses of Johnson-Laird's theory. Indeed, this theory does not make clear the psychological difference between initial and fleshed-out models and their epistemic status.

In order to address Evans et al.'s (2005) criticisms, we have proposed a mental model account for the De Finetti table that combines the mental model theory and Evans' (2006) heuristic-analytic approach. Our integrative approach specifies both the epistemic status of each mental model constructed and the role of heuristic and analytic processes in their construction (Barrouillet,

2011; Barrouillet, Gauffroy, & Lecas, 2008; Gauffroy & Barrouillet, 2009, 2011). According to Evans (2006) and in line with the dual-process approach, two systems coexist when interpreting a conditional statement. The heuristic system (System 1[1]) is automatic, unconscious, and pragmatically cued. As such, heuristic processes should produce an epistemic mental model that is the most plausible and believable with reference to prior knowledge elicited by context and the current goals. This default mental model can be revised or replaced by the intervention of analytic processes (System 2), which are controlled rather than automatic, conscious, slow, and sequential in nature. Evans (2006) assumes that the analytic system may or may not intervene to inhibit default heuristic responses. As Evans suggests, we can easily draw a parallel between the construction of both initial and fleshed-out models on the one hand and heuristic and analytic processes on the other. According to the mental model account, when interpreting a conditional statement, people first construct in a relatively automatic way an initial representation in which most of the information is left implicit. So, the initial representation of conditionals seems to be clearly a product of the heuristic system. On the contrary, the fleshing out may or may not intervene to make explicit the information remained initially implicit, resulting in the construction of $\neg p \neg q$ *and* $\neg p q$ models. This fleshing out is described as controlled, effortful, and constrained by working memory capacities (Johnson-Laird & Byrne, 1991, 2002); this corresponds to the description of the analytic system.

Because the heuristic system produces a default mental model that comes easily to mind, the explicit model in the initial representation would capture its core meaning, that is, $p q$ for basic conditionals. Accordingly, the conditional "If the piece is a square, then it is red" would be evaluated as true for a red square. Possibilities that are not part of the initial representation remain initially implicit because they do not make the conditional true, but are nonetheless compatible with it. So, the fleshing out may intervene to make explicit $\neg p \neg q$ and $\neg p q$ models that are not part of the core meaning of the conditional, but are compatible with it (i.e., blue and red circles). Within this account, fleshing out is a process by which individuals extend the initial meaning of an assertion beyond the states of affairs that make it true to those states of affairs that are only compatible with it. Thus, when presented with these states of affairs and asked to evaluate the truth of a basic conditional, adults who are able to construct the complete three-model representation would deem the conditional true for $p q$ cases, its truth-value remaining indeterminate for cases matching the fleshed-out models (i.e., $\neg p \neg q$ and $\neg p q$ cases). By contrast, those states of affairs that do not correspond to any model, even when the fleshing out process has been completed (i.e., $p \neg q$, the blue square in our example), are considered as incompatible with the sentence and as falsifying it. This conception is coherent with the developmental model outlined above. Indeed, as the heuristic processes are automatic, and not demanding in working memory capacity, they should be efficient early in development. By contrast, the analytic processes, which are attention-demanding and effortful, should develop later. Accordingly, even young children can construct the $p q$ model resulting from heuristic processes, whereas the $\neg p \neg q$ model is constructed by young adolescents and the complete three-model representation does not seem available before the end of adolescence. In a series of experiments, we tested our assumption of different systems underpinning the construction of mental models and resulting in different epistemological status.

We focused on two types of tasks preferentially used by the critics of the mental model theory, the truth-table task and the probability task. In the truth-table task, participants are asked to judge for each of the four logical cases (i.e., red square, blue square, blue circle, red circle) if the conditional ("If the piece is a square then it is red") is true or false, or if the case under consideration does not permit to judge the truth-value of the conditional. In the probability task, participants are informed about the relative frequencies of the four logical cases (i.e., 3 black cards with a circle printed on them, 2 black cards with a square, 3 white cards with a circle, 3 white cards with a square) and have to evaluate the probability that a claim like "If the card is black then it has a circle printed on it" is true for a card drawn at random from the pack. In the same way as the $\neg p$ cases are judged irrelevant to evaluate the truth-value of the conditional in the truth-table task, several studies have demonstrated that the $\neg p$ cases are disregarded when evaluating the probability of conditionals (Evans et al., 2003; Oberauer & Wilhem, 2003). Adults often base their evaluation on the sole p cases and evaluate the probability of the conditional as the conditional probability $p (q/p) = p (p\ q) / [p (p\ q) + p (p\ \neg q)]$. In our example, this corresponds to the probability of finding a circle on a black card (3/5). Thus, these two tasks seemed to be particularly adapted to test our assumption of a different epistemic status between initial and fleshed-out models. More importantly, the developmental course of reasoning about the truth-value of conditionals had never been studied by critics or defenders of the mental model theory.

Barrouillet et al. (2008) proposed a truth-table task to third, sixth, ninth graders and adults. Participants were presented with a conditional statement that described the content of a box, in which there was always a colored circle on the left and a colored star on the right (e.g., "If the circle is red, then the star is yellow"). The correspondence between the color of the circle and the star in the box and those stipulated in the conditional statement was manipulated to form the four logical cases. Participants were instructed to judge if the content of the box made the statement true or false, or if it left its truth-value indeterminate (one cannot know if the sentence is true or false). Our developmental theory makes clear predictions concerning the expected response patterns. Young children often adopt a conjunctive interpretation, constructing only the explicit model (i.e., $p\ q$) and failing to flesh out the other possibilities. Thus, they should consider the $p\ q$ case as making the conditional true and the three other possibilities as rendering it false. At the biconditional level, adolescents are able to flesh out the initial representation and construct the $\neg p\ \neg q$ model. In doing so, they should judge the conditional true for $p\ q$ cases, the $\neg p\ \neg q$ cases as irrelevant to judge the truth-value and the two other possibilities as rendering it false, leading to a defective biconditional interpretation. Finally, the defective conditional level, which corresponds to the construction of the complete three-model representation, should lead to judging *p q* cases as rendering the conditional true, ¬*p* cases constructed through flesh-ing out as irrelevant to judge its truth-value and *p* ¬*q* cases as rendering it false (i.e., the De Finetti table). The results confirmed our predictions. The conjunctive interpretation was mainly produced by younger participants. The defective bicon-ditional interpretation constituted an intermediate level and finally the defective conditional interpretation was predominant only in adults.

The same developmental trend was expected when evaluating the probability of the conditional. Gauffroy and Barrouillet (2009) tested this prediction with a para-digm inspired from Evans et al. (2003). Sixth graders, ninth graders, and adults[2] were presented with problems concerning a pack of cards either black or white, with either a circle or a square printed on them. Participants were instructed to respond to a question of the form: "How likely is the following statement to be true of a card drawn at random from the pack? If the card is black then there is a square printed on it". In the same way that the evaluation of the truth-value of conditional relies on the mental models constructed, people should evaluate the probability of a given conditional from the mental models they have constructed by focusing on those cases that are relevant for the truth or falsity of this conditional. So, for conjunctive responders, all the cases should be considered relevant. The conjunc-tive probability of the conditional to be true is then $P(p\,q)\,/\,[P(p\,q)+P(\neg p\,q)+P(p\,\neg q)+P(\neg p\,\neg q)]$. At the defective biconditional level, adolescents are able to construct through fleshing out the ¬*p* ¬*q* model so the corresponding cases should be disregarded from their probability evaluation. Thus, the defective biconditional probability of the conditional to be true should be $P(p\,q)\,/\,[P(p\,q)+P(\neg p\,q)+P(p\,\neg q)]$. Finally, for individuals who are able to construct the complete three-model representation, the two ¬*p* cases are considered as irrelevant to evaluate the truth or falsity of a conditional. As such, they should evaluate the probability of the conditional to be true as the conditional probability, $P(p\,q)\,/\,[P(p\,q)+P(p\,\neg q)]$. Table 4.2 summarizes and gives an example for these three interpreta-tions. Our results showed that, as for the evaluation of the truth-value, individuals

Table 4.2 Probabilities for the conditionals to be true or false for the different interpreta-tions of basic conditionals with the corresponding probability for the following example: Probability of "If the card is black then there is a square printed on it" from a card drawn at random in a pack containing 2 black cards with a square (i.e., *p q*), 4 black cards with a circle (i.e., *p* ¬*q*), 3 white cards with a circle (i.e., ¬*p* ¬*q*), and 3 white cards with a square (i.e., ¬*p q*)

Interpretation	Probability	
	True	*False*
Conjunctive	P(p q)	P(p ¬q) + P(p q) + P (¬p ¬q)
	2/12	10/12
Defective Biconditional	P(p q) / [P(p q) + P(p ¬q) + P(¬p q)]	[P(p ¬q) + P(¬p q)]/
	2/9	[P(p q) + P(p ¬q) + P(¬p q)
		7/9
Defective Conditional	P(p q) / [P(p q) + P(p ¬q)]	P(p ¬q) / [P(p q) + P(p ¬q)]
	2/6	4/6

evaluated the probability of a conditional statement from the mental models they have constructed. Sixth graders predominantly gave conjunctive responses that became less frequent in older groups. The defective biconditional responses exhibited the predicted quadratic trend, being rare in the younger group, more frequent in ninth graders before disappearing in adults, whereas defective conditional responses appeared in ninth graders to become predominant in adults.

We have seen above that the three hierarchical levels theory perfectly integrated the semantic and pragmatic modulations described by the standard mental model theory (Johnson-Laird & Byrne, 2002). These two modulation mechanisms can either facilitate or block the construction of mental models. We recently suggested that semantic and pragmatic effects can provide another strong support to our assumptions about the epistemic status of initial and fleshed-out models and the different systems underlying their construction.

Concerning semantic modulation, Barrouillet and Lecas (1998) showed that introducing binary terms in the antecedent and the consequent induces a strong tendency towards biconditional reading, abolishing developmental differences between adolescents and adults. The same phenomenon should be observed in the truth-table task and in the probability task. According to Barrouillet and Lecas (1998), the structure of semantic memory for *BB* conditionals affects the fleshing-out process by blocking the construction of the $\neg p\ q$ model. So, binary terms would affect the output of the analytic system. Consequently, if *BB* conditionals block the construction of the $\neg p\ q$ model, the construction of fleshed-out models should remain at the defective biconditional level for *BB* conditionals for older participants, although they should still be able to construct the complete three-model representation for *NN* conditionals. Nonetheless, *BB* and *NN* conditionals should induce the same conjunctive interpretation in young children who are not able to initiate a fleshing-out process. We tested the prediction of predominant defective biconditional patterns for *BB* conditionals in truth-table tasks and probability tasks. For both types of tasks, we compared conditionals involving binary terms with conditionals involving non-binary terms.

In the truth-table task (Gauffroy & Barrouillet, 2009), third, sixth, ninth graders and adults were informed that the conditional statement displayed on the top of the screen (e.g., "if the pupil is a boy then he wears glasses") described a pictured scene representing one of the four logical cases presented under the statement (e.g., a boy wearing glasses). By looking at the pictures, participants had to decide if the sentence was either true or false, or if the picture did not permit to know whether it was true or false. We used a nearly identical experimental design for the probability task (Gauffroy and Barrouillet, in preparation). Participants were presented with a conditional statement and with different cases representing either boys or girls who wear glasses or not (e. g., one boy with glasses, one boy without glasses, three girls with glasses, and one girl without glasses). They were asked to evaluate the probability that the statement was either true or false for a pupil taken at random from the classroom. Once again, results confirmed our predictions. In both tasks, performance on *NN* conditionals replicated the conjunctive–defective biconditional–defective conditional developmental trend that we previously observed. However, as predicted, *BB* conditionals mainly elicited defective biconditional responses that were predominant in all the participants that are known to be able to flesh out the initial representation (i.e., sixth graders, ninth graders, and adults).

Pragmatic modulations induced by promises and threats recently allowed us to test our assumption that the core meaning of the conditional corresponds to the initial representation constructed by heuristic processes. Newstead, Ellis, Evans, and Dennis (1997) observed that, in adults, promises and threats elicit equivalence readings in which both $p\ q$ and $\neg p\ \neg q$ cases are considered as making these conditionals true, whereas $\neg p\ q$ and $p\ \neg q$ cases make them false. According to our theory, this suggests that promises and threats involve a two-model initial representation (i.e., $p\ q$ and $\neg p\ \neg q$) representing cases that make the conditional true. This second model (i.e., $\neg p\ \neg q$) would be present in the initial model representation because pragmatic implicatures are part of the core meaning of any inducement. For example, a promise like "if you mow the lawn, then I'll give you five euros" will only be effective if the listener understands that the promised reward will not be forthcoming if the action is not performed. Thus, the pragmatic implicature "if you don't, I'll give you nothing" is not optional but inherent to the core meaning of this kind of speech act and should be represented in the initial model. This initial representation in turn would block any further construction of models by the analytic system. The original promise "if you mow the lawn, then I'll give you five euros" dismisses the $p\ \neg q$ possibility of mowing the lawn without being rewarded, while the implicature "if you don't mow the lawn, then I won't give you five euros" dismisses the possibility of being rewarded without mowing the lawn. Thus, any intervention of the analytic system would remain fruitless. According to our theory, those states of affairs that make a sentence true are represented in the initial model, whose construction depends on heuristic processes that are not strongly affected by individual or developmental differences. A direct consequence of this proposal is that there should be no difference between younger and older children in the number of models produced by the heuristic system. Thus, whereas an inefficient analytic system limits young children to a one-model representation for the basic conditionals, resulting in a conjunctive reading, this limitation might be overcome for conditionals eliciting multi-model initial representations. Thus, all participants should adopt an equivalence reading. It is exactly what we observed in the truth-table task (Gauffroy & Barrouillet, 2009) and in the probability task (Gauffroy & Barrouillet, in preparation).

Overall, the developmental findings are in line with the hypothesis that heuristic and analytic processes respectively underlie the construction of initial and fleshed-out models. We recently tested this hypothesis through chronometric studies. If the initial model is constructed though heuristic processes that are automatic and unconscious, its construction should be faster than that of those models constructed though analytic processes. As a consequence, in a truth-table task, the cases matching the initial representation should be processed faster than the others, and especially faster than those that are constructed through fleshing out. This general prediction should lead to different patterns of response times as a function of the different types of interpretations. For basic conditionals, we have predicted that a three-model representation underlies the defective conditional response pattern. Responses of irrelevance to $\neg p \neg q$ and $\neg p q$ cases, which require a fleshing out of the initial model $p q$, should take longer than the responses supported by this initial model such as the "true" responses to $p q$ cases. However, the response of irrelevance to $\neg p q$ cases, which necessitates the construction of the complete three-model representation, should take longer than the same response on $\neg p \neg q$ cases, that can be reached with a two-model representation (i.e., $p q$ and $\neg p \neg q$). Thus, at this interpretational level, responses to $p q$ ("true"), $\neg p \neg q$ ("indeterminate"), and $\neg p q$ ("indeterminate") that require one, two, and three models respectively should take increasingly longer with each level. Concerning the defective biconditional response pattern ("true", "irrelevant", "false", and "false" to $p q$, $\neg p \neg q$, $\neg p q$, and $p \neg q$ cases respectively), responses of irrelevance on $\neg p \neg q$ cases, which necessitate the construction of the $\neg p \neg q$ model through fleshing out, should take longer than the "true" responses on $p q$ cases. However, the two-model representation that underlies "irrelevant" responses on $\neg p \neg q$ cases should also lead these reasoners to produce "false" responses on $\neg p q$ cases that are not represented in the most complete representation they are able to construct. As a consequence, the time needed to produce the two types of responses on $\neg p$ cases should not differ. Finally, reasoners who adopt a conjunctive interpretation construct a single $p q$ model representation. So, our theory predicts that all their responses should be based on this one-model representation and, as a consequence, they should not strongly differ from each other in latencies. Concerning "false" responses on $p \neg q$ cases, they can be reached by two different routes. A fast route would consist of drawing "false" responses from the initial representation. Because p is associated with q in the initial model, its association with $\neg q$ can lead to the "false" response. However, a slow route would consist in deducing the "false" response by verifying that the $p \neg q$ case does not match any of the models constructed at the end of the fleshing out process. Because the number of models constructed depends on the kind of interpretation adopted, this slow route should take longer for defective conditional reasoners who construct three models than for defective biconditional reasoners who only construct two models. Unfortunately, the relative weight of these two routes in the evaluation process cannot be predicted with certainty. Thus, we adopted the conservative hypothesis of a mix between the two routes, with the response times for "false" to $p \neg q$ being intermediate between one-model and two-model responses for the biconditional responders, and between one-model and three-model responses for the conditional responders. These predictions are summarized in Figure 4.2.

To test these predictions Vergauwe, Gauffroy, Morsanyi, Dagry, and Barrouillet (2013) had adults complete a computerized version of the truth-table task (Barrouillet et al., 2008). As expected, response times on the different cases varied as a function of the interpretation of the conditional and the number of models it involved (Figure 4.2). Considering the defective conditional responders, as we predicted, their "true" responses on $p q$ cases were faster than their "indeterminate" responses on $\neg p \neg q$ cases (two models needed), which were in turn faster

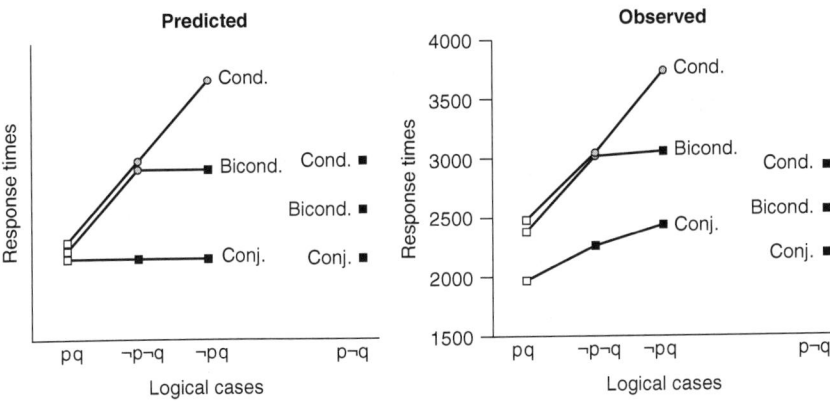

Figure 4.2 Predicted and observed mean response times as a function of logical cases and level of interpretation (Conj., Bicond., and Cond. for conjunctive, defective biconditional and defective conditional interpretations respectively). White squares, black squares, and grey circles refer to "true", "false", and "indeterminate" responses respectively. Mean response times on *p q*, ¬*p* ¬*q*, and ¬*p q* cases are predicted from the number of models they involve. Mean response times on *p* ¬*q* cases are predicted as intermediate between the fastest and slowest responses in each group (see text for explanations about fast and slow routes for "false" responses in these cases)

than their "indeterminate" responses on ¬*p* q cases (three-model representation). In the same way, for defective biconditional responders, "true" responses on *p q* cases were faster than "irrelevant" responses on ¬*p* ¬*q* cases that did not differ from "false" responses to ¬*p q* cases. Finally, concerning conjunctive responses, results were only indicative since only seven adults exhibited this interpretation. As for the two other interpretations, responding "true" on *p q* cases was faster than responding "false" on the three other cases for which response times did not significantly vary. To conclude, the different patterns of response times fit our predictions according to which response times are a function of the number of models each response involved. However, developmental studies focusing on age groups in which conjunctive and defective biconditional interpretations are predominant, such as children or adolescents (Gauffroy & Barrouillet, 2009, 2011), would constitute a necessary complement to this study.

Conclusion

In this chapter, we have reviewed the successive versions of a developmental theory of conditional reasoning based on Johnson-Laird's mental model theory, which assumes that people understand conditionals statements by representing the states of affairs that can occur when these statements are true. As we have seen, the mental model theory provides a heuristic framework within which we elaborated models accounting for the successive interpretations of the "*if . . . then*" condition-als endorsed by children, adolescents, and adults. Especially suited for integrat-ing content and context effects through semantic and pragmatic modulations, our developmental mental model theory is able to account for developmental find-ings concerning a variety of tasks including the identification of cases compatible or incompatible with a conditional statement, the production and evaluation of inferences, truth-table tasks and the evaluation of the probability of the condi-tional. To the best of our knowledge, there is no other theory able to explain such a variety of phenomena revealed through the complete range of paradigms used to study conditional reasoning.

The developmental inquiry reveals that the way adults understand and reason from conditionals is preceded by a series of developmental levels that lead chil-dren and adolescents to process conditionals as conjunctions and then bicondition-als. Interestingly, even if the way adults reason often departs from the norms of formal logic, the development of conditional reasoning can be characterized as converging towards these norms with the capacity to construct representations of the conditional that correspond to the three cases of the material implication (i.e., $p\ q$, $\neg p\ \neg q$, and $\neg p\ q$). At the same time, when people evaluate the truth-value of conditionals, they rely on procedures akin to the Ramsey test and exhibit interpretations conforming to the De Finetti table, on which the suppositional and probabilistic accounts of conditional are based (Evans, 2007; Fugard, Pfeifer, Mayerhofer, & Kleiter, 2011; Oaksford & Chater, 2007). However, the evalua-tion of the probability of the conditional as the conditional probability that has been consistently found in adults appears as a developmental achievement pro-ceeded by the same conjunctive and biconditional interpretations observed with other tasks like inference production or the identification of permissible cases. This succession of the same three developmental levels whatever the task under study suggests that the extensional and probabilistic approaches of the conditional could be closer from each other than usually assumed. Our hypothesis is that these approaches represent two formal descriptions of the same psychological process of constructing mental models of possibilities, this representation increasing in complexity with age.

Notes

1 Recent versions of dual-process models (Evans, 2008, 2009; Stanovitch, 2011) have moved away from the System 1/System 2 terminology to adopt a Type 1/Type 2 process-ing distinction. This is due to the fact that the terms System 1 and System 2 suggested singular systems that could be neurally distinguished, whereas it is now assumed that both systems include a variety of processes. Nonetheless, we will here keep the com-monly used terminology of Systems 1 and 2 without any underlying assumption of sin-gularity at the cognitive neural levels.
2 The task was also proposed to third graders but they usually failed to grasp the notion of probability.

References

Andrews, G., & Halford, G. S. (1998). Children's ability to make transitive inferences: The importance of premise integration and structural complexity. *Cognitive Development, 13*, 479–513.

Barrouillet, P. (2011). Dual-process theories of reasoning: The test of development. *Developmental Review, 31*(2–3), 151–179.

Barrouillet, P., & Gauffroy, C. (2011). Dual processes in the development of understanding conditionals. In K. Manketelow, D. Over & S. Elqayam (Eds.) *The science of reason* (pp 191–215). Hove, UK: Psychology Press.

Barrouillet, P., Gauffroy, C., & Lecas, J. F. (2008). Mental models and the suppositional account of conditionals. *Psychological Review, 115*(3), 760–771.

Barrouillet, P., Gavens, N., Vergauwe, E., Gaillard, V., & Camos, V. (2009). Working memory span development: A time-based resource-sharing model account. *Developmental Psychology, 45*(2), 477–490.

Barrouillet, P., Grosset, N., & Lecas, J. F. (2000). Conditional reasoning by mental models: Chronometric and developmental evidence. *Cognition, 75*, 237–266.

Barrouillet, P., & Lecas, J. F. (1998). How can mental models account for content effects in conditional reasoning? A developmental perspective. *Cognition, 67*, 209–253.

Barrouillet, P., & Lecas, J. F. (1999). Mental models in conditional reasoning and working memory. *Thinking & Reasoning, 5*, 289–302.

Barrouillet, P., & Lecas, J. F. (2002). Content and context effects in children's and adults' conditional reasoning. *Quarterly Journal of Experimental Psychology, 55*(3), 839–854.

Barrouillet, P., Markovits, H., & Quinn, S. (2001). Developmental and content effects in reasoning with causal conditionals. *Journal of Experimental Child Psychology, 81*(3), 235–248.

Braine, M. D. S. (1990). The "natural logic" approach to reasoning. In W. F. Overton (Ed.), *Reasoning, necessity and logic: Developmental perspectives.* Hillsdale, NJ: Erlbaum.

Braine, M. D. S., & O'Brien, D. P. (1991). A theory of If: A lexical entry, reasoning program, and pragmatic principles. *Psychological Review, 98*, 182–203.

Case, R., Kurland, D. M., & Goldberg, J. (1982). Operational efficiency and the growth of short-term-memory span. *Journal of Experimental Child Psychology, 33*(3), 386–404.

Cheng, P. W., & Holyoak, K. J. (1985). Pragmatic reasoning schemas. *Cognitive Psychology, 17*, 391–416.

Cummins, D. D. (1996). Evidence of deontic reasoning in 3- and 4-year-old children. *Cognition, 31*, 187–276.

Dias, M. G., & Harris, P. L. (1988). The effect of make-believe play on deductive reasoning. *British Journal of Developmental Psychology, 6*, 207–221.

Dias, M. G., & Harris, P. L. (1990). The influence of the imagination on reasoning. *British Journal of Developmental Psychology, 8*, 305–318.

Evans, J. St. B. T. (1977). Linguistic factors in reasoning. *Quarterly Journal of Experimental Psychology, 29*, 297–306.

Evans, J. St. B. T. (1989). *Bias in human reasoning: Causes and consequences.* Hillsdale, NJ: Lawrence Erlbaum Associates.

Evans, J. St. B. T. (2006). The heuristic-analytic theory of reasoning: Extension and evaluation. *Psychonomic Bulletin & Review, 13*(3), 378–395.

Evans, J. St. B. T. (2007). *Hypothetical thinking: Dual processes in reasoning and judgment.* Hove, UK: Psychology Press.

Evans, J. St. B. T. (2008). Dual processing accounts of reasoning, judgment and social cognition. *Annual Review of Psychology, 59*, 255–278.

Evans, J. St. B. T., & Handley, S. J. (1999). The role of negation in conditional inference. *Quarterly Journal of Experimental Psychology Section A—Human Experimental Psychology, 52*(3), 739–769.

Evans, J. St. B. T., Handley, S. J., & Over, D. E. (2003). Conditionals and conditional probability. *Journal of Experimental Psychology: Learning, Memory and Cognition, 29*(2), 331–335.

Evans, J. St. B. T., Over, D. E., & Handley, S. J. (2005). Suppositions, extensionality and conditionals: A critique of the mental model theory of Johnson-Laird and Byrne (2002). *Psychological Review, 112*, 1040–1052.

Fugard, A. J. B., Pfeifer, N., Mayerhofer, B., & Kleiter, G. D. (2011). How people interpret conditionals: Shifts toward the conditional event. *Journal of Experimental Psychology: Learning, Memory, and Cognition, 37*, 635–648.

Gauffroy, C., & Barrouillet, P. (2009). Heuristic and analytic processes in mental models for conditionals: An integrative developmental theory. *Developmental Review, 29*, 249–282.

Gauffroy, C., & Barrouillet, P. (2011). The primacy of thinking about possibilities in the development of reasoning. *Developmental Psychology, 47*, 1000–1011.

Gauffroy, C., & Barrouillet, P. (in preparation). Semantic and pragmatic modulation in the evaluation of probability of conditionals.

Halford, G. S., Bain, J. D., Maybery, M. T., & Andrews, G. (1998). Induction of relational schemas: Common processes in reasoning and complex learning. *Cognitive Psychology, 35*(3), 201–245.

Halford, G. S., Wilson, W. H., & Phillips, S. (1998). Processing capacity defined by relational complexity: Implications for comparative, developmental, and cognitive psychology. *Behavorial and Brain Sciences, 21*(6), 803–864.

Harris, P. L., & Nunez, M. (1996). Understanding of permission rules by preschool children. *Child Development, 67*, 1572–1591.

Inhelder, B., & Piaget, J. (1958). *The growth of logical thinking from childhood to adolescence.* Basic Books, New York.

Johnson-Laird, P. N. (1983). *Mental models.* Cambridge, MA: Harvard University Press.

Johnson-Laird, P. N., & Byrne, R. M. J. (1991). *Deduction.* Hillsdale, NJ: Lawrence Erlbaum Associates.

Johnson-Laird, P. N., & Byrne, R. M. J. (2002). Conditionals: A theory of meaning, pragmatics and inference. *Psychological Review, 109*(4), 646–678.

Kuhn, D. (1977). Conditional reasoning in children. *Developmental Psychology, 13*, 342–353.

Kuhn, D., Amsel, E., & O'Loughlin, M. (1988). *The development of scientific thinking skills.* San Diego, CA: Academic Press.

Lecas, J. F., & Barrouillet, P. (1999). Understanding of conditional rules in childhood and adolescence: A mental models approach. *Current Psychology of Cognition, 18*, 363–396.

Light, P., Blaye, A., Gilly, M., & Girotto, V. (1989). Pragmatic schemas and logical reasoning in 6- to 8-year-old children. *Cognitive Development, 4*, 49–64.

Macnamara, J. (1986). *A border dispute: The place of logic in psychology.* Cambridge, MA: Bradford Books/MIT Press.

Markovits, H., & Barrouillet, P. (2002). The development of conditional reasoning: A mental model account. *Developmental Review, 22*(1), 5–36.

Markovits, H., & Vachon, R. (1990). Conditional reasoning, representation, and level of abstraction. *Developmental Psychology, 26*(6), 942–951.

Mueller, U., Overton, W. F., & Reene, K. (2001). Development of conditional reasoning: A longitudinal study. *Journal of Cognition and Development, 2*, 27–49.

Newstead, H. E., Ellis, M. C., Evans, J. St. B. T., & Dennis, I. (1997). Conditional reasoning with realistic material. *Thinking & Reasoning, 3*(1), 49–76.

Oaksford, M., & Chater, N. (2007). *Bayesian rationality: The probabilistic approach to human reasoning*. Oxford: Oxford University Press.

O'Brien, D. P., & Overton, W. F. (1980). Conditional reasoning following contradictory evidence: A developmental analysis. *Journal of Experimental Child Psychology, 30*, 44–61.

O'Brien, D. P., & Overton, W. F. (1982). Conditional reasoning and the competence performance issue: A developmental analysis of a training task. *Journal of Experimental Child Psychology, 34*, 274–290.

Oberauer, K., & Wilhelm, O. (2003). The meaning(s) of conditionals: Conditional probabilities, mental models, and personal utilities. *Journal of Experimental Psychology: Learning, Memory and Cognition, 29*(4), 680–693.

Overton, W. F., Byrnes, J. P., & O'Brien, D. P. (1985). Developmental and individual differences in conditional reasoning: The role of contradiction training and cognitive style. *Developmental Psychology, 21*, 692–701.

Overton, W. F., Ward, S. L., Noveck, I. A., Black, J., & O'Brien, D. P. (1987). Form and content in the development of deductive reasoning. *Developmental Psychology, 23*, 22–30.

Pollard, P., & Evans, J. St. B. T. (1980). The influence of logic on conditional reasoning performance. *Quarterly Journal of Experimental Psychology, 32*(4), 605–624.

Quinn, S., & Markovits, H. (1998). Conditional reasoning, causality, and the structure of semantic memory: Strength of association as a predictive factor for content effects. *Cognition, 68*(3), 93–101.

Richards, C. A. & Sanderson, J. A. (1999). The role of imagination in facilitating deductive reasoning in 2-, 3-, and 4-year-olds. *Cognition, 72*, 81–89.

Rips, L. J. (1994). *The psychology of proof: Deductive reasoning in human thinking*. Cambridge, MA: MIT Press.

Stanovitch, K. E. (2011). *Rationality and the reflective mind*. New York: Oxford University Press.

Vergauwe, E., Gauffroy, C., Morsanyi, K., Dagry, I., & Barrouillet, P. (2013). Chronometric evidence for dual process mental model theory of conditional. *Journal of Cognitive Psychology, 25*(2), 174–182.

Wildman, T. M., & Fletcher, H. J. (1977). Developmental increases and decreases in solutions of conditional syllogism problems. *Developmental Psychology, 13*, 630–636.

5 Heuristics and biases during adolescence

Developmental reversals and individual differences

Paul A. Klaczynski and Wejdan S. Felmban

In recent years, interest in the developmental heuristics and biases ("DHB") research has risen substantially (see Barrouillet & Gauffroy, 2013). Several reviewers of this literature have concluded that although age is sometimes positively associated with heuristic judgments during childhood, age is not related to heuristic judgments during adolescence. This conclusion provided the impetus for our first major goal: To challenge this conclusion by demonstrating that, in some social domains, heuristic judgments increase from late childhood through adolescence. Also expressed in recent reviews is the concern that DHB researchers have paid scant attention to the individual differences in the development of heuristics. This concern led to our second major goal: To show that individual difference variables not only "explain" variance in heuristic use above and beyond that "explained" by age, but also suggest individual differences in the *trajectories* of heuristic and bias development. A final purpose was to discuss briefly directions and methodological issues in DHB research.

To achieve these goals, the chapter is broken into five sections. In a brief introduction, we outline findings from the adult heuristics and biases literature, define terms important to our goals, and discuss the implications of DHB research for theories of cognitive and social cognitive development. The second section provides background information necessary for understanding the origins of claims about heuristic development during adolescence. Thus, we review DHB research with children, concentrating on studies that demonstrated age-related increases in heuristic use, and briefly review adolescent DHB research, highlighting differences between DHB findings with children and adolescents. The gist of this section is that counterintuitive age trends (i.e., "developmental reversals," defined subsequently) have been reported during childhood, but not during adolescence. These findings set the stage for the third section, wherein we present the conclusions noted previously that heuristics develop little during adolescence.

We dedicated the fourth section to our two primary goals. (1) We demonstrate that the conclusions discussed in the third section are not entirely accurate by presenting evidence that in three domains (e.g., obesity, gender) heuristics are used more by older adolescents than younger adolescents and children. (2) The same data are used to show how individual difference variables may predict differences in the developmental trajectories of heuristics. In the concluding section, we suggest directions for additional research and argue for confronting several design and methodological challenges that hinder progress in DHB research.

Introduction: Heuristics, the "normative/descriptive" gap, and developmental reversals

On numerous HB tasks, adults' responses deviate from traditionally prescribed norms (e.g., Kahneman, Slovic, & Tversky, 1982; Stanovich, 1999, 2004). These deviations between normative ideals and performance, indicating a sizable "normative/descriptive gap" (Baron, 1985, 1988) and discrepancies between competence and performance, have been attributed to tendencies to forego deliberative analyses and instead rely on heuristics to draw inferences and make decisions. Despite the potential that developmental research offers for answering questions about the causes and origins of the normative/descriptive gap (i.e., NDG), competence-performance discrepancies, heuristics, and reasoning fallacies, that potential has not yet been realized. For instance, developmental research may show that age is positively associated with normative responses on most heuristics and biases tasks. Would such findings indicate that, despite adults' typically poor performance, the NDG decreases with age? Similarly, would such findings support assumptions common to several prominent theories of cognitive development (e.g., information processing, Neo-Piagetian, behavior decision theories)? Two important assumptions are that development entails progressions toward increasing complexity (see Overton, 1985; Reyna & Farley, 2006) and that the discrepancy between competence and performance (DC-P) decreases with age.[1]

Supporting the first assumption is an impressive evidential corpus indicating that most basic (e.g., processing speed, working memory) and higher-order (e.g., reasoning, metacognitive) abilities improve with age. Although evidence for age increases in HB performance would appear to provide additional support for the "development-as-progression" assumption, the same evidence does not necessarily support the hypothesized decreases in the DC-P. Specifically, most adults acquire the requisite competencies for responding normatively on most HB tasks. However, poor performance on HB problems implies that because these competencies are infrequently instantiated in performance, any observed age improvements are necessarily modest. Because the progressions in the requisite competencies (e.g., reasoning, inhibition) for normative responses outpace gains in performance, modest gains in HB performance do *not* support the expected decreases in the NDG and DC-P. Instead, such gains must reflect age increases in the DC-P.

Yet, more profound implications for theories of cognitive development—and stronger evidence that the NDG and DC-P increase with age—come from evidence of developmental reversals (Brainerd, Reyna, & Ceci, 2008; Gomes & Brainerd, 2013; Reyna, 2013). Developmental reversals are counterintuitive age trends that occur when competence increases with age (or is stable) and performance declines with age. Developmental reversals imply that, under some conditions, children are more rational than adults and that the NGD increases with age. Developmental reversals, particularly if they occur frequently, cannot be readily explained by "bounded rationality" theories of heuristics and biases or most theories of cognitive and social cognitive development. However, if developmental reversals are uncommon, their implications for the assumptions underlying most developmental theories diminish considerably. The question then arises: How common are developmental reversals?

In the following section, we provide an indication of the frequency of reversals in the DHB literature. DHB research with children is reviewed first, followed by a review of DHB research with adolescents. Our brief review is consistent with other reviews in establishing the basis for the conclusions about heuristic development presented in the third section.

Developments in heuristics and biases

To preface, note that our review of DHB research is not comprehensive (for other reviews, see Barrouillet, 2011b; Barrouillet & Gauffroy, 2013; Klaczynski, 2013a; Morsanyi & Handley, 2013; Reyna & Brainerd, 2011; Ricco & Overton, 2011; Strough, Karns, & Schlosnagle, 2011). We focus on developmental reversals in childhood to illustrate that the evidential corpus for developmental reversals is abundant and show that reversals occur on numerous tasks (including tasks not traditionally used in HB research). Note also that we do not believe that reversals are the norm in development; nonetheless, whether the substantial literature indicating progressions in basic and higher-order cognitive competencies (e.g., processing speed, working memory, reasoning) is sufficient to support conclusions that normative responses (i.e., performance) characterize development and that the NGC decreases with age are open questions. Lastly, note that our goals led us to limit our review to middle/late childhood and adolescence. Absent for our review (and other DHB reviews) is research with preschoolers (see Klaczynski, 2013a).[2]

Heuristic development in childhood

In this subsection, we hope to: (1) indicate the frequency with which developmental reversals have been found, (2) illustrate the range of tasks on which reversals have been reported, and (3) provide a basis for comparing DHB childhood research with DHB adolescent research. Studies not cited often as DHB studies, and studies of the "representativeness" heuristic, are discussed in more depth to increase awareness that DHB research is not restricted to tasks derived from adult research and provide a background for several of our adolescent studies.

The range of tasks on which reversals have been observed is impressive and includes problems involving sunk costs, framings, the "conjunction fallacy," belief-bias syllogisms, if-only thinking, social transitive inferences, beverage preferences, and base rate (BR) neglect. For instance, in an early study, Reyna and Ellis (1994) found that investigations' susceptibility to framing effects (i.e., changes in the phrasing of objectively identical responses lead to different decisions) increased with age. Although subsequent research has provided only partial support for this general conclusion, the more general finding—that children are less susceptible to framing effects than adults and adolescents—has been replicated (Strough et al., 2011; Weller, Levin, & Denburg, 2009). Developmental reversals have been found in two studies on "sunk cost" decisions, such that age related positively to fallacious decisions (Krouse, 1986; Webley & Plaisier, 1998). In the third study (Morsanyi & Handley, 2008), the age trend was not significant but, despite a more restricted age range, the age findings paralleled those reported in earlier studies.

Developmental reversals have also been found in the "conjunction fallacy." In a particularly interesting study, Chiesi, Gronchi, and Primi (2008) found that 7-year-olds were less likely than 10-year-olds who were less likely than adults to commit the conjunction fallacy (i.e., judging p [A&B] > p [A] and/or p [B]). This work was novel because the reversal was on "stereotype-free" problems (i.e., coins lost beneath blue flowers [i.e., "A"] and blue flowers with bees on them [i.e., "A&B"]) and occurred when "A&~B" (i.e., blue flowers without bees) was more frequent than "A&B," but not when "A&B" occurred more than "A&~B." Chiesi et al. thus found counterintuitive age trends in the conjunction fallacy *and* framing effects. Preceding this finding were those of Davidson (1995) and Morsanyi and Handley (2008), who found conjunction fallacy reversals problems with stereotype-activating content. Morsanyi and Handley (2008) also found reversals on belief-bias syllogisms and "if-only" (i.e., "if-only" a different action had been taken, a negative outcome would not have occurred) problems. In sum, on various tasks adapted from the adult literature, these studies (typically of 5- to 12-year-olds) indicated reversals in sunk cost decisions, framing effects, the conjunction fallacy, and "if-only" thinking.

Often excluded from DHB reviews, for no compelling theoretical reason, are reversals observed on "non-traditional" HB tasks. An example is Markovits and Dumas' (1999) fascinating study of 6- to 11-year-olds' responses on traditional (A > B; B > C; therefore, A > C) and "social" transitive inference problems. Although age related positively to normative responses on the traditional problems, more interesting were responses on structurally isomorphic social problems (involving "friends" and "not friends") because no conclusions logically followed on these problems (e.g., "A is a friend of B"; "B is a friend of C"). Nonetheless, as age increased so too did non-logical "transitive" inferences on "friends" problems ("A and C are friends"). On the "not friends" problems (e.g., "A is quarreling with B," "B is quarreling with C), age was positively related to "anti-transitive" inferences: Older children inferred that "A *likes* C" more than younger children. Markovits and Dumas' findings indicate age increases in judgments based on, respectively, "friends of friends are friends" heuristic and an "enemies of enemies are friends" heuristic (reminiscent of proverb, often attributed to Sun Tzu, *The enemy of my enemy is my friend*). That neither heuristic related to inferences on the traditional problems indicates that these reversals were not overgeneralizations of emerging transitive reasoning abilities.[3]

In another study with a non-traditional task, Klaczynski (2008) had 7- to 10-year-old Chinese and American children taste drinks purportedly created by obese and average-weight "peers." When the association between ingestion and contagious illnesses was primed, anti-obesity biases (e.g., low flavor ratings, stronger beliefs that "obese-created" drinks could result in sickness) increased with age. In an extension to Chinese and American 4- to 10-year-olds, Klaczynski (2013a) replicated this reversal, discovered that biases against drinks "created" by child amputees also increased with age, *and* found reversals in false memories for "worst tasting" drinks. Specifically, in a subsequent memory test wherein children recalled the drink they liked least, older children (in both countries) misremembered obese- and (to a lesser extent) amputee-created drinks as the worst-tasting drinks, more than younger children (see Gomes & Brainerd, 2013, for discussion and review of reversals in false memories).

Because of the attention it has attracted and its relevance to the research we present, this subsection concludes with studies of the representativeness heuristic on BR neglect problems. On "social" BR problems, "individuating" information, indicating that "targets" possess stereotype-consistent qualities (i.e., targets appears to "represent" stereotyped groups), conflicts with statistical base rate evidence. For instance, Davidson (1995), discussed previously because she found a conjunction fallacy reversal, also found a reversal on BR problems. Informed that more elderly people engaged in stereotype-inconsistent activities (e.g., bicycling) than stereotype-consistent activities (e.g., strolling), 10- and 12-year-olds more often ignored base rates, judged that elderly "targets" engaged in the stereotypical activity, and justified their judgments by reference to stereotypes more than 8-year-olds.

Davidson's work was based on Jacobs and Potenza's (1991) widely cited study. Presented with stereotype-relevant information about targets (e.g., Juanita is popular, attractive, etc.) that conflicted with base rates (e.g., 10 girls want to be cheerleaders, 20 want to join the band), older children (11-year-olds) and adults relied on representativeness (i.e., stereotype-consistent information), and ignored base rates, more than 7- and 9-year-olds. By contrast, when base rates conflicted with individuating information (e.g., a friend's testimony that bicycle brand B is superior to brand A) on problems about objects, base rate judgments increased with age (Jacobs & Potenza, 1991).

Because of its impact on recent research, including several of our studies, we note the question Stanovich, Toplak, and West (2008) raised about Jacobs and Potenza's (1991) seemingly impressive evidence for a developmental reversal. Operating on the assumption that younger children probably had less knowledge of relevant stereotypes than older children and adults, Stanovich et al. conjectured that this reversal in BR neglect—and other reversals based on accrued social knowledge—could have been an artifact of age differences in stereotype knowledge (see note 2). Simply, representativeness cannot underlie judgments in the absence of relevant stereotype knowledge (e.g., cheerleaders). Presumably, if younger children knew the requisite stereotypes, they would be as, and probably more, susceptible to BR neglect as older children.

Although a "knowledge difference" explanation cannot adequately explain reversals on "non-social" tasks (e.g., framing; see Reyna, 2012), the Stanovich et al. (2008) argument provided the impetus for one of the most important DHB studies in recent years. To test the "stereotype knowledge" hypothesis directly, De Neys and Vanderputte (2011) examined 5- and 8-year-olds' responses to BR neglect problems with familiar or unfamiliar stereotypes. Critically, on the conflict problems, wherein information that activated familiar stereotypes conflicted with base rate data, age negatively correlated with normative responses. Thus, De Neys and Vanderputte showed that, despite having as much stereotype knowledge as older children, younger children were less likely to ignore base rates. This finding—together with evidence that (a) developmental reversals occur on stereotype-free conjunction (Chiesi et al., 2008), framing, "if-only," and sunk cost problems, (b) during adolescence, BR neglect and stereotype are unrelated (Klaczynski, 2013b), and (c) there are reversals in false memories—renders less plausible explanations of developmental reversals that hinge on stereotype knowledge.[4]

We have summarized evidence for reversals found in 12 studies. Considering the relatively small size of the DHB literature, and substantial evidence for memory reversals (see Gomes & Brainerd, 2013), the proportion of reversals is substantial. Arguments reducing developmental reversals to "interesting anomalies" are diminished further by the array of tasks on which reversals have been reported. These reversals indicate that, on a number of tasks, the NDG and discrepancies between competence and performance increase between (approximately) 5 and 12 years of age. The theoretical issues implied by development reversals would be quite serious if reversal were also observed from late childhood through adolescence. We next review evidence bearing on the question, have developmental reversals been found (and, if so, how often) between late childhood and late adolescence?

Heuristic development in adolescence

The preceding question has fueled claims about the development of heuristics beyond childhood and therefore is directly relevant to one of our central goals: Challenging the answers several theorists have given recently. The review that follows is intended to illustrate the evidentiary basis on which those answers rest and therefore serves as a preview for the more detailed discussion of those conclusions that form the core of the next section.

Adolescent DHB research can be roughly classified into three categories: (1) "Single-task" research: Investigations of age differences on a single task; (2) "Multiple-task" research: Studies of age differences on multiple HB problems; (3) Research on belief-biased or "motivated" reasoning. We first review several single-task investigations and then discuss findings from multiple-task studies. Immediately preceding a summary of the findings is an overview of developmental research on belief-biased reasoning.

Of the single-task adolescent DHB studies, several concerned the relationship between age and the "ratio bias" (RB) effect. The RB effect is indicated by judgments that "targets" (e.g., winning lottery tickets) are more likely from large denominator/large numerator samples (e.g., 10 winners/100 lottery tickets) than from small denominator/small numerator samples, even though the objective probabilities are identical (1/10) in, or favor (e.g., 2/10), the small sample. In brief, these researches have produced somewhat mixed results: Both positive associations between age and normative responses and null relationships between age and normative responding have been reported. For instance, from early adolescence to adulthood (Klaczynski, 2001b) and late childhood to early adolescence (Klaczynski & Amsel, in press) age and normative responses correlated positively. However, despite examining similar ages, age and normative responses have not been associated in other studies (e.g., Amsel et al., 2008, Exp. 2; Kokis, MacPherson, Toplak, West, & Stanovich, 2002). Other "single task" investigations have yielded more straightforward findings. For instance, normative decisions to avoid sunk costs (Klaczynski & Cottrell, 2004), establish positive precedents (Klaczynski, 2011, Exp. 1), and avoid negative precedents (Klaczynski, 2011, Exp. 2) increase from childhood through adolescence.

The latter findings generally parallel those from multiple-task studies. Several multiple-task investigations have compared early (i.e., 12 to 13 years), middle (i.e., 15 to 16 years), and/or late adolescents (17 to 18 years) and adults. Klaczynski (2001a, 2001b), for instance, found that middle adolescents outperformed early adolescents on 8 of 10 HB tasks (e.g., gambler's fallacy, contingency detection) and that adults and older adolescents selected normative responses more often than early adolescents on ratio bias, sunk cost, and "if-only" problems. On none of the 13 tasks in these 2 studies were developmental reversals reported. The results of several more recent investigations have been similar. For instance, Chiesi, Prime, and Morsanyi (2011) found that age related positively to probabilistic reasoning scores aggregated across several problems (e.g., BR neglect). Likewise, in De Neys, Cromheeke, and Osman (2011, Exp. 3), normative response to conjunction fallacy and BR neglect problems related positively to age (see also Morsanyi & Handley, 2013). In an investigation of 10- to 13 year-olds, Kokis et al. (2002) found that age associated positively with normative responses on belief-bias deductive reasoning (e.g., All mammals walk; whales are mammals; can whales walk?) and statistical reasoning problems.

Although little studied during childhood (e.g., Klaczynski & Aneja, 2002), several studies of belief-biased reasoning involved older children, adolescents, and adults. These researches have consistently yielded two findings. First, Kuhn and her colleagues (e.g., Kuhn, 1989, 1991, 1993; Kuhn, Amsel, & O'Loughlin, 1988) reported modest declines in reasoning biases (i.e., increases in "objective"/ normative reasoning) with age. Second, Klaczynski (e.g., Klaczynski, 1997, 2000; Klaczynski & Narasimham, 1998) found that, in general, age and reasoning biases were unrelated.

To summarize: In 12 of 14 DHB investigations with at least one adolescent group, age and normative responses positively correlated on most tasks. A similar number of belief-biased reasoning investigations indicate that age and biases are unrelated or related negatively. In marked contrast to childhood DHB research, extant research provides no basis for expecting developmental reversals during adolescence. Does this evidence provide a sufficiently strong foundation for conclusions about developmental trends in heuristics and biases during adolescence? In the next section, we present several scholars' affirmative answers to this question.[5]

Conclusions about heuristic development during adolescence

Our review of over 20 investigations of adolescent heuristics and belief-biased reasoning indicates that on numerous (but perhaps not all) tasks, normative responses increase from late childhood through late adolescence. Consistent with other reviews (e.g., Albert & Steinberg, 2011; Barrouillet, 2011b; Morsanyi & Handley, 2013), our review suggests that, if reversals occur during adolescence, they are less common than during childhood. Yet, as we make apparent in the next section, we are reluctant to draw this conclusion. Despite our reluctance and several cautionary notes (e.g., Strough et al., 2011; Stanovich et al., 2008), several scholars have relied on extant evidence to conclude that reversals, although sometimes found in childhood, do not continue into adolescence. For example, citing Davidson (1995) and Jacobs and Potenza, Kuhn (2006) acknowledged that reversals, although occasionally reported during childhood, had not been found in adolescent DHB research. Instead, "The typical picture . . . is one of modest improvement during the teen years, with performance moving toward an asymptote characteristic of the modest level of performance in the adult population" (p. 62). In arguing for the general rule that reliance on heuristics declines or stabilizes after childhood, Ricco and Overton (2011, p. 134) wrote, "age-related increases in heuristic-based responding appear limited to research with children from the early to late elementary years rather than adolescence."

A similar position is evident in Gauffroy and Barrouillet's (2009, p. 255) statement: ". . . though a tendency exists for a developmental increase in heuristic responding in reasoning tasks, it is mainly observed in childhood and on tasks requiring the retrieval and integration of social knowledge."

Similarly, Barrouillet (2011a, p. 156) argued that, whereas the processes underlying higher-order reasoning and decision making continue developing through adolescence, processes responsible for heuristics conclude developing by late childhood; reversals, therefore, are unlikely after childhood. Finally, Evans (2011) proposed that the inhibitory skills critical to suppressing the pragmatic cues that trigger heuristics develop during adolescence. Consequently, "belief biases and other contextual effects may be expected to increase from early to late childhood and then decrease again in later adolescence and early adulthood" (p. 99).

Implicitly or explicitly, these claims reflect the underlying sentiment that defining characteristics of post-childhood are *domain-general decreases* in heuristics and increases in normative responding. We would be remiss, however, if we did not add that qualifications accompanied most of these claims. For instance, Barrouillet (2011b) recognized that some age increases in biases cannot readily be attributed to age differences in knowledge (e.g., framing effects; Reyna & Ellis, 1994; the conjunction fallacy on unfamiliar problems; e.g., Chiesi et al., 2011). Evans (2011, p. 98) noted the need to "tread carefully" because the processes that underlie adult performance may develop at different rates and interact in different ways for younger children, older children, and adults. Although Ricco and Overton considered adolescent developmental reversals "exceptions" to the general rule noted above, they recognized the possibility "of increased use of specific social heuristics [that] might be learned at a particular point in development" (p. 134). Similarly, Morsanyi and Handley (2013) argued that heuristic use increases with age during childhood and decreases in adolescence, but acknowledged occasional exceptions on certain problems. However, although these qualifications suggest several avenues for future research, they do little to diminish the essence of the conclusion these theorists share: Reversals in heuristics and biases are largely limited to childhood.[6]

Developmental reversals and individual differences during adolescence

However guarded they appear, we are wary of these conclusions for several reasons. First, drawing conclusions does not seem prudent because the adolescent DHB database remains impoverished (Kuhn, 2006; Strough et al., 2011). We concur with Stanovich et al.'s (2008) sentiment that adolescent DHB research "is spread widely, but it is thin" (p. 267). Second, in the concluding section, we list a number of methodological problems that cast doubt on some findings and, by extension, conclusions based on these findings. Third, heuristic-based judgments may result from reflective analysis or automatically activated strategies (employed with little or no conscious deliberation). The critical point is that repeated practice/usage can transform deliberate strategies into automatically activated heuristics at virtually any point of the life course (Reyna & Farley, 2006; Stanovich et al., 2011). Therefore, it is not unreasonable to expect adolescent reversals in specific domains. Despite support from studies of expertise, this conjecture has not received the consideration it merits, although Klaczynski (2013a) recently summarized evidence for adolescent reversals in the domain of obesity.

On the following pages, we extend Klaczynski's (2013a) analysis by demonstrating adolescent reversals in several domains that increase in salience during adolescence and thus render the aforementioned "adolescent heuristic" conclusions more dubitable. In addition, we also wholly endorse Morsanyi and Handley's (2013) admonition that DHB researchers have paid scant attention to individual differences. Consequently, accompanying our presentation of data on developmental reversals are analyses suggesting individual differences in the trajectories of heuristics and biases developments.

Because previous investigations of the relationships among age, individual difference, and heuristics did not address hypotheses derived from a domain-specific approach to adolescent reversals and relied on statistical analyses that did not afford examination of differences in developmental trajectories, our synopsis of this work is brief. The variables most often studied by DHB researchers have been intelligence/intellectual capacity, thinking dispositions/epistemic understanding, and (particularly in studies of reasoning) inhibition. For instance, most developmental studies indicate that intelligence is not associated with belief-biased reasoning, but that thinking dispositions correlate negatively with belief-biased reasoning (see Klaczynski, 2009). Individual difference studies of responses on HB tasks have not been as consistent, however. Whereas Klaczynski (2001a) found no relationship between verbal ability and heuristic responses, Handley and Morsanyi found that intelligence and working memory correlated positively with children's heuristic responses, but negatively with adolescents' heuristic responses (Morsanyi & Handley, 2008, 2013). Others (e.g., Kokis et al., 2002) observed that composite normative scores related positively to intelligence and, indeed, that ability explained the correlation between age and normative responses. By contrast, although Chiesi et al. (2011) reported that age and ability correlated positively with probabilistic reasoning scores, ability did not account for the age-normative response association. Similarly, Kokis et al. (2002) found that thinking dispositions explained variance in their aggregative score above and beyond the variance explained by ability, but Chiesi et al. (2011) found that only one (i.e., superstitious thinking) of two measures of dispositions explained variance in probabilistic reasoning. Nonetheless, the most common findings from this research are that ability and thinking dispositions correlate positively with normative responses and negatively with heuristic responses (e.g., Chiesi et al., 2011; Klaczynski, 2000, 2001a; Kokis et al., 2002).

Issues we raise in the Conclusion, data analytic concerns discussed below, evidence that ability-normative response and thinking disposition-normative response relationships are (to some extent) task-specific among adults (Stanovich et al., 2008; Stanovich & West, 2008), and the paucity of DHB research, indicates the inadvisability of drawing conclusions about individual differences and development. Despite our sympathy with Morsanyi and Handley's (2013) concerns, we suggest that DBH researchers consider seriously at least some of the issues raised in the Conclusion and the value of the data analytic techniques typically used in DHB research before undertaking additional studies of age and individual differences,

Concerning the latter issue, neither the results of partial correlational nor multiple regression analyses allow for inferences about individual differences in developmental trajectories. For instance, results of hierarchical multiple regression analyses sometimes imply that an individual difference variable mediates age-heuristic relationships (e.g., Kokis et al., 2002). Are multiple regression analyses useful in testing an alternative possibility? What if ability "explains" the age-heuristic relationships for one (e.g., high ability) or more (moderate and high ability) subgroups, but does not explain such relationships for all (e.g., low ability) subgroups. Because regression and other time-honored analytic approaches are inadequate to this task, more sophisticated techniques (i.e., mediation, moderation, moderated mediation) are required. Consequently, we conducted moderated mediation analyses of the investigations presented subsequently.

However, we accessed several individual difference variables in each study. Consequently, although the findings are considerably more complex than described below, a complete discussion is beyond the scope of this chapter. Because our purpose is best served by discussing evidence that individual difference variables moderated age differences in responses, a brief overview of moderation (and moderated mediation) is in order. In our data, moderation occurred when "effects" associated with age depended (or were "conditional") on "level" (in our analyses, these were always "low," moderate," and "high") of one or more individual difference (or experimental) variables. Suppose that thinking dispositions moderated a positive relationship between age and BR neglect. Follow-up analyses could show, for example, that the age increase in BR neglect was significant only for adolescents with low thinking disposition scores. Such a finding implies limitations on the generalizability of observed developmental reversal in BR neglect such that the reversal is characteristic of adolescents who are low (but not moderate or high) in thinking dispositions. The same example can be used to describe moderated mediation. In moderated mediation, at some—but not all—levels of the moderating variable, another individual difference variable partially or fully "explains" age differences. Thus, for instance, at the lowest level of thinking dispositions, stereotypical beliefs could account for (i.e., mediate) age differences in BR neglect.

This overview, when coupled with our descriptions of the findings (and accompanying figures), should illustrate the value of our analytic approach (for complete descriptions, see Hayes (2012, 2013), Hayes & Preacher (in press), and Fairchild & MacKinnon (2009)). Before presenting our investigations, note that references to "different developmental trajectories" are meant to suggest possible differences that should be treated cautiously. In fact, the cross-sectional designs we used prohibit such strong developmental inferences. Nonetheless, an advantage of moderation and moderation-mediation analyses is that they can, in longitudinal research, uncover different developmental trajectories. Thus, the possible developmental trajectories we mention are merely intended to convey our speculations at this time.

Our hypotheses derived from the view that adolescent reversals are domain-specific; that is, reversals during adolescence occur in specific social domains (Klaczynski, 2013a). Specifically, changes in "socio-cultural atmosphere" of adolescence sometimes lead to age differences in the salience and strength of beliefs and stereotypes in specific domains. Outcomes of these increases include age increases in the ease with which relevant beliefs and stereotypes are activated and age decreases in inhibiting these beliefs/stereotypes. Consequently, judgments based on "social" heuristics (e.g., representativeness) sometimes increase with age (Klaczynski, 2013a; Klaczynski et al., 2009). However, (a) belief changes are not equally extensive within age groups and (b) although heuristic-inhibiting abilities (e.g., both general (e.g., inhibition) and specific (e.g., numeracy)) may develop during the same period, the rate and degree of those developments vary across adolescents. Consequently, increases in heuristics are most likely among adolescents with the strongest beliefs/stereotypes and the least developed "heuristic-inhibiting" abilities. Consistent with this general approach, we conducted five investigations (Ns ranged from 158 to 308) of age and individual differences in heuristics and biases in three social domains: Obesity, gender, and juvenile justice. Ages ranged from approximately 10 to 17 years (the gender and juvenile justice studies were exceptions; ranges = 9 to 14 years and 10 to 19 years, respectively).

Obesity: Reversals in generalization biases and representativeness

Appearance concerns increase from childhood to adolescence, suggesting obesity as an ideal starting point for this research program. In a preliminary investigation, shown pictures of obese and average-weight "targets" and informed that targets had negative characteristics, adolescents indicated the generalizability of those characteristics to others who "looked like" the targets (Klaczynski et al., 2009). As in the research outlined subsequently, generalization biases were computed by subtracting average target generalizations from obese target generalization. Klaczynski et al. initially reported a developmental reversal in generalization biases that, in a reanalysis of the original data, remained significant after controlling for variance associated with stereotyping (see Klaczynski, 2013a). In a second reanalysis, we entered "thin idealization" (i.e., beliefs that thinness/attractiveness determines social and economic success) as a potential moderator of the age-generalization bias association. The results in Figure 5.1 indicate that thin idealization moderated the relationship between age and biases. Specifically, when the "value" (level) of thin idealization was low, age related weakly and negatively to biases. When thin ideal beliefs were moderate, age and generalization biases were unrelated. However, at high levels of idealization, the age-bias relationship was positive and strong. Thus, the reversal in Klaczynski, Daniel, and Keller (2009) was not typical of adolescents, but was restricted to adolescents who most valued the thin ideal.

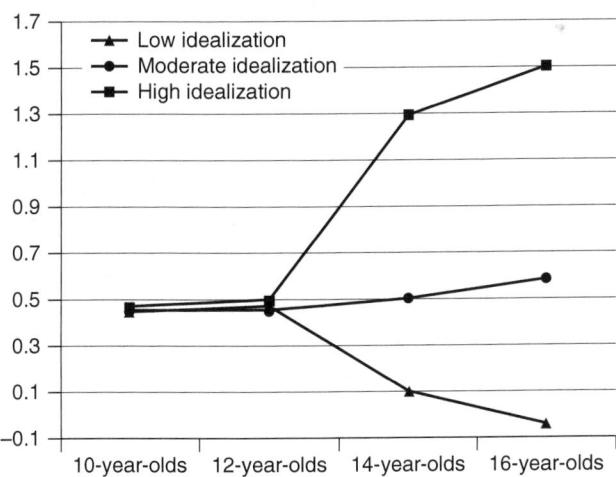

Figure 5.1 Age differences in biased generalizations by level of thin idealization (adjusted for causal attributions, body esteem, and obesity stereotypes; based on Klaczynski et al., 2009)

Recently, Klaczynski (2013b) explored the relationships among age, statistical reasoning (an index of numeracy, discussed subsequently), and obesity biases on problems wherein stereotypicality and sample size conflicted. On the statistical reasoning problems, participants indicated whether decisions should be based on relatively vivid individuating information or relatively pallid large samples of evidence. On the "appearance/sample size" problems, participants rated the strength of arguments, based on large or small samples, that obese or thin "peers" had stereotypically positive or stereotypically negative qualities. "Small sample, positive trait biases" arose when small sample arguments that thin peers had positive qualities were considered stronger than small sample arguments that obese peers had positive qualities. "Large sample, negative trait biases" arose when large sample arguments that obese peers had more negative traits were rated stronger than identical large sample arguments about thin peers.

Two important findings emerged. First, on a task different from that used by Klaczynski et al. (2009), we found developmental reversals on each bias index. Second, independently of cognitive ability and obesity stereotypes, statistical reasoning moderated the age-bias relationships. Because the findings were similar (although not identical) across bias indexes, we summarize only the findings for large sample, negative trait biases.

Figure 5.2 shows the age-bias relationships by "level" of statistical reasoning. When statistical reasoning was low, the age-bias relationship was positive and strong. However, at moderate and high levels of statistical reasoning, age and biases were not related. As in the reanalysis of Klaczynski et al. (2009), these developmental reversals in obesity biases were limited to adolescents with poor statistical reasoning skills (however, see our earlier note cautioning against drawing developmental conclusions).

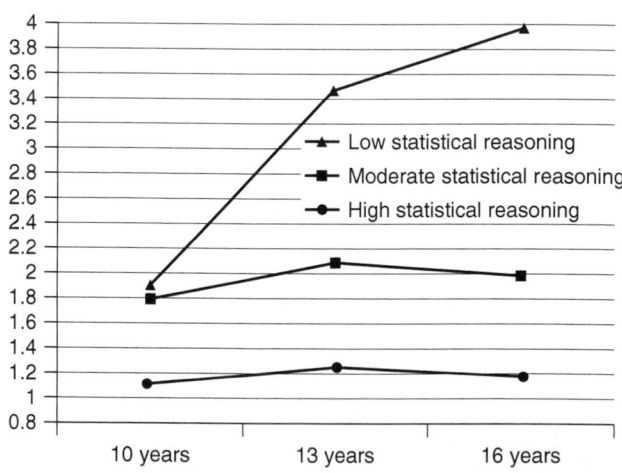

Figure 5.2 Age differences in biased ratings of large sample arguments that obese and thin "peers" had negative traits by level of statistical reasoning (adjusted for causal attributions, intelligence, and obesity stereotypes; Klaczynski, 2013b)

In a study of "obesity base rate neglect," age, and numeracy (i.e., understanding probabilities, numerical relations, etc.), Klaczynski (in press) introduced a modest methodological innovation to BR problems. In most BR studies, no-conflict problems typically include high base rates and stereotype-consistent individuating information; conflict problems pit high base rates (e.g., 20 girls, 5 boys) against stereotype-relevant information (e.g., Child A plays with trucks). Klaczynski added no-conflict problems with low base rates and stereotype-inconsistent information and conflict problems pitting low base rates against stereotype-consistent information. Table 5.1 shows how obesity base rate information and individuating information were varied to create different types of conflict and no-conflict problems.

Below is an abbreviated example of a BR-high/REP-low problem:

> In Jennifer's lunch period, 62 girls are obese and 18 girls are mostly thin. Jennifer is active and liked by other students. She is popular and has good friends. One student likes Jennifer because "she's happy and makes *me* feel happy."

On each problem, Hispanic and Caucasian adolescents indicated the likelihood that "targets" (e.g., Jennifer) were obese. Because base rates and individuating information "pulled" for the same response, the general absence of age differences on no-conflict problems was unsurprising. More critical were the developmental reversals found on the conflict problems. When statistical evidence supported "not obese" judgments, but individuating information was stereotype-consistent (i.e., BR-low/REP-high problems), obesity ratings increased with age. By contrast, when base rates supported (or "pulled" for) obese judgments and individuating evidence was stereotype-inconsistent (i.e., BR-high/REP-low problems), obesity ratings decreased with age. Despite age-related increases on BR-low/REP-high problems and age decreases on BR-high/REP-low problems, the findings indicate reversals in BR neglect *and* obesity biases on both types of conflict problem.

Because other findings were similar (e.g., conflict rated were related to stereotype endorsement and thinking dispositions) for the two types of conflict problem, we summarize only the key findings for BR-high/REP-low problems. Figure 5.3 shows that numeracy moderated the age-BR neglect relationship such that, when numeric ability was low, age "directly" affected ratings (i.e., BR neglect increased with age). When, however, numeracy was moderate or high, age was unrelated to BR neglect.

Table 5.1 The conflict and no-conflict problems in Klaczynski (in press)

Obesity base rates	Obesity representativeness (individuating information)	
	High	Low
High	No-conflict: BR-high/REP-high	Conflict: BR-high/REP-low
Low	Conflict: BR-low/REP-high	No-conflict: BR-low/REP-low

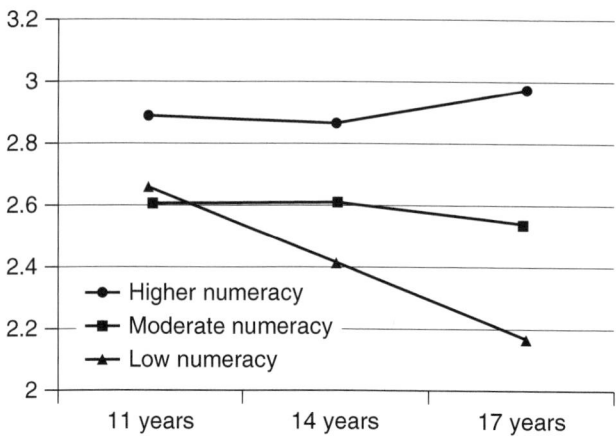

Figure 5.3 Age differences in obesity representativeness ratings on BR-high/REP-low problems by level of numeracy

Not only do these investigations illustrate developmental reversals during adolescence, but they imply that the foundation for conclusions (reviewed previously) that heuristic judgments do not increase during adolescence was inadequate. Although the data only suggest developmental trajectories, each reversal we documented was limited to specific groups, providing preliminary evidence that developmental reversals in this domain are not generalizable to all (or most) adolescents.

Limitations of this research include: (1) The designs were cross-sectional, (2) each study concerned obesity, and (3) the biases we studied implicated (directly and indirectly) representativeness. To address limitations (2) and (3), we examined gender and juvenile justice biases. Our questions were: Would we find adolescent reversals in other social domains? Do reversals in other domains occur on covariation detection, "scientific reasoning," and BR neglect problems? Are there individual difference variables that moderate any observed relationships between age and the heuristics and biases we examined?

Gender: Numeracy and reversals in covariation detection biases

In general, gender stereotypes decline with age; however, a provocative hypothesis—the "gender intensification hypothesis" (i.e., GIH)—is that the physical and cultural transitions (e.g., appearance focus, relationship/dating interests) accompanying the onset of adolescence increase pressures to adopt culturally sanctioned gender roles (Hill & Lynch, 1983; Galambos, Almeida, & Petersen, 1990). Despite rather weak evidence for the GIH, there is some evidence that stereotypes linking gender to science occupations (e.g., engineering) and specific performance areas (e.g., math) strengthen in early adolescence. This evidence led us to hypothesize

(1) an age increase in own-gender biases on "covariation detection" problems and (2) the anticipated reversal in gender covariation biases would be found only among adolescents of low numeric ability.

Numeric ability and responses to "own-gender" and "other-gender" covariation problems of children and early-mid adolescents were assessed. Based on a 2 (sex: boy or girl) × 2 (desirable/undesirable outcome) matrix, we created 12 "own-" and "other-gender" problems, wherein the desirable/undesirable outcome *ratio* was higher for one sex, but the *absolute number* of desirable outcomes (i.e., the numerator) was higher for the other sex. On "own-gender" problems for girls ("other-gender" problems for boys), as in the example below, the desirable outcome was more likely for girls than for boys: Girls' high/low score ratio was higher than boys' ratio.

> To figure out which students were most likely to succeed in college, a principal gave a class of 21 boys and 14 girls a "college prep" exam. The table below shows how many boys and girls had high scores and how many had low scores on the test. Look closely at the numbers in the table.

	Boys	Girls
High scores	12	10
Low scores	9	4

> Based *only* on the test scores in the table, who has a better chance of being successful in college, boys or girls?

Participants indicated whether the desirable outcome was more common to boys or girls. On "own-gender" problems for boys, desirable outcomes were more likely for boys than for girls, but the absolute frequency of desirable outcomes was higher for girls. On own-gender problems, normative responses, which depended on accurately comparing ratios, led to favorable characterizations of participants' genders. By contrast, normative responses on other-gender problems implied associations between participants' genders and an undesirable behavior/trait. However, by ignoring "unsuccessful" cases (i.e., denominators) on other-gender favorable problems—and comparing only numerators—participants could draw inferences favorable to their genders. In the example, comparing only positive outcomes for girls and boys "supports" the (boy-favorable, but inaccurate) inference that boys are better prepared than girls.

An "own-gender" bias score (normative other-gender responses minus normative own-gender responses) was computed to illustrate the main findings. In support of hypothesis (1), gender biases in covariation detection increased with age. In support of hypothesis (2) and consistent with the obesity bias-representativeness findings, numeracy moderated the age-gender bias relationship. Specifically, as illustrated in Figure 5.4, age was "directly" related to gender covariation biases when numeracy was moderate and low. When numeracy was high, age and biases were unrelated.

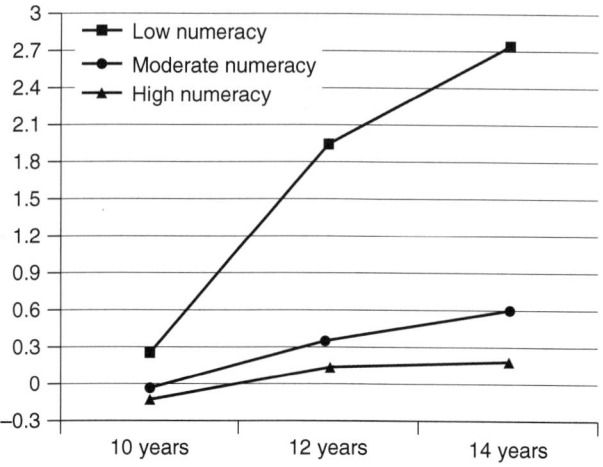

Figure 5.4 Age differences in gender biases in covariation detection by level of numeracy (adjusted for gender attitudes and sex)

Despite its brevity, this summary provides additional evidence for reversals during adolescence and extends the obesity findings to covariation detection problems in the domain of gender.

Juvenile justice: Beliefs, thinking dispositions, and developmental reversals in reasoning

In an extension to another domain, Klaczynski and Felmban (2013) examined the associations among age, juvenile justice beliefs, and two forms of bias: Biased judgments based on representativeness, and belief-biased reasoning. Literature relevant to juvenile justice system beliefs indicated that age relates positively to media exposure of teen violence and negatively to judgments that authorities enforce rules unfairly (e.g., Cauffman & Woolard, 2005; Fagan, & Tyler, 2005; Tang, Nunez, & Bourgeois, 2009; Woolard, Harvell, & Graham, 2008). We therefore suspected age increases in cynicism regarding the juvenile justice system's efficacy.

Because the findings for biased representativeness judgments and reasoning biases were similar, we believed evidence suggesting a reversal on another HB task was important. Since this study was the first showing a reversal in belief-biased reasoning, we describe only the key reasoning biases findings. To assess reasoning biases, vignettes describing evidence based on flawed "research" were presented to participants in each of two "ethnicity" conditions (Klaczynski & Felmban, 2013). In one condition, Hispanic juveniles were "research participants"; in the other, Caucasian juveniles were "participants." In both conditions, "pro-juvenile" evidence showed the juvenile system as more effective than the adult system (e.g., lower probability of recidivism); "anti-juvenile" evidence indicated that the adult system was more effective. Reasoning biases favoring the adult justice system occurred when flaws were detected more often, and "research" validity ratings were lower, on "pro-juvenile" problems than on "anti-juvenile" problems. Biases supporting the juvenile system were revealed when validity ratings were lower and flaws were detected more often on "anti-juvenile" problems. The scores that indexed biases were calculated such that negative scores indicated pro-adult justice system biases and positive scores indicated pro-juvenile justice reasoning biases.

As expected, preliminary analyses showed age increases in reasoning biases. However, the direction of biases (i.e., "pro-adult" or "pro-juvenile" justice) was dramatically influenced by ethnicity condition. Whereas pro-adult justice system reasoning biases increased with age in the Hispanic condition, pro-juvenile justice biases increased with age in the Caucasian condition. Moderated mediation analyses showed, first, that ethnicity condition moderated the age-bias relationship and, second, different variables mediated the age-bias relationship in the two conditions. Specifically, in the Hispanic condition, juvenile justice beliefs mediated the age-reasoning bias relationship; in the Caucasian condition, thinking dispositions mediated the link between age-reasoning biases.

As shown in the upper graph of Figure 5.5, bias scores decreased with age— indicating, in fact, age increases in pro-adult justice biases—in the Hispanic condition. Yet, the correlation between age and reasoning biases was strongest when adolescents had strong anti-juvenile justice beliefs, somewhat weaker (but nonetheless significant) when adolescents had relatively moderate anti-juvenile justice beliefs, and not significant when adolescents had relatively weak anti-juvenile justice beliefs. In the Caucasian condition, thinking dispositions mediated the age-bias relationship: Only when thinking dispositions scores were high did pro-juvenile justice biases increase with age.

These findings extended the previous research in several ways. First, they revealed developmental reversals in reasoning biases and biases in judgments based on representativeness (the latter were not discussed here). Second, the direction of the age-bias association depended on ethnicity condition and, within conditions, on juvenile justice beliefs and thinking dispositions. Although beliefs correlated with biases in the Caucasian condition, their role was modest relative to that of thinking dispositions. The thinking disposition findings are particularly intriguing because, in contrast with the typical finding that thinking dispositions relate negatively to reasoning biases, more advanced thinking dispositions related positively to biases (unfortunately, we have no ready explanation for this unusual finding).

Conclusions

Our reviews indicated that whereas a substantial proportion of DHB investigations revealed developmental reversals in childhood, few studied indicated reversals during adolescence. From similar reviews, several scholars concluded that age

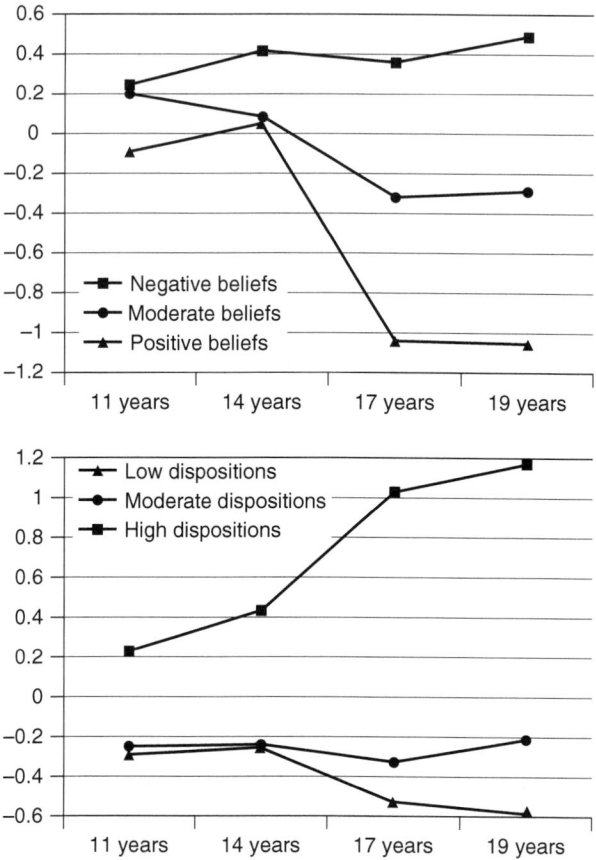

Figure 5.5 Age differences in belief-biased reasoning by (a) belief strength in the Hispanic condition (upper panel) and (b) thinking dispositions in the Caucasian condition (lower panel)

increases in heuristic judgments are largely limited to childhood. Wariness of these conclusions (see also Stanovich et al., 2011; Strough et al., 2011) led to a central goal of this chapter: Presenting evidence that they were premature. We achieved this goal with five studies demonstrating adolescent developmental reversals in three social domains. On the one hand, these reversals were observed on five tasks (i.e., generalizations, biased arguments ratings, BR neglect, covariation detection, belief-biased reasoning), indicating that they were not task-specific. On the other hand, our domain-specific approach dictated the use of "social" tasks (see Barrouillet, 2011b). For this reason, we have not argued that reversals are likely on relatively less "social" tasks, or tasks that do not tap belief systems that are particularly salient during adolescence (see Ricco & Overton, 2011). Neither have we ruled out reversals on "non-social" tasks (e.g., sunk costs, outcome bias, "if-only," conditional reasoning) constructed to activate beliefs and stereotypes that increase in salience during adolescence.

Throughout this chapter, we focused on age differences in *performance*. We have not argued against theories, such as those of Moshman (2004, 2009, 2013), Markovits (2004, Markovits & Lortie-Forgues, 2011), Overton (1990; Ricco & Overton, 2011), and Barrouillet and Gauffroy (2013), that emphasize *competence* development. Instead, findings such as those we presented, together with an impressive literature on adolescent competence development, imply that adolescent development entails progressions in the processes that underlie reasoning and changes in the conditions that activate domain-specific biases and heuristics.

Data intended to achieve our second goal—addressing concerns that DHB research has lagged behind adult research in the study of individual differences (Morsanyi & Handley, 2013; Stanovich et al., 2008, 2011)—support conjectures that adolescent development does not proceed in a uniform manner (Moshman, 2013). As opposed to showing individual difference variables that "explain" age-related variance in heuristics, we provided suggestive evidence that individual differences (e.g., thin idealization, numeracy) are linked to different trajectories of heuristic development. We again advocate interpreting the potentially moderating roles of these variables cautiously because our research was cross-sectional. Nonetheless, the statistical methods we used allowed us to provide the strongest evidence to date that heuristics develop along multiple trajectories and that reversals are limited to specific subgroups of adolescence.

Of the individual difference variables discussed by DHB theorists, we assessed thinking dispositions and general ability, as well as a specific ability (numeracy), in several studies. Although the importance of thinking dispositions was most evident in Klaczynski and Felmban (2013), our focus on moderation precluded discussing findings that thinking dispositions partially mediate the age-heuristic/bias relationships in two investigations (i.e., Klaczynski, 2013b, in press). Cognitive ability was mentioned only briefly, primarily because cognitive ability did not mediate any relationships between age and heuristic or reasoning biases (Klaczynski, 2013b, in press; Klaczynski & Felmban, 2013). The general absence of cognitive ability effects, the role of thin idealization in moderating the age-obesity generalization bias relationship, and data (not reported here) that other "non-cognitive" variables (e.g., attributions, gender stereotypes, obesity stereotypes) mediated several of the reported age-heuristic associations led to several recommendations for future research.

First, to better understand heuristic development, we advise greater consideration than prior research implies of the influences of "social" (e.g., thin idealization, beliefs) variables in examinations of relationships between age and heuristics. We are not arguing that general cognitive abilities do not influence heuristic development; although we later discuss specific abilities, general ability may influence mediated age differences in heuristic judgments on problems, the content of which has less bearing on issues salient to adolescents than the problems we used. Our point is that the findings cited previously provide compelling reasons for considering seriously the possibility that, in certain domains, social variables are better predictors of age differences in heuristics and biases than cognitive abilities. Despite concurring with Morsanyi and Handley (2013) that the individual differences have been understudied in DHB research, we are concerned that theorists may overly focus on cognitive (e.g., inhibition) variables. If a cost of this emphasis is downplaying, dismissing, or relegating social variables to secondary status, the price may be too high.

Second, we advocate additional research on the relationships among age, heuristics, biases, and numeracy. It is quite possible that one of our most important discoveries was that numeracy moderated the age-obesity BR neglect and the age-gender covariation bias associations. Concerns about mathematical literacy have led to increased interest, by researchers and policy makers, in numeracy. Unfortunately, this interest—and evidence that numeracy predicts adult performance on several HB tasks (Liberali, Reyna, Furlan, Stein, & Pardo, 2011; Toplak, West, & Stanovich, 2011)—has not significantly affected DHB researchers, a claim supported by the scarcity of relevant research.

Several recurrent methodological issues prompted us toward our final recommendations. We are not the first to argue that DHB research suffers from a number of theoretical and methodological weaknesses (e.g., Evans, 2011; Kuhn, 2006; Morsanyi & Handley, 2013; Stanovich et al., 2011) and recognize that some of the issues we raise are applicable to our own research. Nonetheless, despite the expansion of DHB research, we are dismayed that methodological and theoretical issues that characterize early DHB work continue plaguing the field. With few exceptions (e.g., De Neys & Vanderputte, 2011), attempts to replicate, extend, and resolve issues with early DHB research are rare. This failure has hindered advances in the field and hampered attempts to bridge gaps between DHB research and other areas of developmental inquiry (e.g., social development). Although space limitations preclude a complete discussion, brevity does not diminish the importance of working toward resolving the limitations and weaknesses, listed below, that we perceive in DHB research.

- Sample size. Some rather important claims about heuristic development have come from research with small samples. Our concern with repeated reliance on small samples stems, to some extent, from its connection to other recurrent issues in DHB research. Although we oversimplify, the reason age and heuristics are sometimes unrelated may sometimes be insufficient power. However, more disconcerting is the tendency, found in several papers, to increase an age group's size by combining ages traditionally considered distinct (e.g., categorizing 10- to 14-year-olds as "adolescents"). Potentially offsetting the resultant increase in power are problems interpreting age differences (or the lack thereof).
- Sample/theory justifications. It may be obvious that age group selection should be guided by theory or, in the absence of relevant theories, prior research. Yet, justifications for selecting and comparing age groups are often vague or not specified. If sample selection is not adequately justified, it may be difficult (or impossible) to understand the basis for developmental hypotheses.

- Median splits. In several papers reviewed, age groups were based on median splits. Median splits can be useful for descriptive purposes (e.g., readers can inspect, at a course level, group means) when distinct age groups are not sampled. Because most statistical analyses of split-created groups are less powerful than analyses of continuous data, analyses should focus on the continuous data; however, at times only analyses of arbitrary (or artificial) age groups are presented. This artificiality amplifies concerns with justifying samples and the hypotheses purportedly being tested.
- Reliability/validity/scoring. Obtaining developmental samples is often difficult, a difficulty compounded by time limitations, whether imposed by guardians or schools, or necessitated by children's abilities to attend for prolonged periods. The concern that arises is often relevant to "multiple-task" research. Decisions about numbers of problems per task (e.g., BR neglect, conjunction) are critical. When, for instance, participants respond to only one or two problems per task, reliability and generalizability are questionable. To deal with these issues, researchers sometimes analyse aggregated scores (i.e., summed across problems and tasks). Without evidence that responses tap the same underlying construct, the aggregate's meaning is questionable. When analyses of aggregates are not accompanied by analyses of individual tasks—and mean task scores are not available—determining whether significant/nonsignificant age differences resulted primarily from one or two tasks is impossible. If aggregates are based on neither factor scores, nor standardized scores, interpretative issues become more problematic.
- Two-group comparisons. Related to justifying sample selection, an issue that appears not to have overly concerned DHB researchers—if it has been considered at all—arises when researchers compare only two age groups. Assume, for instance, that the age differences Klaczynski (2001a) found reflect actual development. Because Klaczynski did not include children and/or adults (or a middle age), we cannot know whether those developments were linear or curvilinear or both. The research could have been more informative. Yet, over a decade has passed and "two-age" studies are still common in DHB research.
- Statistical approaches. Those interested in individual and group differences in development will likely benefit from studying moderation, mediation, and moderated mediation data analytic techniques. The spread of these statistics in psychological science (Bauer, 2011), however, has yet to reach DHB research.

Voicing these concerns was a goal because their recurring nature slows advances in research and theory. One cannot assume that increases in interest, visibility, and DHB publications indicate an increased understanding of heuristics and biases and development. But, the challenges facing DHB researchers can be overcome; indeed, they must be confronted to ensure progress. Increased communication and discussion among DHB researchers will likely lead to improved research and facilitate the field's development beyond its current status.

Notes

1 We use the term "normative" in referring to responses considered correct or rational by traditional standards of reasoning and decision making. In the heuristics and biases literature, "normative" implies ideal and not typical or average (Reyna & Farley, 2006). Although debates over the rationality and adaptive value of heuristics are plentiful (see Kahneman & Tversky, 1996; Hutchinson & Gigerenzer, 2005; Reyna & Farley, 2006), responses traditionally considered normative in the heuristics and biases literature are also considered correct in most cognitive developmental theories. We do not equate normative responses with adaptive responses or non-normative responses with maladaptive responses: Under some conditions, normative responses may be maladaptive and non-normative responses may be adaptive. Also, although we refer to age increases and decreases, these terms do not imply age-related *changes* because the studies we review are almost entirely cross-sectional. Finally, readers unfamiliar with the tasks reviewed subsequently can find examples in myriad sources (e.g., references cited).

2 Although we restricted our review to middle-late childhood and early-late adolescence, several DHB studies indicate that preschoolers are susceptible to framing effects, hindsight biases, and appearance-based biases (Bernstein, Erdfelder, Meltzoff, Peria, & Loftus, 2010; Klaczynski, 2013a; Levin & Hart, 2003; Moreira, Matsushita, & Da Silva, 2010). These findings suggest greater caution in making claims about heuristic developments in children. For instance, De Neys & Vanderputte (2011) asserted that their findings with 5- and 8-year-olds illustrated heuristics in "the *youngest age range*" (p. 10, italics added), a claim not supported by the preschooler research. Indeed, researchers studying DHB in preschoolers have questioned the view that most DHB research has been with older children and adolescents (e.g., Morsanyi & Handley, 2013). The theoretical implications of DHB research with young children are considerable, yet this literature appears somewhat neglected (see Klaczynski, 2013a).

3 Sun Tzu (Sunzi, a Chinese general during the Zhou dynasty; ~1100–221 BCE) is best known as the author of *The Art of War* (written between 600 and 500 BCE; see Cleary, trans. 2005), an ancient text that has influenced modern business and military philosophy. However, whether Sun Tzu authored or quoted this proverb is a matter of some dispute. The proverb may originally have been Arabic, Chinese, or originated (albeit in rather different forms) in both areas.

4 Reyna & Brainerd (2011; Chick & Reyna, 2012) provide additional arguments against the knowledge-reversal argument; Klaczynski (2013a) suggests interpreting data that apparently contravene the knowledge-reversal hypothesis cautiously until data with more elaborate measures of knowledge are available.

5 We excluded several reports of adolescent reversals in conditional reasoning (e.g., Janveau-Brennan & Markovits, 1999; Klaczynski & Narasimham, 1998; Wildman & Fletcher, 1977; see Klaczynski, 2013a). The conditions under which these reversals occurred are worthy of additional study. At present, however, these findings should be considered in the context of an expansive literature on conditional reasoning and its development. In general, that literature indicates that normative responses increase during childhood and subsequently either increase with age or stabilize (Barrouillet & Gauffroy, 2013; Markovits, 2013; Markovits & Barrouillet, 2002; Moshman, 2013; Overton, 1990; Ricco & Overton 2011).

6 Klaczynski (2013a) observed that many of the conclusions presented in this section seemed to be based on confusing processes and products. Just as the processes responsible for *producing* heuristic may sometimes be conscious, deliberative, and analytic, the processes underlying normative responses are sometimes relatively implicit. Sometimes resulting from these confusions (e.g., between "heuristic" or implicit processes and heuristic judgments/products) are "face value" interpretations, wherein age differences in products are taken to reflect age differences in processes and vice versa.

References

Albert, D., & Steinberg, L. (2011). Judgment and decision making in adolescence. *Journal of Research on Adolescence, 21*, 211–224.

Amsel, E., Klaczynski, P. A., Johnston, A., Bench, S., Close, J., Sadler, E., & Walker, R. (2008). A dual-process account of the development of scientific reasoning: The nature and development of metacognitive intercession skills. *Cognitive Development, 23*, 451–471.

Baron, J. (1985). *Rationality and intelligence*. Cambridge: Cambridge University Press.

Baron, J. (1988). *Thinking and deciding*. Cambridge: Cambridge University Press.

Barrouillet, P. (2011a). Dual-process theories and cognitive development: Advances and challenges. *Developmental Review, 31*, 79–85.

Barrouillet, P. (2011b). Dual-process theories of reasoning: The test of development. *Developmental Review, 31*, 151–179.

Barrouillet, P. & Gauffroy, C. (2013). Dual process and mental models in the development of conditional reasoning. In P. Barrouillet & C. Gauffroy (Eds.), *Thinking, reasoning, and development* (pp. 95–121). New York: Psychology Press.

Bauer, D. J. (2011). Evaluating individual differences in psychological processes. *Current Directions in Psychological Science, 20*, 115–118.

Bernstein, D. M., Erdfelder, E., Meltzoff, A. N., Peria, W., & Loftus, G. R. (2011). Hindsight bias from 3 to 95 years of age. *Journal of Experimental Psychology: Learning Memory and Cognition, 37*, 378.

Brainerd, C. J., Reyna, V. F., & Ceci, S. J. (2008). Developmental reversals in false memory: A review of data and theory. *Psychological Bulletin, 134*, 343–382.

Cauffman, E., & Woolard, J. (2005). Crime, competence, and culpability: Adolescent judgment in the justice system. In J. E. Jacobs & P. A. Klaczynski (Eds.), *The development of judgment and decision making in children and adolescents* (pp. 279–301). Mahwah, NJ: Erlbaum.

Chiesi, F., Gronchi, G., & Primi, C. (2008). Age-trend-related differences in tasks involving conjunctive probabilistic reasoning. *Canadian Journal of Experimental Psychology, 62*, 188.

Chiesi, F., Primi, C., & Morsanyi, K. (2011). Developmental changes in probabilistic reasoning: The role of cognitive capacity, instructions, thinking styles, and relevant knowledge. *Thinking & Reasoning, 17*, 315–350.

Davidson, D. (1995). The representativeness heuristic and the conjunction fallacy effect in children's decision making. *Merrill-Palmer Quarterly, 41*, 328–346.

De Neys, W., Cromheeke, S., & Osman, M. (2011) Biased but in doubt: Conflict and decision confidence. *PLoS ONE 6*: e15954. doi:10.1371/journal pone.0015954

De Neys, W., & Vanderputte, K. (2011). When less is not always more: Stereotype knowledge and reasoning development. *Developmental Psychology, 47*, 432–441.

Evans, J. St. B. T. (2011). Dual process theories of reasoning: Contemporary issues and developmental applications. *Developmental Review, 31*, 86–102.

Fagan, J., & Tyler, T. R. (2005). Legal socialization of children and adolescents. *Social Justice Research, 18*, 217–241.

Fairchild, A. J., & MacKinnon, D. P. (2009). A general model for testing mediation and moderation effects. *Prevention Science, 10*, 87–99.

Galambos, N. L., Almeida, D. M., & Petersen, A. C. (1990). Masculinity, femininity, and sex role attitudes in early adolescence: Exploring gender intensification. *Child Development, 61*, 1905–1914.

Gauffroy, C., & Barrouillet, P. (2009). Heuristic and analytic processes in mental models for conditionals: An integrative developmental theory. *Developmental Review, 29*, 249–282.

Gomes, C. F., & Brainerd, C. J. (2013). Dual processes in the development of reasoning: The memory side of the theory. In P. Barrouillet & C. Gauffroy (Eds.), *Thinking, reasoning, and development* (pp. 221–242). New York: Psychology Press.

Hayes, A. F. (2012). Process: A versatile computational tool for observed variable mediation, moderation, and conditional process modeling. Unpublished manuscript. University of Kansas.

Hayes, A. F. (2013). *An introduction to mediation, moderation, and conditional process analysis: A regression-based approach.* New York: Guilford Press.

Hayes, A. F., & Preacher, K. J. (in press). Statistical mediation analysis with a multicategorical independent variable. Submitted for publication.

Hill, J. P., & Lynch, M. E. (1983). The intensification of gender-related role expectations during early adolescence. In Brooks-Gunn, J. & Petersen, A. C. (Eds.), *Girls at puberty: Biological and psychosocial perspectives* (pp. 201–228). New York: Plenum Press.

Hutchinson, J., & Gigerenzer, G. (2005). Simple heuristics and rules of thumb: Where psychologists and behavioural biologists might meet. *Behavioural Processes, 69*, 97–124.

Jacobs, J. E., & Potenza, M. (1991). The use of judgment heuristics to make social and object decisions: A developmental perspective. *Child Development, 62*, 166–178.

Janveau-Brennan, G., & Markovits, H. (1999). The development of reasoning with causal conditionals. *Developmental Psychology, 35*, 904–911.

Kahneman, D., Slovic, P., & Tversky, A. (Eds.) (1982). *Judgment under uncertainty: Heuristics and biases.* Cambridge, MA: Cambridge University Press.

Kahneman, D., & Tversky, A. (1996). On the reality of cognitive illusions. *Psychological Review, 103*, 582–591.

Klaczynski, P. A. (1997). Bias in adolescents' everyday reasoning and its relationship with intellectual ability, personal theories, and self-serving motivation. *Developmental Psychology, 33*, 273–283.

Klaczynski, P. A. (2000). Motivated scientific reasoning biases, epistemological beliefs, and theory polarization: A two-process approach to adolescent cognition. *Child Development, 71*, 1347–1366.

Klaczynski, P. A. (2001a). Analytic and heuristic processing influences on adolescent reasoning and decision making. *Child Development, 72*, 844–861.

Klaczynski, P. A. (2001b). Framing effects on adolescent task representations, analytic and heuristic processing, and decision making: Implications for the normative-descriptive gap. *Journal of Applied Developmental Psychology, 22*, 289–309.

Klaczynski, P. A. (2008). There's something about obesity: Culture, contagion, rationality, and children's responses to drinks "created" by obese children. *Journal of Experimental Child Psychology, 99*, 58–74.

Klaczynski, P. A. (2009). Cognitive and social cognitive development: Dual-process research and theory. J. B. St. T. Evans & K. Frankish (Eds.), *In two minds: Psychological and philosophical theories of dual processing* (pp. 265–292). Oxford: Oxford University Press.

Klaczynski, P. A. (2011). Age differences in understanding precedent-setting decisions and authorities' responses to violations of deontic rules. *Journal of Experimental Child Psychology, 129*, 1–24.

Klaczynski, P. A. (2013a). Culture and the development of heuristics and biases: Implications for developmental dual-process theories. In P. Barrouillet & C. Gauffroy (Eds.),

The development in thinking and reasoning (pp. 150–192). London, UK: Psychology Press.

Klaczynski, P. A. (2013b). A moderator-mediator analysis of adolescents' obesity stereotypes and obesity representativeness heuristic: Age and individual differences in statistical reasoning, body image, appearance-related beliefs. Unpublished manuscript.

Klaczynski, P. A. (in press). Obesity and biases in heuristic judgments: Relations to age, ethnicity, gender, stereotype endorsement, and stereotype knowledge. Submitted.

Klaczynski, P. A., & Amsel, E. A. (in press). Numeracy, priming, and ratio biases in Chinese and American children. Submitted.

Klaczynski, P. A., & Aneja, A. (2002). The development of quantitative reasoning and gender biases. *Developmental Psychology, 38*, 208–221.

Klaczynski, P. A., & Cottrell, J. E. (2004). A dual-process approach to cognitive development: The case of children's understanding of sunk cost decisions. *Thinking & Reasoning, 10*, 147–174.

Klaczynski, P. A., Daniel, D. B., & Keller, P. S. (2009). Appearance idealization, body esteem, causal attributions, and ethnic variations in the development of obesity stereotypes. *Journal of Applied Developmental Psychology, 30*, 537–551.

Klaczynski, P. A., & Felmban, W. (2013). Age increases in reasoning and heuristics biases: The roles of juvenile justice beliefs, psychosocial maturity, and offender ethnicity. Unpublished manuscript.

Klaczynski, P. A., & Narasimham, G. (1998). Development of scientific reasoning biases: Ego-protective versus cognitive explanations. *Developmental Psychology, 34*, 175–187.

Kokis, J. V., MacPherson, R., Toplak, M. E., West, R. F., & Stanovich, K. E. (2002). Heuristic and analytic processing: Age trends and associations with cognitive ability and cognitive styles. *Journal of Experimental Child Psychology, 83*, 26–52.

Krouse, H. J. (1986). Use of decision frames by elementary school children. *Perceptual and Motor Skills, 63*, 1107–1112.

Kuhn, D. (1989). Children and adults as intuitive scientists. *Psychological Review, 96*, 674–689.

Kuhn, D. (1991). *The skills of argument.* Cambridge, MA: Cambridge University Press.

Kuhn, D. (1993). Science as argument: Implications for teaching and learning scientific thinking. *Science Education, 77*, 319–337.

Kuhn, D. (2006). Do cognitive changes accompany developments in the adolescent brain? *Perspectives on Psychological Science, 1*, 59–67.

Kuhn, D., Amsel, E., & O'Loughlin, M. (1988). *The development of scientific thinking.* San Diego, CA: Academic Press.

Levin, I. P., & Hart, S. S. (2003). Risk preferences in young children: Early evidence of individual differences in reaction to potential gains and losses. *Journal of Behavioral Decision Making, 16*, 397–413.

Liberali, J. M., Reyna, V. E., Furlan, S., Stein, L. M., & Pardo, S. T. (2011). Individual differences in numeracy and cognitive reflection, with implications for biases and fallacies in probability judgment. *Journal of Behavioral Decision Making, 25*, 361–381.

Markovits, H. (2004). The development of deductive reasoning. In J. P. Leighton & R. J. Sternberg (Eds.), *The nature of reasoning* (pp. 313–338). Cambridge: Cambridge University Press.

Markovits, H. (2013). The development of abstract conditional reasoning. In P. Barrouillet & C. Gauffroy (Eds.), *The development of thinking and reasoning* (pp. 71–91). New York: Psychology Press.

Markovits, H., & Barrouillet, P. (2002). The development of conditional reasoning: A mental model account. *Developmental Review, 22*, 5–36.

Markovits, H., & Dumas, C. (1999). Developmental patterns in the understanding of social and physical transitivity. *Journal of Experimental Child Psychology, 73*, 95–114.

Markovits, H., Lortie-Forgues, H., & Brunet, M.-L. (2012). More evidence for a dual-process model of conditional reasoning. *Memory & Cognition, 40*, 736–747.

Moreira, B., Matsushita, R., & Da Silva, S. (2010). Risk seeking behavior of preschool children in a gambling task. *Journal of Economic Psychology, 31*, 794–801.

Morsanyi, K., & Handley, S. J. (2008). How smart do you need to be to get it wrong? The role of cognitive capacity in the development of heuristic-based judgment. *Journal of Experimental Child Psychology, 99*, 18–36.

Morsanyi, K., & Handley, S. (2013). Heuristics and biases: Insights from developmental studies. In P. Barrouillet & C. Gauffroy (Eds.), *The development of thinking and reasoning* (pp. 122–149). New York: Psychology Press.

Moshman, D. (2004). From inference to reasoning: The construction of rationality. *Thinking & Reasoning, 10*, 221–239.

Moshman, D. (2009). The development of rationality. In H. Siegel (Ed.), *Oxford handbook of philosophy of education* (pp. 145–161). Oxford: Oxford University Press.

Moshman, D. (2013). Epistemic cognition and development. In P. Barrouillet & C. Gauffroy (Eds.), *The development of thinking and reasoning* (pp. 13–33). New York: Psychology Press.

Overton, W. E. (1985). Scientific methodologies and the competence-moderator performance issue. In E. D. Neimark, R. DeLisi, & J. L. Newman (Eds.), *Moderators of competence* (pp. 15–41). Hillsdale, NJ: Erlbaum.

Overton, W. E. (1990). Competence and procedures: Constraints on the development of logical reasoning. In W. E. Overton (Ed.), *Reasoning, necessity, and logic* (pp. 1–32). Hillsdale, NJ: Erlbaum.

Reyna, V. F. (2012). A new intuitionism: Meaning, memory, and development in fuzzy-trace theory. *Judgment and Decision Making, 7*, 332–359.

Reyna, V. F. (2013). Intuition, reasoning, and development: A fuzzy-trace theory approach. In P. Barrouillet & C. Gauffroy (Eds.), *Thinking, reasoning, and development* (pp. 193–220). New York: Psychology Press.

Reyna, V. F., & Brainerd, C. J. (2011). Dual processes in decision making and developmental neuroscience: A fuzzy-trace model. *Developmental Review, 31*, 180–206.

Reyna, V. F. & Ellis, S. C. (1994). Fuzzy-trace theory and framing effects in children's risky decision making. *Psychological Science, 5*, 275–279.

Reyna, V. F., & Farley, F. (2006). Risk and rationality in adolescent decision making: Implications for theory, practice, and public policy. *Psychological Science in the Public Interest, 7*, 1–43.

Ricco, R. B., & Overton, W. F. (2011). Dual systems competence ←-→ Procedural processing: A relational developmental systems approach to reasoning. *Developmental Review, 31*, 119–150.

Stanovich, K. E. (1999). *Who is rational? Studies of individual differences in reasoning.* Mahwah, NJ: Lawrence Erlbaum Associates.

Stanovich, K. E. (2004). *The robot's rebellion: Finding meaning in the age of Darwin.* Chicago: The Chicago University Press.

Stanovich, K. E., Toplak, M. E., & West, R. F. (2008). The development of rational thought: A taxonomy of heuristics and biases. *Advances in Child Development and Behavior, 36*, 251–285.

Stanovich, K. E., & West, R. F. (2008). On the relative independence of thinking biases and cognitive ability. *Journal of Personality and Social Psychology, 94,* 672.

Stanovich, K. E., West, R. F., & Toplak, M. E. (2011). The complexity of developmental predictions from dual process models. *Developmental Review, 31,* 103–118.

Strough, J., Karns, T. E., & Schlosnagle, L. (2011). Decision making heuristics and biases across the life span. *Annals of the New York Academy of Sciences, 1235,* 57–74.

Tang, C. M., Nunez, N., & Bourgeois, M. (2009). Effects of trial venue and pretrial bias on the evaluation of juvenile defendants. *Criminal Justice Review, 34,* 210–225.

Toplak, M. E., West, R. F., & Stanovich, K. E. (2011). The cognitive reflection test as a predictor of performance on heuristics-and-biases tasks. *Memory & Cognition, 39,* 1275–1289.

Webley, P., & Plaisier, Z. (1998). Mental accounting in childhood. *Children's Social and Economics Education, 3,* 55–63.

Weller, J. A., Levin, I. P., & Denburg, N. L. (2009). Trajectory of adaptive decision making for risky gains and losses from ages 5 to 85. *Journal of Behavioral Decision Making, 22,* 1–14.

Wildman, T. M., & Fletcher, H. J. (1977). Developmental increases and decreases in solutions of conditional syllogism problems. *Developmental Psychology, 13,* 630–636.

Woolard, J. L., Harvell, S., & Graham, S. (2008). Anticipatory injustice among adolescents: Age and racial/ethnic differences in perceived unfairness of the justice system. *Behavioral Sciences and the Law, 26,* 207–226.

Part II

Development of specific competencies

6 Epistemic domains of reasoning

David Moshman

There appears to be a consensus among cognitive psychologists that inference is in large part domain-specific and that thinking is in large part a function of domain. I argue in this chapter that reasoning is also domain-specific but in a different sense that remains mostly unrecognized. I distinguish several domains of reasoning and discuss the potential for research on how adolescents and adults reflect on these distinctions at advanced levels of epistemic development.

Inference, thinking, and reasoning

The terms "inference," "thinking," and "reasoning" are sometimes used interchangeably but the literature manifests some degree of consensus that reasoning is a subset of thinking, which in turn is a subset of inference. To reason is to think, but not all thinking is reasoning. Similarly, to think is to infer, but not all inference is thinking (Moshman, 2004, 2011a, 2013).

I define *inference* as *going beyond the data*. To infer is to go beyond the raw facts. Cognition, however, is intrinsically inferential. To know is to go beyond the data. Even what seem to be raw facts are the result of assimilating reality to our theories, narratives, frameworks, structures, concepts, and processes. People of all ages rely in large degree on automatic inferences, for better and for worse. I infer from your smile that you are happy, for example, without intending to make an inference and without realizing I have done so. Our automatic and intuitive inferences often embody heuristic knowledge that guides us well within familiar domains, such as the interpretation of human facial expressions with respect to associated emotions. But there is no guarantee these processes will always serve us well, and often they don't.

I define *thinking* as *the deliberate application and coordination of one's inferences to serve one's purposes*. This includes a variety of interrelated mental actions such as problem solving, decision making, judgment, and planning. But our ability to apply and coordinate inferences to solve problems, make decisions, evaluate, and plan is in part a function of the sort of inferences we are able to make, which depends in large part on the topic we are thinking about. We will return in the next section to the question of domain specificity.

Finally, I define *reasoning* as *epistemologically self-constrained thinking—that is, thinking aimed at reaching true or justifiable conclusions*. This includes logical reasoning, scientific reasoning, moral reasoning, and argumentation. Reasoning is a type of thinking and is domain-specific in the same sense that most thinking is domain-specific: we make better inferences about some things than others. As we will see, however, reasoning is also domain-specific in another way that is specifically epistemological.

Over the course of development our automatic inferences are increasingly supplemented by acts of thinking and our thinking increasingly takes the form of reasoning. That is, there are developmental trends in the direction of more thinking and, especially, more reasoning over the course of childhood and often beyond. The developmental trend toward thinking consists of an increase in the deliberate application and coordination of inferences to serve one's purposes (Kuhn, 2009). The developmental trend toward reasoning consists of the increasing ability to constrain one's inferences in the interest of justification and truth (Moshman, 2004, 2011a). The developmental trends toward more thinking and reasoning are not a stagelike progression from inference to thinking to reasoning, however. Neither thinking nor reasoning replaces automatic inference. Even among high-functioning adults, thinking and reasoning remain the rational tip of the iceberg of cognition.

This conception of inference, thinking, and reasoning is fully consistent with dual processing theories, which generally see most of our cognitive processing as automatic and intuitive rather than deliberate and reflective (Kahneman, 2011). It brings in an epistemological dimension, however, in its distinction of reasoning from thinking in general.

Domains of knowledge and inference

Knowledge is in large part domain-specific. Our knowledge about facial expressions is specific to facial expressions; it cannot be used for mathematical calculations. Our knowledge of number and arithmetic is specific to mathematics; it cannot be used to interpret facial expressions. And our knowledge of grammar is specific to a particular language or perhaps, at a more abstract level, to human language in general; it does not apply to interpreting facial expressions or understanding mathematics.

Inference is also largely domain-specific. Our interpretation of facial expressions involves inferences specific to facial expressions. Our mathematical inferences help us reach mathematical conclusions; they do not help us speak or understand language. Our inferences about the meaning of a sentence are rooted in our domain-specific knowledge of grammar; such inferences do not help us subtract or multiply numbers.

Thinking is in part a function of the inferences to be coordinated. Those inferences are in part domain-specific. Thus thinking is in part domain-specific. This does not rule out the construction and application of, say, general problem-solving skills or general strategies of decision making. But even general skills must be applied in specific contexts, and domain-specific inferences play a major role in such applications. Our deliberate efforts to figure out what someone is feeling may have much in common with our deliberate efforts to figure out the meaning of a sentence, but the two cases involve different sorts of inference appropriate to distinct domains of knowledge.

Domains of truth and justification

Domains of reasoning are domains of truth and justification, which is to say they are epistemic domains. In reasoning about a scientific claim, for example, we would expect arguments that refer, at least in part, to empirical evidence, and we would remain open to further evidence. In reasoning about a mathematical claim, in contrast, we would expect proof.

Epistemic domains of reasoning are distinct from cognitive domains of thinking. Consider physics, biology, and mathematics. In general, we would expect a physicist to be better at solving physics problems than a biologist or mathematician due to greater (domain-specific) expertise. Everyone thinks best about what they know best. But when asked whether reasoning leads to truth, all three, at least upon reflection, would distinguish mathematics from the two scientific disciplines.

Or so I suggest. The epistemological issue quickly gets complex. Fortunately, there is no need for present purposes to settle on a definitive taxonomy of epistemic domains. The issue for us is the psychological issue of whether individuals without specialized education in philosophy make epistemic domain distinctions and, if so, what distinctions they make and how they make progress in their understanding and application of such distinctions and in associated forms of reasoning.

Science as an epistemic domain

Science aims for knowledge, not just belief, and thus cannot avoid issues of truth and justification. The goal of any science (e.g., physics, biology, or sociology) is to understand some aspect of reality (e.g., elementary particles, living organisms, or human societies), which means to have a good theory about it. Science assumes there is a reality sufficiently distinct from our theories of it that our theories could be wrong, thus raising questions of truth and justification. In the domain of science, questions of truth and justification lead to empirical research seeking empirical evidence relevant to our theories.

Empirical hypothesis testing is thus the form of reasoning most central to science. This is not to deny that scientists use many forms of reasoning, nor is it to deny that hypothesis testing is relevant in other epistemic domains. Hypothesis testing is central to science, however, because science relies on putting hypotheses to empirical test.

Scientific reasoning is much more complex than this, however. Theories are not simply hypotheses and they are not immediately abandoned every time they generate a hypothesis that is not confirmed. The coordination of theories and evidence to generate scientific progress is a more subtle matter than the direct testing of an individual hypothesis but still consistent with the empirical nature of science and the empirical aim of scientific inquiry (Koslowski, 1996; Kuhn, 2009).

Developmental changes in understanding the epistemology of science follow the general trends seen in the substantial literature on epistemic development from objectivist to subjectivist to rationalist epistemologies (Chandler, 1987; Chandler, Boyes, & Ball, 1990; Chandler, Hallett, & Sokol, 2002; King & Kitchener, 1994, 2002; Kitchener, 1983; Kuhn, 2009; Kuhn, Cheney, & Weinstock, 2000; Kuhn & Franklin, 2006; Kuhn & Weinstock, 2002; Mansfield & Clinchy, 2002; Moshman, 2008, 2011a, 2011b, 2013). Objectivists, presumably, see hypothesis testing as an objective matter of controlling variables, with truth the reward for proper methodology. Subjectivists recognize that our theories determine the data we seek and drive the interpretation of evidence. This leads them to question the supposed objectivity of science. Rationalists recognize the subjectivity and complexity of scientific reasoning but believe progress in knowledge is nonetheless possible through the reflective coordination of perspectives, theories, and data.

Epistemic cognition in the domain of science has been extensively studied in the science education literature (Sandoval, 2005; Sandoval & Reiser, 2004) as part of a broader literature on students' understanding of the nature of science. Sandoval (2005) defined science as "the effort to explain observations of the natural world" and proposed that students need to understand "that scientific knowledge is constructed by people, not simply discovered out in the world (p. 639)." They must also understand the epistemological basis for their own inquiry in science labs and elsewhere. Research in this area, argued Sandoval (2005), must distinguish students' formal epistemologies of science from their practical epistemologies of their own inquiry and must investigate the interrelations between these.

The logicomathematical domain

Logic and mathematics also raise issues of knowledge, truth, and justification, but they are not generally thought to raise empirical questions that can be answered, even in principle, by getting the right evidence. On the contrary, logical and mathematical claims are proved or disproved. Adding two objects to three results in five objects and taking two away leaves three. If we were to add and subtract two objects and then count a different number than before, we would assume we had miscounted or made some other mistake. We would not conclude that we have evidence contrary to the theory of arithmetic. Rejecting the evidence is contrary to good reasoning in the domain of science but the logicomathematical domain is epistemologically distinct from the domain of science. Logical and mathematical truths are matters of logical necessity rather than empirical evidence (Piaget, 1952, 1987; Smith, 1993, 2009).

Logical and mathematical reasoning are prototypically rule-based in that they involve adhering to strict rules that distinguish right from wrong answers. Disagreement is possible only if someone has made a mistake. At advanced levels, reasoning in the logicomathematical domain may provide a rigorous combinatorial analysis of all possibilities without regard for empirical truth or falsity (Amsel, 2011; Gauffroy & Barrouillet, 2011; Inhelder & Piaget, 1958).

Research shows that children begin to distinguish logical from empirical truths about the age of 6 or 7 and proceed from there to increasingly reflective understanding of the distinction between logical and empirical knowledge (Inhelder & Piaget, 1958, 1964; Miller, Custer, & Nassau, 2000; Moshman, 1990, 2004, 2009, 2013; Moshman & Franks, 1986; Moshman & Timmons, 1982; Piaget, 1952; Piéraut-Le Bonniec, 1980; Pillow, 2002; Pillow & Anderson, 2006). At advanced levels, one can raise questions about whether logical truth is relative to diverse systems of logic (subjectivism) and, beyond that, the possibility that some systems of logic or mathematics may be more defensible than others (rationalism). Thus there may be developmental trends in the logicomathematical domain that parallel the general trend noted with respect to science. Nevertheless, objectivism is more defensible as an epistemology of logic or mathematics than as an epistemology of science. Psychological research on epistemic domains has generally failed to investigate or address this.

Logic and mathematics play crucial roles in science and are certainly no less rigorous than science. In the case of simple hypotheses, for example, strict isolation of variables may be seen as the logic of hypothesis testing, allowing highly defensible conclusions about the causal role of a particular variable. Nevertheless, there is an important epistemic distinction between the necessary logic of a particular research method and the empirical contingency of scientific conclusions. Even as we coordinate the logicomathematical and scientific domains and their corresponding forms of reasoning, it remains important to distinguish the two domains and the corresponding characteristics of knowledge and reasoning in each.

The moral domain

Science includes social science, which is about what people do and how societies are organized. Morality, however, is not the study of what people do or what the social world is really like. Morality is the study of what people ought to do and how the social world ought to be organized. Morality, that is, is distinct from science because it concerns what people should do (not what they actually do) and how things should be (not how they are). Whereas science is empirical, morality is normative (Carpendale, 2009; Gibbs, 2014; Killen & Rutland, 2011; Kohlberg, 1981, 1984; Moshman, 2011a; Piaget, 1932/1965; Smetana, 2011; Turiel, 2008).

Logic is normative too. Morality was, in fact, famously conceptualized as the logic of social action in Piaget's (1932/1965) classic work on the topic, and there is much to say for this (Carpendale, 2009; Gibbs, 2014). But morality is not always so clearly objective as logic. Many deem it a matter of subjective values outside the realm of knowledge, where epistemological questions of truth and justification are simply irrelevant. But many see morality, even to the extent that it is less than fully objective, as nevertheless having a rational basis (Moshman, 2011a, 2013).

Thus morality is arguably a domain of knowledge that lends itself, like the scientific domain, to objectivist, subjectivist, and rationalist epistemologies.

Two major forms of reasoning are strongly associated with the moral domain: Perspective taking and principled reasoning. Perspective taking is not just empathy. It is a cognitive process of recognizing and understanding perspectives other than one's own. This includes not only seeing the world from another perspective but also seeing oneself from the perspective of another, seeing one's relation to another from the perspective of a third party, and complex coordinations of multiple perspectives (Selman, 1980).

A second form of reasoning central to morality is principled reasoning, in which conclusions are justified on the basis of their relation to general principles. Principles, at least in a moral context, are not empirical generalizations; rather they have a rational basis (related, perhaps, to full intercoordination of all possible perspectives). But principles are not rules; their application involves matters of interpretation on which rational individuals may differ (Moshman, 1995, 1998). We expect full agreement in a matter involving an even division of some number of objects (if not, there has been a mistake) but we do not expect full agreement on what constitutes "the equal protection of the law," a principle reasonably subject to multiple interpretations.

The development of moral epistemology was investigated in a study by Krettenauer (2004), who used the term "meta-ethical cognition" to refer to knowledge about the basis for and justification of moral judgments. Drawing on the general epistemological trend from objectivism to subjectivism to rationalism and the results of a series of pilot studies, he identified three moral epistemologies, which he labeled *intuitionism*, *subjectivism*, and *transsubjectivism*. Intuitionism maintains that moral rightness or wrongness can be determined by moral intuitions, which allow us to perceive truth in the moral domain in much the way that the evidence of our senses enables us to perceive empirical truths in the domain of science. Subjectivism maintains that moral judgments are simply matters of preference or taste, neither right nor wrong. Subjectivism questions the possibility of truth or rational justification, at least in the moral domain. Finally, transsubjectivism deems moral judgments to be justifiable but fallible, consistent with a rationalist stance in the domain of science.

Krettenauer (2004) assessed the moral epistemologies of 200 German high school students (ages 13–19). Students made judgments about moral dilemmas and were then asked about the sources, certainty, and justification of their judgments and the possibility of equally justifiable alternatives. Responses could be classified reliably with respect to the three moral epistemologies identified above. Individual adolescents showed some (but not perfect) consistency across dilemmas in their moral epistemologies. Age differences were consistent with developmental expectations of a general trend from intuitionism to subjectivism, with evidence of transsubjectivism in some of the older students. A comparison group of graduate students with expertise in moral philosophy responded mostly at the transsubjectivist level. Moral epistemologies were substantially (but not perfectly) correlated with epistemologies of science.

The domain of social convention

Social conventions are norms of behavior. Like moral norms, they dictate what we should do; they are arguably something more than empirical generalizations of how we actually behave. Morality and social convention differ epistemologically, however, in that morality has a universal rational basis and is thus obligatory for everyone, whereas social convention is always relative to a particular social system and thus binding, if at all, only within that social system. Each social system has its own history and thus its own conventional norms, which are relative to that history in a way that moral norms are not. Moral norms can be justified on grounds outside the social system in a way that conventional norms cannot.

Social conventional norms are generally discussed in the developmental literature in the context of distinguishing them from moral norms. Kohlberg (1984) proposed that the disentangling of genuine morality from adherence to the conventions of a particular social system is a project that potentially extends well into adulthood, leading to a social contract morality that many individuals, perhaps most, never achieve. Social domain theorists have provided evidence that, to the contrary, the epistemological distinction between morality and social convention is understood by age 4 or 5 years (Killen & Rutland, 2011; Smetana, 2011; Turiel, 2008). Social conventions, in this view, are not just the background social obligations from which morality must be distinguished but compose a domain in their own right with its own developmental trends. Consistent with this view, I suggest that the social conventional domain is an epistemic domain with its own form of reasoning.

The core form of social conventional reasoning is precedent-based reasoning, a type of case-based reasoning (Klaczynski, 2011; Moshman, 1998). Case-based reasoning is thinking constrained by attention to concrete manifestations (cases) that are deemed relevant to achieving a justifiable cognitive outcome in the case at hand. This includes analogical reasoning and precedent-based reasoning. In analogical reasoning a case reflectively deemed analogous is deliberately taken as the basis for achieving a justifiable resolution to a present case (as in solving a problem in a manner that yielded a correct solution to a previous problem because we see the previous problem as relevantly similar). Precedent-based reasoning also takes analogous instances as a basis for constraining one's thinking. In analogical reasoning, however, the analogous instances are merely heuristic. In precedent-based reasoning, the constraint imposed on the basis of the precedent is stricter. Fidelity to precedent is not just useful; we must adhere to precedent unless we have specific and strong justification for doing otherwise. Precedent-based reasoning is central, for example, to constitutional law. In resolving a complex case with more than one potentially justifiable outcome, the previous resolution of a relevantly similar case is not merely an example of how the present case could be handled; rather, it is a fundamental constraint on the legitimacy of any solution (Planned Parenthood v. Casey, 1992).

Social conventional reasoning addresses the present on the basis of the past; in other words, previous cases deemed sufficiently analogous are binding, not just helpful. Note that precedent-based reasoning is largely irrelevant or antithetical to logic, science, and morality. The fact that nearly all of us have believed something for a long time does not make it true and the fact that we have all behaved in certain ways does not make those modes of behavior moral. Social conventional reasoning is not limited to precedent-based reasoning, but respect for precedent has a special epistemic status in the domain of social convention that it lacks in the domains of logic, science, or morality. This supports the identification of social convention as an epistemic domain with its own prototypical form of reasoning.

The domain of history

One last potential domain for consideration is history (Maggioni, 2010; Maggioni & Parkinson, 2008; Maggioni, VanSledright, & Alexander, 2009; Moshman, 2008). History is empirical like science rather than normative like logic, morality, or convention. Historians rely on archival and other data, not on logical proof. A work of history is about what actually happened in the past, not what morally should have happened or what convention demanded. Of course, historians use logical reasoning and study morality and social conventions. But their epistemological approach is empirical, like that of scientists.

Does history, then, fall within the epistemic domain of science? Epistemologies of history, like those of science, do plausibly show a developmental transition from objectivism to subjectivism to rationalism. The objectivist believes historical truth is there to be found in the archives of history. The subjectivist believes individuals and social groups construct their own histories, none of which are, in any objective sense, better or worse than any others. Rationalists, in contrast, believe the subjective construction of history is potentially a rational process that leads to justifiable knowledge of the past, albeit not to final truths.

There is, however, a potentially important, and potentially epistemic, difference between history and science. Science aims to explain and predict, whereas history, arguably, has no such aims. Science aims for general theories, whereas history is satisfied with contingent facts. Scientific accounts consist of theoretical explanations, whereas historical accounts consist of narratives.

History, then, may be seen as a domain of its own with its own core form of reasoning: Narrative reasoning. Narratives are judged in part on the basis of coherence across time. But is this specific to historical reasoning? Developmental biology and developmental psychology both provide theories that consist in part of narratives of change over time. Such theories may be regarded as scientific in that they are judged not just on the coherence of the narrative—does it tell a good story?—but also on its relation to data. But this is true of historical narratives as well.

It is thus unclear whether history is best regarded as a topic of scientific investigation or as a distinct epistemic domain. History students and developing individuals may have ideas of their own about this, which may greatly influence how they reason about history.

Are there more epistemic domains?

As we have seen, there is room for disagreement as to whether history is a domain of its own. Thus, while I do not rule out the possibility of additional domains, I do not assume the number of epistemic domains is even as great as five, and urge caution about a proliferation of domains (Siegel, 2006). The mere fact that we think differently about some topic does not make it an epistemic domain. For two domains to be epistemologically distinct they must employ qualitatively different standards of truth and justification.

It must be remembered, however, that as individuals at various levels of development reason about various topics in various contexts, they may posit more, fewer, or different epistemic domains than philosophers. The study of epistemic development must acknowledge and investigate all epistemologies while differentiating higher and lower levels of epistemic understanding.

Reflection on epistemic domains

There is no evidence that children reflect on the distinctions between epistemic domains. Children reason *within* domains, thus implicitly distinguishing them, but they do not identify, compare, analyze, or coordinate the domains themselves.

For example, children beginning about age 6 or 7 understand the logical necessity of deductive reasoning and mathematical calculations (Miller, Custer, & Nassau, 2000; Moshman, 1990, 2004, 2009, 2013; Moshman & Franks, 1986; Moshman & Timmons, 1982; Nicholls & Thorkildsen, 1988; Piaget, 1952, 1987; Pillow, 2002; Pillow & Anderson, 2006). They also understand that empirical beliefs about the world can be wrong for a variety of reasons (Carpendale & Chandler, 1996; Doherty, 2009; Lalonde & Chandler, 2002; Miller, 2012; Pillow and Henrichon, 1996; Rowley & Robinson, 2007; Wimmer & Doherty, 2011). It is not until at least age 11 or 12, however, that they reflect on the epistemological intuitions implicit in their distinction between logical and empirical knowledge (Moshman, 1990; Moshman & Franks, 1986).

Similarly, children as young as age 4 distinguish moral matters of justice, care, harm, and rights from social conventions that vary across cultural contexts (Killen & Rutland, 2011; Smetana, 2011; Turiel, 2008). That is, they respond differently to matters of morality than to matters of convention and can explain the rational basis for their moral judgments. Their explanations, however, are limited to the case at hand. Only in adolescence and beyond do people consider, in the abstract, the nature of the moral domain in relation to the domain of social convention, as in Kohlberg's (1984) conception of Stage 5 (postconventional social contract) reasoning (for a neoKohlbergian alternative, see Gibbs, 2014).

We doubtless continue throughout our lives to address epistemological issues within fundamental domains such as science, logic, and morality that were constructed in early childhood. In adolescence and beyond, reflection on the domains themselves, including their defining characteristics and distinctions, may generate advanced epistemic development, including the construction of reflective epistemologies.

There is thus a great need for research on reflective understanding of epistemic domains and their distinctions and interrelations and on development of the ability to coordinate epistemic domains. I suggest in the next section some possibilities for research.

Research on epistemic domains

There already exists substantial research on differences in knowledge, inference, and thinking across a variety of topics and academic disciplines, including research addressing epistemologically meaningful distinctions with important implications for reasoning (Chandler & Proulx, 2010; Flavell, Flavell, Green, & Moses, 1990; Flavell, Mumme, Green, & Flavell, 1992; Kuhn et al., 2000; Muis, Bendixen, & Haerle, 2006; Nicholls & Thorkildsen, 1988; Wainryb, Shaw, Langley, Cottam, & Lewis, 2004). There is also substantial research on reasoning within the domains of science, logic, and morality and on epistemic cognition and development within each, beginning in childhood (much of it discussed above). What is lacking in the literature is research on the development of epistemic reflection on these epistemic distinctions.

Consider this research question: What epistemic domain distinctions do adolescents and adults make? In seeking to answer that question we must steer a course between two extremes. On the one hand, if we simply look for whether people understand the domain distinctions we find important, we may find that they do but we would remain ignorant of other epistemic distinctions they may consider more important. On the other hand, we can't simply ask people to tell us their epistemologies. Most wouldn't know what we were talking about. Even if people did tell us their epistemologies, moreover, we would have no way of interpreting them or identifying developmental progress without an epistemological framework of our own.

Thus we need a methodology that permits people to make and explain epistemic domain distinctions but also permits researchers to focus people's attention on potentially important distinctions and domains. A useful possibility is the "Rep Test," a methodology devised by the constructivist personality theorist George Kelly (1955) to identify an individual's spontaneous concepts. A concept is assumed to require at least three cases, two that have something in common and a third that differs in that regard. Conceptualization can thus be studied by presenting three cases to be classified.

Moshman and Franks (1986) used Kelly's Rep Test methodology to study the spontaneous distinction of logic from empirical truth. Logical arguments were presented three at a time to: individual fourth graders (ages 9–10 years); seventh graders (ages 12–13 years); and college students. The arguments varied with respect to (a) truth of the premises, (b) truth of the conclusion, (c) validity of the argument form, and (d) topic. Individuals of all ages sorted on the basis of truth and topic but only the seventh graders and college students distinguished valid from invalid arguments and explained this distinction as different from the distinction between true and false premises or conclusions by distinguishing logic from empirical truth.

This methodology could readily be extended to a broader array of epistemic domains. Here is a collection of statements, varying in topic, truth status, and epistemic domain:

Elephants are larger than mice.
Mice are larger than elephants.
There are more dimes than nickels in Fargo, North Dakota.
There are more dimes than coins in Fargo, North Dakota.
People who do equal work equally well should receive equal pay.
People should be free to pursue their own lives.
People should stop at red lights and go on green lights.
People should stop at green lights and go on red lights.
You shouldn't hit other people without good reason.
You should never hurt other people.
All triangles have three sides.
Some triangles have four sides.
All triangles have equal sides.
Human activity is causing global climate change.
We should be concerned about future generations.
The earth is billions of years old.
World War I began in 1914.
World War I made the world safe for democracy.
The U.S. Civil War ended slavery in the United States.
The North fought the Civil War to end slavery in the United States.
God intended the Civil War to end slavery in the United States.
Slavery should be ended.

Statements of this sort could be presented three or more at a time to research participants with instructions to sort the statements into two groups, explain their sorting, sort into two different groups with explanation, and continue the process for all possible sortings and explanations. The task can then be repeated for additional sets of statements. Research participants can be asked to clarify and expand on their explanations as needed to determine their meaning.

Participants can be expected to distinguish true statements from false and, perhaps, justifiable statements from those without rational basis. The question of interest is whether and how they also distinguish claims on the more subtle epistemic bases of whether they are (a) subject to empirical test; (b) necessary, provable, or impossible; (c) potentially part of a coherent narrative; (d) potentially consistent with precedent; (e) potentially consistent with relevant principles; or (f) the result of coordinating multiple perspectives. Questions to be addressed would include (a) what domains are distinguished; (b) how such distinctions are explained; (c) how such distinctions and explanations relate to age, education, and other variables; and (d) what developmental trends can be seen, even if they are not universal or tied to age.

Of course this is just a start. Further research would need to consider how we coordinate forms of reasoning that differ in their epistemic goals and assumptions.

The study of reasoning is much enriched by considering its nature and development with respect to discrete epistemic domains.

Conclusion

Epistemic cognition is knowledge about the nature of knowledge, especially about the justification and truth of beliefs and claims. With this in mind, reasoning can be defined as epistemologically self-constrained thinking—that is, thinking aimed at reaching true, or at least justifiable, conclusions. Reasoning, I have argued, generally occurs within epistemic domains, which have different means and standards of justification associated with different conceptions of truth. Empirical and logicomathematical knowledge are standard examples of qualitatively distinct epistemic domains, and moral knowledge is commonly seen as a domain of its own. Social conventional knowledge and historical knowledge arguably constitute additional epistemic domains. Each domain is associated with one or two prototypical forms of reasoning, though multiple forms of reasoning are used in each and most forms of reasoning are applicable in multiple epistemic domains.

In adolescence and beyond, I have suggested, some individuals construct epistemologies that coordinate multiple domains and can serve as a basis for advanced forms of reasoning. Although the general transition from objectivist to subjectivist to rationalist epistemologies remains fundamental to understanding developmental change, research on the conceptualization of distinct epistemic domains and the development of an understanding of their differences is crucial to enriching our understanding of human rationality and of the development of diverse forms of reasoning. Such research, I have suggested, has hardly begun.

References

Amsel, E. (2011). Hypothetical thinking in adolescence: Its nature, development, and applications. In E. Amsel & J. G. Smetana (Eds.), *Adolescent vulnerabilities and opportunities: Developmental and constructivist perspectives* (pp. 86–113). New York: Cambridge University Press.

Carpendale, J. I., & Chandler, M. J. (1996). On the distinction between false belief understanding and subscribing to an interpretive theory of mind. *Child Development, 67,* 1686–1706.

Carpendale, J. I. M. (2009). Piaget's theory of moral development. In U. Müller, J. I. M. Carpendale, & L. Smith (Eds.), *The Cambridge companion to Piaget* (pp. 270–286). Cambridge: Cambridge University Press.

Chandler, M. J. (1987). The Othello effect: Essay on the emergence and eclipse of skeptical doubt. *Human Development, 30,* 137–159.

Chandler, M., Boyes, M., & Ball, L. (1990). Relativism and stations of epistemic doubt. *Journal of Experimental Child Psychology, 50,* 370–395.

Chandler, M. J., Hallett, D., & Sokol, B. W. (2002). Competing claims about competing knowledge claims. In B. K. Hofer & P. R. Pintrich (Eds.), *Personal epistemology: The psychology of beliefs about knowledge and knowing* (pp. 145–168). Mahwah, NJ: Erlbaum.

Chandler, M. J., & Proulx, T. (2010). Stalking young persons' changing beliefs about belief. In L. D. Bendixen & F. C. Feucht (Eds.), *Personal epistemology in the classroom: Theory, research, and implications for practice* (pp. 197–219). New York: Cambridge University Press.

Doherty, M. J. (2009). *Theory of mind: How children understand others' thoughts and feelings*. New York: Psychology Press.

Flavell, J. H., Flavell, E. R., Green, F. L., & Moses, L. J. (1990). Young children's understanding of fact beliefs versus value beliefs. *Child Development, 61*, 915–928.

Flavell, J. H., Mumme, D. L., Green, F. L., & Flavell, E. R. (1992). Young children's understanding of different types of beliefs. *Child Development, 63*, 960–977.

Gauffroy, C., & Barrouillet, P. (2011). The primacy of thinking about possibilities in the development of reasoning. *Developmental Psychology, 47*, 1000–1011.

Gibbs, J. C. (2014). *Moral development and reality: Beyond the theories of Kohlberg, Hoffman, and Haidt* (3rd edn.). Oxford: Oxford University Press.

Inhelder, B., & Piaget, J. (1958). *The growth of logical thinking from childhood to adolescence*. New York: Basic Books.

Inhelder, B., & Piaget, J. (1964). *The early growth of logic in the child: Classification and seriation*. London: Routledge.

Kahneman, D. (2011). *Thinking, fast and slow*. New York: Farrar, Straus & Giroux.

Kelly, G. A. (1955). *The psychology of personal constructs*. New York: Norton.

Killen, M., & Rutland, A. (2011). *Children and social exclusion: Morality, prejudice, and group identity*. Malden, MA: Wiley-Blackwell.

King, P. M., & Kitchener, K. S. (1994). *Developing reflective judgment: Understanding and promoting intellectual growth and critical thinking in adolescents and adults*. San Francisco, CA: Jossey-Bass.

King, P. M., & Kitchener, K. S. (2002). The reflective judgment model: Twenty years of research on epistemic cognition. In B. K. Hofer & P. K. Pintrich (Eds.), *Personal epistemology: The psychology of beliefs about knowledge and knowing* (pp. 37–61). Mahwah, NJ: Erlbaum.

Kitchener, K. S. (1983). Cognition, metacognition, and epistemic cognition: A three-level model of cognitive processing. *Human Development, 26*, 222–232.

Klaczynski, P. A. (2011). Age differences in understanding precedent-setting decisions and authorities' responses to violations of deontic rules. *Journal of Experimental Child Psychology, 109*, 1–24.

Kohlberg, L. (1981). *The philosophy of moral development*. San Francisco, CA: Harper & Row.

Kohlberg, L. (1984). *The psychology of moral development*. San Francisco, CA: Harper & Row.

Koslowski, B. (1996). *Theory and evidence: The development of scientific reasoning*. Cambridge, MA: MIT Press.

Krettenauer, T. (2004). Metaethical cognition and epistemic reasoning development in adolescence. *International Journal of Behavioral Development, 28*, 461–470.

Kuhn, D. (2009). Adolescent thinking. In R. M. Lerner & L. Steinberg (Eds.), *Handbook of adolescent psychology* (3rd edn., Vol. 1, pp. 152–186). Hoboken, NJ: Wiley.

Kuhn, D., Cheney, R., & Weinstock, M. (2000). The development of epistemological understanding. *Cognitive Development, 15*, 309–328.

Kuhn, D. & Franklin, S. (2006). The second decade: What develops (and how)? In W. Damon & R. M. Lerner (Series Eds.) & D. Kuhn & R. Siegler (Vol. Eds.), *Handbook of child psychology, Vol. 2: Cognition, perception, and language* (6th edn., pp. 953–993). Hoboken, NJ: Wiley.

Kuhn, D. & Weinstock, M. (2002). What is epistemological thinking and why does it matter? In B. K. Hofer & P. R. Pintrich (Eds.), *Personal epistemology: The psychology of beliefs about knowledge and knowing* (pp. 121–144). Mahwah, NJ: Erlbaum.

Lalonde, C. E., & Chandler, M. J. (2002). Children's understanding of interpretation. *New Ideas in Psychology, 20*, 163–198.

Maggioni, L. (2010). *Studying epistemic cognition in the history classroom: Cases of teaching and learning to think historically.* Dissertation, University of Maryland, College Park.

Maggioni, L., & Parkinson, M. M. (2008). The role of teacher epistemic cognition, epistemic beliefs, and calibration in instruction. *Educational Psychology Review, 20*, 445–461.

Maggioni, L., VanSledright, B., & Alexander, P. A. (2009). Walking on the borders: A measure of epistemic cognition in history. *Journal of Experimental Education, 77*, 187–213.

Mansfield, A. F., & Clinchy, B. M. (2002). Toward the integration of objectivity and subjectivity: Epistemological development from 10 to 16. *New Ideas in Psychology, 20*, 225–262.

Miller, S. A. (2012). *Theory of mind: Beyond the preschool years.* New York: Psychology Press.

Miller, S. A., Custer, W. L., & Nassau, G. (2000). Children's understanding of the necessity of logically necessary truths. *Cognitive Development, 15*, 383–403.

Moshman, D. (1990). The development of metalogical understanding. In W. F. Overton (Ed.), *Reasoning, necessity, and logic: Developmental perspectives* (pp. 205–225). Hillsdale, NJ: Erlbaum.

Moshman, D. (1995). The construction of moral rationality. *Human Development, 38*, 265–281.

Moshman, D. (1998). Cognitive development beyond childhood. In W. Damon (Series Ed.) & D. Kuhn & R. Siegler (Vol. Eds.), *Handbook of child psychology: Vol. 2. Cognition, perception, and language* (5th edn., pp. 947–978). New York: Wiley.

Moshman, D. (2004). From inference to reasoning: The construction of rationality. *Thinking & Reasoning, 10*, 221–239.

Moshman, D. (2008). Epistemic development and the perils of Pluto. In M. F. Shaughnessy, M. V. J. Veenman, & C. Kleyn-Kennedy (Eds.), *Meta-cognition: A recent review of research, theory and perspectives* (pp. 161–174). New York: Nova Science.

Moshman, D. (2009). The development of rationality. In H. Siegel (Ed.), *Oxford handbook of philosophy of education* (pp. 145–161). Oxford: Oxford University Press.

Moshman, D. (2011a). *Adolescent rationality and development: Cognition, morality, and identity* (3rd edn.). New York: Psychology Press.

Moshman, D. (2011b). Epistemic cognition. In R. J. R. Levesque (Ed.), *Encyclopedia of adolescence* (pp. 847–853). New York: Springer.

Moshman, D. (2013). Epistemic cognition and development. In P. Barrouillet & C. Gauffroy (Eds.), *The development of thinking and reasoning* (pp. 13–33). New York: Psychology Press.

Moshman, D., & Franks, B. A. (1986). Development of the concept of inferential validity. *Child Development, 57*, 153–165.

Moshman, D., & Timmons, M. (1982). The construction of logical necessity. *Human Development, 25*, 309–324.

Muis, K. R., Bendixen, L. D., & Haerle, F. C. (2006). Domain-generality and domain-specificity in personal epistemology research: Philosophical and empirical reflections in the development of a theoretical framework. *Educational Psychology Review, 18*, 3–54.

Nicholls, J. G., & Thorkildsen, T. A. (1988). Children's distinctions among matters of intellectual convention, logic, fact, and personal choice. *Child Development, 59*, 939–949.

Piaget, J. (1952). *The child's conception of number.* London: Routledge & Kegan Paul.

Piaget, J. (1965). *The moral judgment of the child.* New York: Free Press. (Orig. work published 1932.)

Piaget, J. (1987). *Possibility and necessity* (two volumes). Minneapolis: University of Minnesota Press.

Piéraut-Le Bonniec, G. (1980). *The development of modal reasoning: Genesis of necessity and possibility notions.* New York: Academic Press.

Pillow, B. H. (2002). Children's and adults' evaluation of the certainty of deductive inferences, inductive inferences, and guesses. *Child Development, 73*, 779–792.

Pillow, B. H., & Anderson, K. L. (2006). Children's awareness of their own certainty and understanding of deduction and guessing. *British Journal of Developmental Psychology, 24*, 823–849.

Pillow, B. H., & Henrichon, A. J. (1996). There's more to the picture than meets the eye: Young children's difficulty understanding biased interpretation. *Child Development, 67*, 803–819.

Planned Parenthood v. Casey, 505 U. S. 833 (1992).

Rowley, M., & Robinson, E. J. (2007). Understanding the truth about subjectivity. *Social Development, 16*, 741–757.

Sandoval, W. A. (2005). Understanding students' practical epistemologies and their influence on learning through inquiry. *Science Education, 89*, 634–656.

Sandoval, W. A., & Reiser, B. J. (2004). Explanation-driven inquiry: Integrating conceptual and epistemic scaffolds for scientific inquiry. *Science Education, 88*, 345–372.

Selman, R. L. (1980). *The growth of interpersonal understanding: Developmental and clinical analyses.* New York: Academic Press.

Siegel, H. (2006). Epistemological diversity and education research: Much ado about nothing much? *Educational Researcher, 35*(2), 3–12.

Smetana, J. G. (2011). *Adolescents, families, and social development: How teens construct their worlds.* Malden, MA: Wiley-Blackwell.

Smith, L. (1993). *Necessary knowledge: Piagetian perspectives on constructivism.* Hillsdale, NJ: Erlbaum.

Smith, L. (2009). Piaget's developmental epistemology. In U. Müller, J. I. M. Carpendale, & L. Smith (Eds.), *The Cambridge companion to Piaget* (pp. 64–93). Cambridge: Cambridge University Press.

Turiel, E. (2008). The development of children's orientations toward moral, social, and personal orders: More than a sequence in development. *Human Development, 51*, 21–39.

Wainryb, C., Shaw, L. A., Langley, M., Cottam, K., & Lewis, R. (2004). Children's thinking about diversity of belief in the early school years: Judgments of relativism, tolerance, and disagreeing persons. *Child Development, 75*, 687–703.

Wimmer, M. C., & Doherty, M. J. (2011). The development of ambiguous figure perception. *Monographs of the Society for Research in Child Development, 76*(1), Serial No. 298.

7 Heuristics, biases and the development of conflict detection during reasoning

Wim De Neys

Human judgment is easily biased. Consider, for example, the controversy that surrounded the introduction of beach volleyball as an Olympic sport at the Atlanta 1996 games. A lot of critics objected and argued that they simply could not rate beach volleyball as a real sport. It was considered to be nothing more than a fun pastime that you play on the beach on holiday (Coren, 2012). I've always found this striking because beach volleyball is both physically and mentally one of the most demanding sports that I know. To excel players need speed, strength, excellent technical skills, and the ability to play tactically as a pair. Indeed, a close look at the impressive physique of the top players makes it clear that—in contrast with, let's say, the average slugger in baseball or lineman in football—you need to be a highly trained athlete to make it in this game. Hence, if you deliberately reflect on it for a minute, there are very good reasons to classify beach volleyball as a real sport. The problem, however, seems to be that intuitively, beach volleyball is readily associated with prototypical "leisure" concepts such as "beach," "fun," and "holiday." After all, the game is played on a sand court, players dress in typical beachwear, and major tournaments are held at exotic destinations such as Rio de Janeiro, Hawaii, or Santa Barbara. These automatic intuitive associations seem to have an irresistible biasing pull on people's judgment (Lewis, 2008).

Decades of reasoning and decision-making research have shown that similar intuitive thinking is biasing people's reasoning in a wide range of logical and probabilistic reasoning tasks (Evans, 2008; Evans & Over, 1996; Kahneman & Frederick, 2005). Consider, for example, the following adaptation of the famous base-rate neglect (Kahneman & Tversky, 1973) problem:

> A psychologist wrote thumbnail descriptions of a sample of 1000 participants consisting of 5 women and 995 men. The description below was drawn randomly from the 1000 available descriptions.
>
> Sam is a 25 year old writer who lives in Toronto. Sam likes to shop and spends a lot of money on clothes.
>
> What is most likely?
> a. Sam is a woman.
> b. Sam is a man.

Intuitively, many people will be tempted to conclude that Sam is a woman based on stereotypical beliefs cued by the description. However, given that there are far more males than females in the sample (i.e., 995 out of 1000) the statistical base-rates favor the conclusion that a randomly drawn individual will most likely be a man. Hence, logically speaking, taking the base-rate into account should push the scale to the "man" side. Unfortunately, just as in the beach volley case, educated reasoners are typically tricked by their intuition and fail to solve the problem correctly (e.g., De Neys & Glumicic, 2008). In general, human reasoners seem to have a strong tendency to base their judgment on fast intuitive impressions rather than on more demanding, deliberative reasoning. Although this intuitive or so-called "heuristic" thinking might sometimes be useful, it can also cue responses that conflict with more logical or probabilistic considerations and bias our thinking (Evans, 2003, 2010; Kahneman, 2011; Stanovich & West, 2000).

Interestingly, however, recent studies on conflict detection during thinking show that despite the omnipresent bias, adults demonstrate a remarkable sensitivity to violations of logical and probabilistic principles when they reason (e.g., Bonner & Newell, 2010; De Neys & Franssens, 2009; De Neys & Glumicic, 2008; Handley, Newstead, & Trippas, 2011; Morsanyi & Handley, 2012; Stupple & Ball, 2008; Villejoubert, 2009). That is, although people are often biased and fail to give the correct response, they at least seem to detect that their intuitive heuristic response is questionable. For example, giving an erroneous heuristic response has been shown to result in increased autonomic activation (e.g., De Neys, Moyens, & Vansteenwegen, 2010), increased activation of brain regions supposed to be mediating conflict detection (e.g., De Neys, Vartanian, & Goel, 2008), and decreased response confidence (De Neys, Cromheeke, & Osman, 2011). Bluntly put, although reasoners might be biased, they at least seem to sense that they are erring. In this chapter I present emerging work on the development of this critical conflict or bias sensitivity process. I will try to clarify that the efficiency of the conflict detection process might be a key factor that distinguishes older and younger reasoners. The chapter starts with an overview of the core findings of the conflict detection studies with adults. Next, I review the developmental findings. I conclude the chapter by discussing limitations of the presented developmental framework and sketch directions for further research.

For clarity, the reader might want to note that I will be using the label "correct" or "logical" response as a handy shortcut to refer to "the response that has traditionally been considered as correct or normative according to standard logic or probability theory." The appropriateness of these traditional norms has sometimes been questioned in the reasoning field (e.g., see Stanovich & West, 2000, for a review). Under this interpretation, the heuristic response should not be labeled as "incorrect" or "biased." For the sake of simplicity I stick to the traditional labeling. In the same vein, I use the term "logical" as a general header to refer both to standard logic and probability theory.

Conflict detection studies with adults

Research on conflict detection during thinking has focused on people's processing of the infamous classic reasoning tasks that have been studied for decades in the reasoning and decision-making field (e.g., base-rate neglect tasks, ratio-bias tasks, conjunction fallacy, belief bias syllogisms; see De Neys, 2012, for examples). Giving the correct response in these tasks requires only the application of some very basic logical or probabilistic principles. However, as the introductory base-rate neglect example illustrated, the tasks are constructed such that they intuitively cue a tempting heuristic response that conflicts with these principles. The basic question that the detection studies have been trying to answer is whether people are sensitive to this conflict and notice that their heuristic response is questionable. Therefore, the studies typically contrast people's processing of the classic problems with newly constructed control versions. In the control or no-conflict versions the conflict is removed and the cued heuristic response is consistent with the logical response. For example, a no-conflict control version of the introductory base-rate problem would simply switch the base-rates around (i.e., the problem would state that there are 995 women and 5 men in the sample). Everything else stays the same. Consider this example:

> A psychologist wrote thumbnail descriptions of a sample of 1000 participants consisting of 5 men and 995 women. The description below was drawn randomly from the 1000 available descriptions.
>
> Sam is a 25 year old writer who lives in Toronto. Sam likes to shop and spends a lot of money on clothes.
>
> What is most likely?
> a. Sam is a woman.
> b. Sam is a man.

Hence, both heuristic considerations based on the description and logical ratio considerations cue the exact same response.

In a nutshell, the conflict detection studies have introduced a wide range of subtle processing measures to examine whether people process the conflict and no-conflict versions differently. For example, one basic procedure has been to simply look at people's response latencies: A number of studies reported that people need typically more time to solve the conflict than the control versions (e.g., Bonner & Newell, 2010; De Neys & Glumicic, 2008; Stupple & Ball, 2008; Thompson, Striemer, Reikoff, Gunter, & Campbell, 2003; Villejoubert, 2009). Now, the only difference between the two versions is whether the cued heuristic response is consistent with the correct logical response or not. For example, in the base-rate problem the only modified factor in the control version is the fact that the base-rates were switched around. If biased reasoners were really mere heuristic thinkers who neglected the base-rate information, they should not process the two types of problems any differently. Hence, the latency findings support the idea that people are sensitive to the logical status of their judgment: If people's intuitive heuristic answer conflicts with the logical norm, their problem processing time will increase.

Further support for this claim has come from gaze and eye-tracking studies that showed that the longer latencies are specifically accompanied by a longer inspection of logically critical problem information. For example, Ball, Philips, Wade, and Quayle (2006) observed that after participants read the conclusion of a conflict syllogism in which the conclusion believability conflicts with its logical validity (e.g., a problem with a valid but unbelievable conclusion), they make saccades to the major and minor premises and start re-inspecting this information. Such "reviewing" was found to be much less pronounced on the no-conflict problems. De Neys and Glumicic (2008) observed a similar gaze trend with base-rate problems: When solving conflict versions, participants showed an increased tendency to re-view the paragraph with the base-rate information after they had read the personality description.

In a surprise recall test that was presented to participants after the study, De Neys and Glumicic (2008) also observed that the increased base-rate inspection was accompanied by a better recall of the base-rate information for the conflict vs. no-conflict problems. Interestingly, in a subsequent study, De Neys & Franssens (2009) showed that in contrast to the logical information, information that was associated with the heuristic response was less accessible in memory after solving conflict problems. Participants in this study were given a lexical decision task in which they had to decide whether a string of letters formed a word or not after each reasoning problem. Results showed that lexical decisions about words that were linked to the cued heuristic response took longer after solving conflict vs. control problems, suggesting that participants had attempted to block this information during reasoning.

The behavioral conflict findings have also been validated with a brain-based approach. For example, De Neys et al. (2008) used fMRI to monitor the activation of a specific brain area, the Anterior Cingulate Cortex (ACC), which is believed to mediate conflict detection during thinking (e.g., Botvinick, Cohen, & Carter, 2004). Participants were given classic conflict base-rate problems and the no-conflict control versions. In line with the behavioral findings, results showed that the ACC was much more activated when people solved the conflict versions than when they solved the control versions. In a subsequent study, participants' skin-conductance was recorded to monitor autonomic nervous system activation while solving conflict and no-conflict syllogisms (De Neys, Moyens, & Vansteenwegen, 2010). Results showed that solving the conflict problems resulted in a clear electrodermal activation spike. Hence, in addition to the ACC activation, solving conflict problems literally aroused participants. These neural conflict signals have also been shown to affect people's subjective response confidence: Participants typically indicate that they feel less confident about their answer after solving conflict problems than after solving the control problems (e.g., De Neys et al., 2011; see also Morsanyi & Handley, 2012, for related findings on people's affective evaluation).

In sum, the conflict detection studies with adults indicate that although people might be often biased and fail to give the correct logical answer on many reasoning tasks, they are not completely oblivious to their bias. Reasoners show some basic sensitivity to the fact that their heuristic answer conflicts with logical considerations. This conflict sensitivity entails that they do not simply disregard the logical implication of their judgments.

Developmental conflict detection studies

Numerous authors have argued that for sound reasoning it is paramount that reasoners monitor their heuristic intuitions for conflict with logical principles and subsequently inhibit the tempting heuristics in case such a conflict is detected (Barrouillet, 2011; Evans, 2010; Stanovich & West, 2000; De Neys & Glumicic, 2008). Therefore, the conflict detection findings that I reviewed above have been taken as support for the idea that heuristic bias typically results from an inhibition failure (e.g., Bonner & Newell, 2010; De Neys & Glumicic, 2008). That is, the problem does not seem to be that people do not detect that the heuristic response is questionable and needs to be discarded, but rather that people fail to complete the demanding inhibition process (e.g., De Neys & Franssens, 2009). This idea fits with the vast literature in the reasoning field that has stressed the critical role of inhibitory processing skills to override erroneous heuristic responses (e.g., Brainerd & Reyna, 2001; De Neys & Van Gelder, 2008; Handley, Capon, Beveridge, Dennis, & Evans, 2004; Houdé, 1997, 2007; Moutier, Plagne-Cayeux, Melot, & Houdé, 2006; Simoneau & Markovits, 2003; Stanovich & West, 2000).

However, it is crucial to stress that the bias detection studies have been typically run with adult participants. In general, developmental psychologists have often stressed that reasoning is a multi-component process and that biased responses might have multiple causes (e.g., Brainerd & Reyna, 2001; Jacobs & Klaczynski, 2002; Markovits & Barrouillet, 2004; Stanovich, West, & Toplak, 2011). Hence, it cannot be excluded that bias detection failures play a more crucial role earlier on in our reasoning development. This hypothesis receives some support from basic neurological studies that suggest that the ACC, the critical brain structure that is supposed to be mediating elementary conflict monitoring, is quite slow to mature and would only reach full functionality late in adolescence (e.g., Davies, Segalowitz, & Gavin, 2004; Fitzgerald et al., 2010; Santesso & Segalowitz, 2008). This tentatively indicates that there might be a critical transition with respect to the locus of heuristic bias in human development. That is, whereas adults would be primarily biased because they fail to inhibit the heuristic response after successful conflict detection, younger reasoners could be biased because they fail to detect the need to inhibit the heuristic response in the first place.

Together with a number of colleagues, I recently started to explore and test this developmental bias detection hypothesis (e.g., De Neys et al., 2011; De Neys & Feremans, 2012; De Neys, Lubin, & Houdé, in press; Steegen & De Neys, 2012). I review our initial findings below.

Adolescents

Based on the neurological evidence that suggests that the ACC slowly develops throughout adolescence (e.g., Davies et al., 2004; Fitzgerald et al., 2010; Santesso & Segalowitz, 2008), we decided to start our developmental work by contrasting the bias detection efficiency of a group of early adolescents (i.e., 13-year-old middle school students) and late adolescents (i.e., 16-year-old high school students). In their studies with adults (De Neys et al., 2011, Experiment 1 and 2), De Neys and colleagues already established that the previously documented neural conflict detection signals were also reflected in people's response confidence. Biased participants typically indicated that they felt less confident about their answer after solving conflict problems than after solving the control problems.[1] This directly indicated that participants questioned the correctness of their erroneous response. We decided to use this confidence measure to test the conflict detection efficiency in our first developmental study (De Neys et al., 2011, Experiment 3). Just as in our work with adults, our adolescents were presented with conflict and control versions of classic tasks (e.g., base-rate and conjunction fallacy problems). After answering each problem they were asked to indicate how confident they were that their answer was correct on a scale ranging from zero to 100 percent.

Analysis of reasoning accuracy showed that, just like most adults, the vast majority of our two adolescents groups were biased and failed to solve the conflict problems correctly. Further in line with the findings in adult groups, the critical confidence findings established that biased late adolescents also showed a confidence drop (i.e., about 10 percent decrease) after solving conflict problems. However, consistent with our developmental working hypothesis, this confidence decrease was less clear for biased early adolescents (i.e., about a 5 percent decrease). Hence, as expected, younger adolescents did seem to have a harder time detecting the biased nature of their judgment.

Pre-adolescents

Our initial study suggested that conflict detection during reasoning was less efficient for early than for late adolescents. However, although the confidence decrease was statistically smaller for early adolescents, it was not completely absent. In a subsequent study (De Neys & Feremans, 2012), we decided to validate our initial findings by focusing on even younger age groups. In theory, conflict detection should be even more problematic in the preadolescent age range, of course. Consequently, we decided to contrast the performance of pre-adolescent third graders (i.e., 9-year-olds) and early adolescent sixth graders (i.e., 12-year-olds).

To make sure that the format of the reasoning task would be suited for the younger children in this study, we decided to adopt the child friendly adaptation of the base-rate task that was introduced by De Neys and Vanderputte (2011). In this task, children are familiarized with the base-rates in a sample by showing them cards that depict characters that belong to one of two groups. For example, nine cards might depict a boy and one card might depict a girl. On the back of the cards, children see a picture of an object that will cue a clear stereotypical association. For example, children would be told that on the back we printed a picture of the boy's or girl's favorite toy (e.g., a toy truck or a doll). Next, children observe how the experimenter shuffles the cards, puts them in a bag, and randomly draws one card from the bag. The experimenter always shows children the back side of the drawn card (e.g., a truck) and then asks them whether there will be a boy or girl on the front. By playing around with the base-rates (e.g., nine girls/one boy or nine boys/one girl) one can easily construct conflict and no-conflict control problems. Hence, this format maintains the crucial characteristics of the original base-rate problems while remaining appropriate for testing younger children.

We measured bias detection sensitivity by asking the children to rate their response confidence on a simplified 4-point rating scale that ranged from 0 (really not sure) to 3 (totally sure). Children were familiarized with the scale and had to put a board game pawn on the number that best reflected their feeling of confidence.

Before presenting the results, I would like to highlight an important methodological issue. A critical prerequisite to study conflict detection in a developmental context is, of course, that all age groups are familiar with the stereotypical material. For example, if children have not yet acquired the typical "girls-like-shopping" stereotype, the base-rate problem that I presented in the introduction will simply not cue a heuristic response in younger age groups and there will be no conflict to detect. Although the absence of a cued intuitive response entails that correct responding no longer requires a demanding inhibition process and has been shown to help children reason more accurately (even far more accurately than adults, e.g., see Davidson, 1995; De Neys & Vanderputte, 2011; Jacobs & Potenza, 1991; Reyna & Brainerd, 1994; Stanovich et al., 2011), it is clear that it would confound the assessment of their conflict detection skills. Clearly, any measured absence of conflict detection in younger age groups would not point to a less developed detection skill under these circumstances. Hence, when drawing conclusions about the efficiency of conflict detection across age groups it is paramount to use stereotypes and materials that are familiar to all age groups (e.g., see De Neys & Vanderputte, 2011, for an extensive discussion of the role of stereotype knowledge development in reasoning). Consequently, all problem content in our studies was carefully pretested to make sure that it evoked the intended heuristic response.

Results of the study were pretty straightforward. As in our first study, biased early adolescent sixth graders still showed a significantly lower confidence rating after solving conflict vs. control problems. However, this effect was no longer observed in the group of third graders. That is, biased third graders were fully confident that their response was correct and did not show any sensitivity to their errors.

At this point it is also useful to discuss a second methodological issue when drawing conclusions about the efficiency of children's conflict detection skills. Just as it is important to make sure that the problems cue a heuristic response, one needs to be sure that children have some basic knowledge about the logical principles that are evoked in the tasks. For example, if third graders do not know that base-rates matter for their judgment, the lack of bias awareness should not be attributed to a conflict detection failure but rather to an insufficiently developed logical/probabilistic knowledge base. To eliminate such a confound, the children in our study were also presented with an abstract version of the problem. In this problem, the cards did not depict a character or object but were simply colored yellow or blue. There were nine yellow cards and one blue card. The back side of all cards was white. The experimenter showed the white back side after drawing it from the bag and asked what color the other side would have. Hence, on this abstract problem, heuristic thinking could not bias (or help) sound reasoning. Solving the problem relies on mere logical thinking about the group sizes. Thereby the problem allowed us to check whether our youngest reasoners had mastered the necessary logical knowledge about the impact of relative group sizes or base-rates on a probability estimate. Results showed that this was indeed the case. Even our third graders solved the abstract problem almost perfectly.[2] This establishes that our observed lack of confidence decrease in third graders indeed resulted from a failed conflict detection and not from a mere logical knowledge gap.

In sum, taken together our initial studies indicate that conflict or bias detection efficiency in classic reasoning tasks shows critical improvement near the start of adolescence. In contrast with older reasoners, young preadolescents do not yet seem to detect that their heuristic response conflicts with logical principles and biases their judgment. These findings fit with the observation that the brain-structure that is believed to mediate conflict detection (i.e., the ACC) is quite late to mature and only starts to reach proper functionality after the onset of adolescence (e.g., Davies et al., 2004; Fitzgerald et al., 2010; Santesso & Segalowitz, 2008).

Cueing detection? Preschoolers and conservation error detection

Do our findings imply that heuristic bias detection is by definition impossible for pre-adolescent reasoners? Not necessarily. In a third study (De Neys et al., in press) we showed that under the right circumstances, even preschoolers can show some sensitivity to their judgment bias. I'll first describe the study and then clarify what I mean by "the right circumstances."

In this study we decided to move away from the typical logical and probabilistic reasoning tasks that were used in our previous detection work. We focused on judgment bias in a different domain, namely number conservation. Number conservation refers to the insight that a numerical quantity will remain the same despite changes in its apparent shape or size. Imagine you are presented with a row of coins that is subsequently stretched out. Adults and older children will have little trouble grasping that although the stretching makes the row longer, it does not increase the number of coins, of course. However, until approximately age 7 children typically fail this task and seem to be convinced that the longer row also contains more coins (e.g., Piaget, 1941/1952; see also Borst, Poirel, Pineau, Cassotti, & Houdé, in press; Houdé, 1997; Ping & Goldin-Meadow, 2008). That is, in the coin-spreading task children tend to be biased by an erroneous intuition that is visuospatial in nature (i.e., a so-called "length-equals-number" intuition).

The goal of the study was to explore young children's possible sensitivity to their number conservation errors. To test our hypothesis we used a method similar to the one we used in the initial bias detection studies with the base-rate problems. Children were given both a classic version of the number conservation task in which the intuitively cued visuospatial length-equals-number response conflicted with the correct conservation response (i.e., conflict version) and a control or no-conflict version in which this conflict was not present. That is, in the conflict version children initially saw two rows of equal length containing the same number of coins. Next, one of the rows was spread apart so that one is longer than the other and children were asked whether the two rows contained the same number of coins. In the no-conflict version the two rows also have the same number of coins but initially differed in length. The longer row is now transformed (i.e., contracted) to give both rows equal length and the child is asked whether the two rows contain an equal number of coins. Hence, the critical difference is that the control problem does not cue an erroneous visuospatial response.

After solving each version, children were asked to indicate their response confidence on a rating scale. Just as in our studies with adolescents and pre-adolescents, this allowed us to measure participants' bias detection sensitivity. We focused on the performance of preschoolers, since older children (e.g., +7 years) have little trouble in answering the conservation task correctly. Obviously, there is little point in studying bias sensitivity if one's judgment is no longer biased.

Results showed that, as expected, the vast majority of our preschoolers failed to solve the conservation task and responded that the longer row also contained more coins. However, similar to older reasoners in our conflict detection work with logical and probabilistic reasoning tasks, preschoolers seemed to detect the erroneous nature of their judgment. Biased (i.e., so-called "non-conserving") preschoolers were significantly less confident about their response on the conflict than on the no-conflict problem. Hence, although our preschoolers did not manage to give the correct conservation response, their confidence indicated that they were not completely oblivious to their error.

To recap, our initial developmental studies suggested that bias detection during logical and probabilistic reasoning is only observed after the onset of adolescence (i.e., by the end of elementary school, e.g., De Neys et al., 2011; De Neys & Feremans, 2012). We linked this developmental pattern to the late maturation of the Anterior Cingulate Cortex (ACC, e.g., Davies et al., 2004; De Neys et al., 2008; Fitzgerald et al., 2010). Given these findings, the successful number conservation error detection at the preschool age might seem somewhat surprising. However, here one needs to take into account that a less developed ACC (i.e., a less efficient detection engine) does not imply a lack of all conflict detection. Indeed, basic error monitoring studies have shown that even 3-year-olds can detect errors in simple tasks that do not cue a strong intuitive response (Lyons & Ghetti, 2011). Arguably, in comparison with logical and probabilistic reasoning tasks in which the cued intuitive response typically entails a semantic prior belief or stereotypical information, the critical physical transformation in conservation tasks might act as a cue that directs children's attention and thereby facilitates monitoring. Hence, detection of intuitive bias in number conservation might be less demanding and occur at a younger age than in logical and probabilistic reasoning tasks.

Note that the idea that monitoring or conflict detection demands can be facilitated receives some support from our previous work with logical and probabilistic reasoning tasks. Here we need to highlight that the conflict factor in these studies was typically manipulated within-subjects. That is, the same participant is presented with multiple conflict and no-conflict problems. Kahneman (2002) has since long argued that such within-subject tests are less demanding because they help to focus people's attention on the conflict. Bluntly put, after a couple of trials people will get the hang of it and notice that they need to pay attention to potential conflict. Hence, the purest (or hardest) test of people's conflict detection capacity concerns the first problems in the series.[3] In our studies with adults and late adolescents we found that the detection effects were indeed present right from the start (e.g., De Neys & Franssens, 2009; De Neys & Glumicic, 2008; De Neys, Moyens, & Vansteenwegen, 2010; De Neys et al., 2011). Hence, for our older reasoners, the observed detection effects did not result from a cueing effect. However, this was no longer the case for our young adolescents. Although they showed a confidence decrease near the end of the experiment, this decreased confidence was not observed on the initial trials (De Neys et al., 2011, Experiment 3). Thus, in line with Kahneman's (2002) claims, attentional cuing resulting from repeated testing does seem to facilitate conflict detection for younger reasoners.

In general, these findings support the idea that task-related attentional cues can boost bias detection in younger age groups; this points to a number of interesting implications. First, the fact that conflict detection can be improved by attentional cues sketches an interesting avenue for future research. Indeed, future studies that directly test which features (e.g., warnings, presentation of multiple problems, highlighting certain content, etc.) do or don't facilitate the detection of conflict between intuitive heuristics and logical knowledge seem specifically promising. At an applied level, this can help to design effective intervention programs to improve young reasoners' thinking despite their intrinsically more limited detection capacities. Second, at a more theoretical level it also indicates that when making general statements about children's bias detection efficiency, it is important to keep in mind that these can be modulated and might differ across domains depending on task demands. Third, in and by itself, the finding that preschoolers show conservation error sensitivity also has direct implications for work on conservation development. For example, in the classic work of Piaget (1941/1952), who introduced the coin-spreading task, number conservation marked a critical transition from a pre-operational to operational stage in children's thinking. According to Piaget, young children before the age of 7 show a structural conservation knowledge deficit. Piaget basically claimed that the young child cannot grasp the conservation principle because she or he is limited to a purely intuitive and perceptual way of processing information. Our confidence data directly argues against Piaget's classic characterization of the preschool child as an illogical reasoner who is bound to rely on mere visuospatial intuitions. If biased non-conservers did not have some elementary understanding of the conservation principle, they should have no reason to doubt their answer. In line with other critiques of Piaget's claim (e.g., Bjorklund & Harnishfeger, 1990; Borst et al., in press; Dempster & Brainerd, 1995; Houdé, 2000; Houdé & Guichart, 2001; Leroux et al., 2006; Poirel et al., in press) this indicates that preschoolers are more knowledgeable than their conservation errors suggest.

Adolescents and inhibition initiation

Our conflict detection study with adolescents indicated that late adolescents showed a bias sensitivity that was comparable to the levels we observed in adults. It is important to stress that this does not necessarily imply that the way that reasoners deal with heuristic bias and conflict shows no further evolution in young adulthood. As I noted in the overview of the adult findings, it has been observed that after detecting conflict, adults also engage in an inhibition process and at least try to discard the erroneous heuristic response (e.g., De Neys & Franssens, 2009). To recap, adults in De Neys and Franssens' study were given a lexical decision task in which they had to decide whether a string of letters formed a word or not after each reasoning problem. Results showed that lexical decisions about words that were linked to the cued heuristic response (e.g., with the introductory base-rate problem these could be the words "purse" or "skirt") took longer after solving conflict vs. control problems. Hence, information that was associated with the heuristic response was less accessible in memory after solving conflict problems. This suggested that participants had attempted to inhibit this information during reasoning.

Steegen and De Neys (2012) recently ran a similar study with adolescents. We observed that adolescents who gave the correct response on conflict problems also showed the impaired access (i.e., longer decision times) to target words that were associated with the cued heuristic response. Not surprisingly, this indicates that sound reasoning in younger reasoners also relies on inhibition of the heuristic response (see also Moutier et al., 2006, for related evidence). However, unlike the findings with adults, we did not observe this memory impairment for biased late (or younger) adolescents. Our initial conflict detection studies showed that at least late adolescents are very good at bias detection. However, the Steegen and De Neys study suggests that unlike in biased adults, this successful bias detection is not yet followed by an inhibition engagement in adolescents. It is well established that inhibitory processing capacity increases from childhood to young adulthood (e.g., Bedart et al., 2002; Christ, White, Mandernach, & Keys, 2001; Dempster & Brainerd, 1995; De Neys & Everaerts, 2008; De Neys & Van Gelder, 2008; Houdé, 2007; Klaczynski & Narashimham, 1998; Kokis, Macpherson, Toplak, West, & Stanovich, 2002). Biased late adolescents' lack of inhibition engagement, despite successful conflict detection, might indicate that the additional inhibition engagement step is still too demanding for them.

Clarifications and future directions

I this last section I would like to clarify some possible misconceptions and sketch directions for future research.

Need for generalization

In this chapter I presented emerging work on the development of conflict or bias detection during thinking. I hope to have clarified that this is an important process that deserves further attention from developmental scientists. However, it will be clear that the framework that I presented here is still in its infancy and will need to be further developed and validated. For example, it will be critical to test the generalizability of the findings across different tasks. In the section on detection cuing, I already noted the importance of generalizing the findings across different domains (e.g., conservation vs. logical and probabilistic reasoning). However, it is important to bear in mind that even within the domains of reasoning and decision-making, our developmental studies have so far only focused on one specific task (e.g., base-rate neglect tasks). One strong point of the conflict detection work with adults is precisely that the findings have been validated with a wide range of tasks (e.g., base-rate neglect, e.g., De Neys & Glumicic, 2008; syllogisms, e.g., De Neys, Moyens, & Vansteenwegen, 2010, De Neys & Franssens, 2009; conjunction fallacy, e.g., De Neys et al., 2011, Villejoubert, 2009; ratio-bias, e.g., Bonner & Newell, 2010; bat-and-ball problem, e.g., De Neys, Rossi, & Houdé, 2013). This establishes that the findings with adults are not driven by confounds or characteristics associated with a specific task (e.g., Klauer & Singmann, 2012; Pennycook, Fugelsang, & Koehler, 2012). Future developmental studies will need to take this task generalization seriously. In addition, a second limitation that needs to be taken into account is that our developmental studies have focused on one specific (behavioral) detection measure (i.e., confidence ratings). Again, conflict detection studies with adults have used a wide-range of methods and techniques to measure detection sensitivity (e.g., latencies, e.g., Bonner & Newell, 2010, De Neys & Glumicic, 2008; eye-tracking, e.g., Ball et al., 2006; memory recall, e.g., Franssens & De Neys, 2009; skin-conductance, e.g., De Neys, Moyens, & Vansteenwegen, 2010; EEG, e.g., De Neys, Novitskiy, Ramautar, & Wagemans, 2010; fMRI, e.g., De Neys et al., 2008). In addition to task generalization, such future method generalization is also critical. Note that a developmental neuroscientific approach would be especially welcome. Indeed, we have hypothesized that our initial findings, pointing to less efficient bias detection for younger reasoners can be linked to the late maturation of the Anterior Cingulate Cortex. In this respect it would be very interesting to run fMRI, EEG, or skin-conductance studies to test directly whether the lack of a confidence drop is accompanied by a less responsive ACC in younger age groups.

In sum, I believe that the emerging framework that I sketched in this chapter is promising "work-in-progress." However, the young nature of the research definitely entails that the initial findings and claims need to be interpreted with some caution.

What do we "know": Implicit bias detection?

It is perhaps also useful to stress that the conflict detection studies with adults have typically characterized the documented bias detection as an implicit process (e.g., De Neys, 2012). That is, the claim that adults know that they are biased and detect logical violations does not entail that they have a fully explicit understanding of the violated principles that they can verbally justify. A key point is that the necessary logical knowledge that allows people to detect a conflict with the cued heuristic response is conceived to be implicit in nature. Consequently, the conflict experience has been described as a "gut feeling" (e.g., Franssens & De Neys, 2009; Thompson, 2009; Thompson, Prowse Turner, & Pennycook, 2011): People will be aware that there is something fishy about their heuristic response, but they will not be able to put their finger on it and explain why their response is questionable. More precisely, the idea is that the conflict between implicitly activated logical knowledge and the cued heuristic response creates arousal. People experience this arousal, this makes them doubt their heuristic response, but they will not be able to justify why their response is questionable. However, the key point is that the implicit knowledge at least suffices to signal that the heuristic response is not fully warranted.

The interested reader can find a detailed discussion of this issue elsewhere (see De Neys, 2012) but I would simply like to stress here that the detection in younger reasoners that I reviewed and documented in this chapter needs to be conceived of at the same level. Obviously, our detection findings do not entail that young adolescents (or non-conserving preschoolers for that matter) have a fully explicit understanding of the logical principles they intuitively sense to be violating.

In closing

Some 10 years ago, guest editors Henry Markovits and Pierre Barrouillet (2004) noted in a special developmental issue of the journal *Thinking & Reasoning* that although reasoning and decision-making were once one of the prime research areas for developmental scientists, interest had faded in more recent years. Markovits and Barrouillet suggested that one of the reasons for this decline was the rise of the "Heuristics and Biases" research program and its demonstration of the widespread bias in human reasoning. This massive bias seemed to point to a developmental standstill in human reasoning. That is, if even the vast majority of educated university students fail to solve basic logical reasoning problems, one might easily get the impression that there doesn't seem to be a lot of development going on. Consequently, as Markovits and Barrouillet put it, many developmental scientists concluded that "there is no point in looking at the development of something that is not present."

I mention Markovits and Barrouillet's special issue here because it actually kick-started my interest in reasoning development. Bluntly put, I guess that some 10 years later, I am in a position to start sketching a way out of the apparent deadlock they mentioned. Looking closely at the conflict detection process suggests that the lack of reasoning development is more apparent than real. Although both adults and younger reasoners are indeed biased most of the time, the findings that I reviewed here indicate that older reasoners at least detect that their responses are biased. Consistent with recent insights in the developmental field (e.g., Brainerd, Reyna, & Ceci, 2008; Klaczynski, Byrnes, & Jacobs, 2001; Reyna & Farley, 2006; Reyna, Lloyd, & Brainerd, 2003) this differential bias awareness argues against the idea of a developmental standstill in human reasoning.

As I stated above, I fully realize that this framework needs to be further validated and caution is needed when interpreting the initial findings. However, I do hope I managed to illustrate that studying the development of conflict detection during thinking holds great promise and deserves to attract more interest from developmental psychologists.

Acknowledgements

Preparation of this manuscript was supported by a grant from the Agence National de la Recherche (ANR-12-JSH2-0007-01).

Notes

1 Not surprisingly, in the rare case that participants answered the conflict problem correctly, the confidence decrease was less clear. That is, adults who give the correct response also seem to know that it is correct.
2 Note that this fits with previous developmental work that established that even infants often show some basic understanding of the logical principles that are evoked in the classic "bias" tasks (e.g., Brainerd & Reyna, 2001; De Neys & Everaerts 2008; Morris, 2000; Téglás, Girotto, Gonzalez, & Bonatti, 2007)
3 More specifically, a between-subject test in which only the first problem that people are presented (e.g., half the sample solves a conflict version first and the other half a no-conflict version) is taken into account.

References

Ball, L. J., Philips, P., Wade, C. N., & Quayle, J. D. (2006). Effects of belief and logic on syllogistic reasoning: Eye-movement evidence for selective processing models. *Experimental Psychology, 53*, 77–86.

Barrouillet, P. (2011). Dual proces theories of reasoning: The test of development. *Developmental Review, 31*, 151–179.

Bedart, A. C., Nichols, S., Barbosa, J. A., Schachar, R., Logan, G. D., & Tannock, R. (2002). The development of selective inhibitory control across the life span. *Developmental Neuropsychology, 21*, 93–111.

Bjorklund, D. F., & Harnishfeger, K. K. (1990). The resources construct in cognitive development: Diverse sources of evidence and a theory of inefficient inhibition. *Developmental Review, 10*, 48–71.

Bonner, C., & Newell, B. R. (2010). In conflict with ourselves? An investigation of heuristic and analytic processes in decision making. *Memory & Cognition, 38*, 186–196.

Borst, G., Poirel, N., Pineau, A., Cassotti, M., & Houdé, O. (in press). Inhibitory control in number conservation and class inclusion tasks: A neo-Piagetian inter-tasks priming study. *Cognitive Development*.

Botvinick, M. M., Cohen, J. D., & Carter, C. S. (2004). Conflict monitoring and anterior cingulate cortex: An update. *Trends in Cognitive Sciences, 12*, 539–546.

Brainerd, C. J., & Reyna, V. F. (2001). Fuzzy-trace theory: Dual processes in memory, reasoning, and cognitive neuroscience. In H. W. Reese & R. Kail (Eds.), *Advances in child development and behavior* (Vol. 28, pp. 41–100). San Diego, CA: Academic Press.

Brainerd, C. J., Reyna, V. F., & Ceci, S. J. (2008). Developmental reversals in false memory: A review of data and theory. *Psychological Bulletin, 134*, 343–382.

Christ, S. E., White, D. A., Mandernach, T., & Keys, B. A. (2001). Inhibitory control across the life span. *Developmental Neuropsychology, 20*, 653–669.

Coren, G. (2012). Why beach volleyball is not a sport. The Australian. Retrieved November 7, 2012, from http://www.theaustralian.com.au/sport/london-games/beach-volleyball-is-not-a-sport/story-fne39r9e-1226438385456

Davidson, D. (1995). The representativeness heuristic and the conjunction fallacy effect in children's decision making. *Merrill-Palmer Quarterly, 41*, 328–346.

Davies, P. L., Segalowitz, S. J., & Gavin, W. J. (2004). Development of response-monitoring ERPs in 7- to 25-year-olds. *Developmental Neuropsychology, 25*, 355–376.

Dempster, F. N., & Brainerd, C. J. (1995). *Interference and inhibition in cognition*. San Diego, CA: Academic Press.

De Neys, W. (2012). Bias and conflict: A case for logical intuitions. *Perspectives on Psychological Science, 7*, 28–38.

De Neys, W., Cromheeke, S., & Osman, M. (2011). Biased but in doubt: Conflict and decision confidence. *PLoS ONE, 6*, e15954.

De Neys, W., & Everaerts, D. (2008). Developmental trends in everyday conditional reasoning: The retrieval and inhibition interplay. *Journal of Experimental Child Psychology, 100*, 252–263.

De Neys, W., & Feremans, V. (2012). Development of heuristic bias detection in elementary school. *Developmental Psychology*. DOI:10.1037/a0028320.

De Neys, W., & Franssens, S. (2009). Belief inhibition during thinking: Not always winning but at least taking part. *Cognition, 113*, 45–61.

De Neys, W., & Glumicic, T. (2008). Conflict monitoring in dual process theories of thinking. *Cognition, 106*, 1248–1299.

De Neys, W., Lubin, A., & Houdé, O. (in press). The smart non-conserver: Preschoolers detect their number conservation error. Manuscript submitted for publication.

De Neys, W., Moyens, E., & Vansteenwegen, D. (2010). Feeling we're biased: Autonomic arousal and reasoning conflict. *Cognitive, Affective, & Behavioral Neuroscience, 10*, 208–216.

De Neys, W., Novitskiy, N., Ramautar, J., & Wagemans, J. (2010). What makes a good reasoner? Brain potentials and heuristic bias susceptibility. *Proceedings of the Annual Conference of the Cognitive Science Society, 32*, 1020–1025.

De Neys, W., Rossi, S., & Houdé, O. (2013). Bats, balls, and substitution sensitivity: Cognitive misers are no happy fools. *Psychonomic Bulletin & Review, 20*, 269–273.

De Neys, W., & Van Gelder, E. (2008). Logic and belief across the life span: The rise and fall of belief inhibition during syllogistic reasoning. *Developmental Science, 12*, 123–130.

De Neys, W., & Vanderputte, K. (2011). When less is not always more: Stereotype knowledge and reasoning development. *Developmental Psychology, 47*, 432–441.

De Neys, W., Vartanian, O., & Goel, V. (2008). Smarter than we think: When our brains detect that we are biased. *Psychological Science, 19*, 483–489.

Evans, J. St. B. T. (2003). In two minds: Dual-process accounts of reasoning. *Trends in Cognitive Sciences, 7*, 454–459.

Evans, J. St. B. T. (2008). Dual-processing accounts of reasoning, judgment and social cognition. *Annual Review of Psychology, 59*, 255–278.

Evans, J. St. B. T. (2010). Intuition and reasoning: A dual process perspective. *Psychological Inquiry, 21*, 313–326.

Evans, J. St. B. T., & Over, D. E. (1996). *Rationality and reasoning.* Hove, UK: Psychology Press.

Fitzgerald, K. D., Perkins, S. C., Angstadt, M., Johnson, T., Stern, E. R., Welsh, R. C., et al. (2010). The development of performance-monitoring function in the posterior medial frontal cortex. *Neuroimage, 49*, 3463–3473.

Franssens, S., & De Neys, W. (2009). The effortless nature of conflict detection during thinking. *Thinking & Reasoning, 15*, 105–128.

Handley, S. J., Capon, A., Beveridge, M., Dennis, I., & Evans, J. St. B. T. (2004) Working memory, inhibitory control, and the development of children's reasoning. *Thinking & Reasoning, 10*, 175–195.

Handley, S. J., Newstead, S. E., & Trippas, D. (2011). Logic, beliefs, and instruction: A test of the default interventionist account of belief bias. *Journal of Experimental Psychology: Learning, Memory, & Cognition, 37*, 28–34.

Houdé, O. (1997). Rationality in reasoning: The problem of deductive competence and the inhibitory control of cognition. *Current Psychology of Cognition, 16*, 108–113.

Houdé, O. (2000). Inhibition and cognitive development: Object, number, categorization, and reasoning. *Cognitive Development, 15*, 63–73.

Houdé, O. (2007). First insights on neuropedagogy of reasoning. *Thinking & Reasoning, 13*, 81–89.

Houdé, O., & Guichart, E. (2001). Negative priming effect after inhibition of number/length interference in a Piaget-like task. *Developmental Science, 4*, 71–74.

Jacobs, J. E., & Klaczynski, P. A. (2002). The development of decision making during childhood and adolescence. *Current Directions in Psychological Science, 4*, 145–149.

Jacobs, J. E., & Potenza, M. (1991). The use of judgment heuristics to make social and object decisions: A developmental perspective. *Child Development, 62*, 166–178.

Kahneman, D. (2002, December). Maps of bounded rationality: A perspective on intuitive judgment and choice. Nobel Prize Lecture. Retrieved January 11, 2006, from http://nobelprize.org/nobel_prizes/economics/laureates/2002/kahnemann-lecture.pdf

Kahneman, D. (2011). *Thinking, fast and slow.* New York: Farrar, Straus, & Giroux.

Kahneman, D. & Frederick, S. (2005). A model of heuristic judgement. In K. J. Holyoak & R. G. Morrison (Eds.), *The Cambridge handbook of thinking and reasoning* (pp. 267–293). Cambridge, MA: Cambridge University Press.

Kahneman, D., & Tversky, A. (1973). On the psychology of prediction. *Psychological Review, 80*, 237–251.

Klaczynski, P. A., Byrnes, J. B., & Jacobs, J. E. (2001). Introduction: Special issue on decision making. *Journal of Applied Developmental Psychology, 22*, 225–236.

Klaczynski, P. A., & Narashimham, G. (1998). Representations as mediators of adolescent deductive reasoning. *Developmental Psychology, 5*, 865–881.

Klauer, K. C., & Singmann, H. (2012). Does logic feel good? Testing for intuitive detection of logicality in syllogistic reasoning. *Journal of Experimental Psychology: Learning, Memory, & Cognition.* Advance online publication. DOI:10.1037/a0030530.

Kokis, J. V., Macpherson, R., Toplak, M. E., West, R. F., & Stanovich, K. E. (2002). Heuristic and analytic processing: Age trends and associations with cognitive ability and cognitive styles. *Journal of Experimental Child Psychology, 83*, 26–52.

Leroux, G., Joliot, M., Dubal, S., Mazoyer, B., Tzourio-Mazoyer, N., & Houdé, O. (2006).

Cognitive inhibition of number/length interference in a Piaget-like task: Evidence from ERP and fMRI. *Human Brain Mapping, 27*, 498–509.

Lewis, P. (2008). Just why is beach volleyball in the Olympics? *The Independent*. Retrieved July 12, 2012, from http://www. independent.co.uk/sport/olympics/just-why-is-beach-volleyball-in-the-olympics-898147.html

Lyons, K. E., & Ghetti, S. (2011). The development of uncertainty monitoring in early childhood. *Child Development, 82*, 1778–1787.

Markovits, H., & Barrouillet, P. (2004). Why is understanding the development of reasoning important? *Thinking & Reasoning, 10*, 113–121.

Morris, A. K. (2000). Development of logical reasoning: Children's ability to verbally explain the nature of the distinction between logical and nonlogical forms of argument. *Developmental Psychology, 36*, 741–758.

Morsanyi, K., & Handley, S. J. (2012). Logic feels so good—I like it! Evidence for intuitive detection of logicality in syllogistic reasoning. *Journal of Experimental Psychology: Learning, Memory, & Cognition*. DOI: 10. 1037/a0026099.

Moutier, S., Plagne-Cayeux, S., Melot, A. M., & Houdé, O. (2006). Syllogistic reasoning and belief-bias inhibition in school children: Evidence from a negative priming paradigm. *Developmental Science, 9*, 166–172.

Pennycook, G., Fugelsang, J. A., & Koehler, D. J. (2012). Are we good at detecting conflict during reasoning. *Cognition, 124*, 101–106.

Piaget, J. (1952/1941). *The child's conception of number*. New York: Routledge & Kegan Paul.

Ping, R. M., & Goldin-Meadow, S. (2008). Hands in the air: Using iconic gestures to teach children conservation of quantity. *Developmental Psychology, 44*, 1277–1287.

Poirel, N., Borst, G., Simon, G., Rossi, S., Cassotti, M., Pineau, A., & Houdé, O. (in press). Number conservation is related to children's prefrontal inhibitory control: An fMRI study of a Piagetian task. *PLoS ONE*.

Reyna, V. F., & Brainerd, C. J. (1994). The origins of probability judgment: A review of data and theories. In G. Wright & P. Ayton (Eds.), *Subjective probability* (pp. 239–272). New York: Wiley.

Reyna, V. F., & Farley, F. (2006). Risk and rationality in adolescent decision making: Implications for theory, practice, and public policy. *Psychological Science in the Public Interest, 7*, 1–44.

Reyna, V. F., Lloyd, F. J., & Brainerd, C. J. (2003). Memory, development, and rationality: An integrative theory of judgement and decision-making. In S. Schneider & J. Shanteau (Eds.), *Emerging perspectives on judgment and decision research* (pp. 201–245). New York: Cambridge University Press.

Santesso, D. L., & Segalowitz, S. J. (2008). Developmental differences in error-related ERPs in middle- to late-adolescent males. *Developmental Psychology, 44*, 205–217.

Simoneau, M., & Markovits, H. (2003). Reasoning with premises that are not empirically true: Evidence for the role of inhibition and retrieval. *Developmental Psychology, 39*, 964–975.

Stanovich, K. E., & West, R. F. (2000). Individual differences in reasoning: Implications for the rationality debate? *Behavioral and Brain Sciences, 23*, 645–726.

Stanovich, K. E., West, R. F., & Toplak, M. E. (2011). The complexity of developmental predictions from dual process models. *Developmental Review, 31*, 103–118.

Steegen, S., & De Neys, W. (2012). Belief inhibition in children's reasoning: Memory-based evidence. *Journal of Expermental Child Psychology, 112*, 231–242.

Stupple, E. J. N., & Ball, L. J. (2008). Belief-logic conflict resolution in syllogistic reasoning: Inspection-time evidence for a parallel-process model. *Thinking & Reasoning, 14,* 168–181.

Téglás, E., Girotto, V., Gonzalez, M., & Bonatti, L. L. (2007). Intuitions of probabilities shape expectations about the future at 12 months and beyond. *Proceedings of the National Academy of Sciences, 104,* 19156–19159.

Thompson, V. A. (2009). Dual process theories: A metacognitive perspective. In J. Evans and K. Frankish (Eds.), *In two minds: Dual processes and beyond.* Oxford: Oxford University Press.

Thompson, V. A., Prowse Turner, J. A., & Pennycook, G. (2011). Intuition, reason, and metacognition. *Cognitive Psychology, 63,* 107–140.

Thompson, V. A., Striemer, C. L., Reikoff, R., Gunter, R. W., & Campbell, J. I. D. (2003). Syllogistic reasoning time: Disconfirmation disconfirmed. *Psychonomic Bulletin & Review, 10,* 184–189.

Villejoubert, G. (2009). Are representativeness judgments automatic and rapid? The effect of time pressure on the conjunction fallacy. *Proceedings of the Annual Meeting of the Cognitive Science Society, 30,* 2980–2985.

8　How to develop a logical reasoner

A hierarchical model of the role of divergent thinking in the development of conditional reasoning

Henry Markovits

Logical deduction involves the ability to distinguish valid from invalid conclusions that can be derived from premises, with no consideration of the empirical status of these premises, or of the conclusion. This allows people to reason with unfamiliar, false, imaginary or nonsensical premises. Logical deduction provides a way to understand the consequences of possible states of the world that we may believe to be wrong, but that, given the uncertain epistemological status of intuition and belief, often end up to be a better approximation to underlying reality than belief. One could well argue that the ability to make logical deductions is, almost paradoxically, the cornerstone to integrating empirical observation into coherent scientific theories. Certainly, being able to make logically valid inferences is of critical importance to understanding mathematics and science. In addition, being able to distinguish logical from merely plausible or believable conclusions is probably essential to being able to navigate through the minefields of politics and opinion.

Given the importance of deduction to scientific and mathematical theories, it is not surprising that research into logical reasoning has a long and complex history. Systematic developmental studies were given an initial impetus by Piaget's formulation of cognitive development, in particular his analysis of the development of formal thought (Inhelder & Piaget, 1958). This sees the ability to make logically valid deductions that are not based on empirical truth or belief as the end-point of a sequence of developmental stages originating from early sensori-motor intelligence. Once the formal operational stage is attained, people should be able to reason consistently in a logical manner irrespective of content, belief, and so on. Empirical studies of reasoning have not supported this particular version of Piaget's theory. This has led to a variety of very different theoretical conceptions, which, while on the surface are completely contradictory, I will argue have captured some important characteristics of reasoning.

Empirical and theoretical approaches to the development of reasoning

Developmental studies within the Piagetian framework provided a mixed profile of results. Many studies have indeed found age-related increases in the ability to give the "logical" response to deductive reasoning problems (Janveau-Brennan & Markovits, 1999; Kuhn, 1977; Markovits & Vachon, 1989; O'Brien & Overton, 1980; Overton, Byrnes, & O'Brien, 1985; Roberge, 1976). However, many studies have found that it is disconcertingly difficult for even presumably well-educated university students to be consistently logical in their deductions (Cummins, Lubart, Alksnis, & Rist, 1991; Evans, Barston, & Pollard, 1983; Markovits, 1985; Oakhill, Johnson-Laird, & Garnham, 1989; Thompson, 1994). Critically, many studies have shown clear patterns of variability in the kinds of inferences that adults and children make to what appear to be logically identical problems, where the sole difference is the specific content of the problems (Cummins et al., 1991; Markovits & Vachon, 1990; Thompson, 1995). Since in theory, at least, formal operations allow making "logical" inferences that are made solely on the basis of the formal structure, and should be impervious to content, these were difficult to assimilate into the formal operational model and consequently led to some important modifications to Piagetian theory. The first of these was the inclusion of the idea of domain familiarity into the formal operational model (Piaget, 1972). The basic idea was that people might find it easier to deploy formal operations within domains where their specific experience makes them more expert. While certainly a possible explanation of some of the results, such a model cannot explain the high degree of variability in reasoning with problems that cannot reasonably be construed as belonging to different domains. In addition, this kind of global explanation provides no specific mechanism that can explain just how familiarity might impact reasoning. In fact, empirical research has not shown that familiarity improves reasoning (Roberge & Richard, 1979), with some results showing the opposite effect (Quinn & Markovits, 1998). Another approach that attempts to reconcile the formal operational model with observed variability is Overton's competence/performance model (O'Brien & Overton, 1982; Overton, Ward, Black, Noveck, & O'Brien, 1987; Overton & Ricco, 2011). This considers that the way people actually reason does not necessarily reflect their level of competence, but is due to a variety of performance-related factors, such as time, level of attention, interpretational factors, and so on. This model highlights the fact that the ability to reason logically does not guarantee use of this ability in a specific content. Such a model can in principle account for variation in reasoning, particularly those related to the conditions in which reasoning is performed. However, it does not really allow for any clear explanation of the consistent patterns of variability found when the same person reasons with what appear to be remarkably similar formal problems in identical conditions.

At the same time, research from a different perspective strongly reinforced the apparent fragility of the formal operational level as a useful model of adult reasoning. Starting from the seminal work of Wason (1968), many studies have found that adults often make non-logical inferences (Cummins et al., 1991; Markovits, 1985; Oberauer, 2006; Roberge, 1982; Thompson & Mann, 1995). Equally disconcerting for a strictly Piagetian point of view are many studies that have found that adults are prone to logical distortions that appear to be unrelated to reasoning. For example, a classical effect in the psychology of reasoning is the belief-bias effect, which shows that people tend to consider that conclusions that are empirically believable are often accepted as logically valid, even when they are not (Evans, 1983; Evans et al., 1983; Markovits & Nantel, 1989). On one level, these kinds of results have led to the construction of dual-process theories of reasoning (Evans, 2007; Sloman, 1996; Stanovich & West, 2000; see also chapters in this book). Such theories consider that reasoning is the product of both a "logical" and a "heuristic" system, which can interact in ways that make people's inferences variable and somewhat unpredictable. However, these same results, along with others showing high rates of content-related variability, have led some researchers to make the more extreme claim that "logical" reasoning is simply not an appropriate description of what people actually do when making inferences. Recent probabilistic approaches to reasoning consider that people make inferences by attempting to estimate the probability that a given conclusion is true, something that is done by accessing knowledge about the real world (Evans, Over, & Handley, 2003; Evans, Over, & Handley, 2005; Oaksford, & Chater, 2007; Oaksford & Chater, 2003). Such theories certainly capture the difficulty that people have in making logical inferences and the clear and predictable effects of content on inferential performance. However, it is simply not clear how they might account for the clear developmental patterns generally observed and, of course, they are not sufficiently well-designed to understand how reasoning can be done with premises which are not reflections of the real world.

Finally, to make this picture even more complicated, researchers from different theoretical perspectives have found results that appeared to show that even young children are able to make logical deductions, especially when helped to overcome the pernicious influence of their real-world knowledge (Dias & Harris, 1988, 1990; Hawkins, Pea, Glick, & Scribner, 1984; Rumain, Connell, & Braine, 1983). This has led to some theorists claiming that at least certain forms of reasoning are developmentally or even biologically primitive (Braine, 1978). Theories that claim that logical reasoning is a fairly primitive cognitive ability capture some important empirical data about the way that young children reason, but it is difficult to see just how to integrate them with the consistent patterns of age-related improvement in reasoning, or the high degree of variability found with adults.

In summary, this very disconcerting variety of results has led researchers to simultaneously conclude that logical reasoning is a very primitive ability, available to even young children, that logical reasoning is difficult, but that the ability to reason logically develops over time, and that logical reasoning is just not within the cognitive abilities of even the most well-educated adults who must instead rely on real-world knowledge to make inferences. Many current theories of reasoning do not really attempt to consider the complete gamut of empirical data, and focus on results that are consistent with their basic assumptions. There is often the presumption that conflicting data are somehow wrong, or irrelevant to understanding the nature of reasoning. But, these variable results have not been found with different species. The same children, who can reason perfectly logically at 4 or 5 years of age, grow up and show gradual increases in logical reasoning abilities through adolescence, and finally become adults who find it difficult to reason logically at any age! These conflicting approaches to reasoning each emphasize aspects of the way that people reason; however, any complete theory of reasoning must be able to account for all of these results. In the following, I will present a developmental model that can in principle do this.

Before continuing, it is useful to review just what is meant by conditional reasoning. Conditional reasoning in its most basic sense involves making inferences with a given major premise of the form "p implies q" and one of four possible minor premises. Modus ponens (MP) is the logical principle that involves reasoning with the premises "p implies q, p is true" and leads to the logically correct conclusion "q is true". Modus tollens (MT) involves reasoning with the premises "p implies q, q is false" and leads to the logically correct conclusion "p is false". These two are valid logical forms, since they both lead to a single, logically correct conclusion. Affirmation of the consequent (AC) involves reasoning with the premises "p implies q, q is true". Denial of the antecedent (DA) involves reasoning with the premises "p implies q, p is false". In both cases the implied conclusions, "p is true" for AC and "q is false" for DA are not logically correct. Neither of these forms leads to a single, logically correct conclusion and the correct response would be to deny the implied (biconditional) conclusion in both cases.

Reasoning strategies

Before examining the model in detail, it is useful to look at a basic distinction that has recently proved to be useful in clarifying some of the variability in adult reasoning. Dual-process theories, which are the basis of several chapters in this book (see Chapters 3, 4, 5 and 7), have been developed in response to many studies that have found that people's reasoning and decision-making processes are often subject to the influence of personal belief or to intuitive heuristics of various kinds. These theories suggest that reasoning is a product of two independent inferential systems. On the one hand, what is frequently referred to as analytic reasoning corresponds to the ability to make logical inferences, which is what we are trying to account for here. The second system, which is referred to as the heuristic system, specializes in the use of heuristics that depend essentially on the ability to quickly access information stored in memory, without the requirement for the kind of working-memory-dependent processing required for analytic reasoning. Now, there are different ways that heuristic processes can function. One way, which is often the main target of dual-process studies, involves using what we might call inferential short-cuts. For example, belief-bias effects produce tendencies to judge inferential validity solely on the basis of the believability of conclusions (Evans et al., 1983). However, more important for our specific context is the existence of another form of heuristic processing leading to probabilistic evaluations of conclusion likelihood. Such evaluations are performed by a rapid, associative scan of real-world knowledge about premises that generate an intuitive evaluation that a given conclusion is more or less probable, given the premises. For example, when given an inference such as: "If a rock is thrown at a window, the window will break. A window is broken. Was a rock thrown at the window?", such a heuristic strategy allows the conclusion that it is relatively unlikely that a rock was thrown at the window, since it is very easy to access many other ways of breaking windows. In fact, probabilistic theories would claim that this kind of intuitive evaluation underlies even "logical" deductions (Oaksford & Chater, 2007). According to these theories, inferring that a conclusion is logically valid is just shorthand for the "real" evaluation that this conclusion is highly probable.

There is, however, another way of conceptualizing how people can use the same information to make a logical inference. What we have referred to as counterexample theories (the best example of which is mental model theory (Johnson-Laird, 2001), as we shall see) consider that a conclusion will be logically valid unless at least one counterexample to this conclusion can be generated. Thus, the conclusion that "a rock was thrown at the window" in the above example would be considered to be invalid if a search for counterexamples turned up at least one such alternative (e.g. throwing a chair at a window).

Although these two conceptions of the inferential process appear to be contradictory, there is an elegant way of reconciling them. Verschueren's dual-process model of conditional reasoning (Verschueren, Schaeken, & d'Ydewalle, 2005a, 2005b) suggests that when adults reason with familiar premises, they can use either one of these two strategies to make inferences. The probabilistic strategy generates a rapid and low-cost evaluation of conclusion likelihood, while a counterexample strategy generates a clear-cut judgment of validity, but requires a working-memory intensive process. In fact, recent results have provided direct evidence that people can switch back and forth between these two strategies, depending on available cognitive resources (Markovits, Brunet, Thompson, & Brisson, in press). Consistent with Verschueren's formulation, people who have relatively little time to process information will tend to use a probabilistic strategy in order to generate what are, on the surface, deductive inferences. When given more time, these same reasoners are capable of using a consistent counterexample-based strategy, which accesses the same information but in a more working-memory intensive analytic fashion. A critical component of this model is the role of metacognitive strategy switching (see Moshman in this volume). In fact, Markovits et al. (in press) found evidence for a clear metacognitive component underlying strategy choice in adults. This shows that use of a more demanding counterexample search strategy requires a form of metacognitive decision.

In other words, "logical" reasoning is not a default, but requires use of the cognitively costly counterexample strategy, which in turn requires some form of metacognitive engagement. Of course, the applicability of this form of variation to children remains an open question. However, recent developmental studies have clearly shown that both probabilistic and counterexample-based strategies can be found in children as young as 6–7 years of age, with the latter coming online somewhat earlier (Markovits & Thompson, 2008). Thus, even 6- and 7-year-old children are able to use directly available information in order to generate a counterexample to a simple conditional conclusion, which allows them to conclude (rightly or wrongly) that this conclusion is certainly true or not. However, for both children and adults, the presence of an alternative strategy implies that a counterexample strategy, which allows a logical conclusion, is not automatic, but requires a strategy choice. Thus, any complete model of inferential performance must contain a specific strategy choice component at all ages.

Content and developmental differences in reasoning

Both the probabilistic and the counterexample strategies described above rely on access to stored information, in order to generate either a likelihood estimation, or a judgment of validity respectively. This brings back the critical issue of just how the effects of content can be explained, something that is at the heart of our developmental model. Most current theories of reasoning rely on some direct measure of the complexity of reasoning to account for differences in the rate of difficulty in different forms of reasoning. Certainly, working-memory load can explain many differences in the ability of people to make logical inferences with reasoning that varies in complexity. For example, studies by Barrouillet & Lecas (1999) have shown consistent effects of complexity in the ability to generate an explicit representation of conditionals. However, if complexity was the most critical component of development, then we would expect to find a developmental pattern that showed younger children were able to reason with simpler forms only, while the ability to reason with more complex forms would slowly increase with age. However, as we shall see, the effects of complexity are far overshadowed by variation due to content. Since this effect is found with arguments that are formally identical, cognitive complexity cannot, even in principle, account for these differences. Most critically, content-related effects underlie important developmental differences.

Before examining these, it is important to clarify what an appropriate measure of the ability to reason logically might be. One common way to look at logical reasoning is to simply present a set of inferential problems and to add up the numbers of "correct" responses. However, this misses a critical distinction. As several studies have shown, adults and especially children are prone to making surface-level inferences that use some form of matching strategy to rate conclusions, which leads to high rates of "correct" acceptance of certain conclusions. Even young children will correctly accept the MP and MT inferences, while "incorrectly" accepting the AC and DA inferences. Does this mean that young children are reasoning logically 50 percent of the time? Similarly, a relatively common response pattern in adults involves rejecting all four inferences (Markovits, 1985). Once again, this implies a 50 percent rate of logically correct responses (on the AC and DA inferences). However, both forms of response patterns are easily explicable by use of some global strategy, which does not require any judgment of validity. I have argued that the best criterion of logical reasoning is the ability to distinguish appropriately between certain and uncertain conclusions. The clearest form of this criterion involves correctly accepting the MP inference, and being able to reject the AC or the DA inference (or both).

If we use this as our definition of logical reasoning with conditional inferences, then we can organize what appears to be a widely divergent set of empirical results into a coherent developmental picture. To do this, we can define a hierarchy of premise types which lead to a consistent developmental pattern, where the ability to reason logically comes online at increasingly later ages. We can summarize this pattern in Table 8.1.

We can then summarize the full array of empirical results by the statement that there is a clear developmental progression in the ability of children to make logical inferences for each of these four premise categories. This developmental pattern clearly shows that reasoning with identical forms of inference shows large developmental divergences when content is varied. How can we understand this?

The first implication of this developmental pattern is that it is difficult to argue that logical reasoning requires using some form of syntactic rule (Braine, 1978; Rips, 1983). In fact, the key to understanding the explanation starts with understanding that logical reasoning requires going beyond the information that is specifically presented in premises. An excellent way of looking at just what is involved in logical reasoning is given by what could be called the "Sherlock Holmes" principle. Holmes once stated that "Eliminate all other factors, and the one which remains must be the truth". In other words, logical reasoning requires being able to generate *all the possibilities* other than a putative conclusion. These possibilities must be inferred since they are not directly accessible. If these can be eliminated, then the conclusion is valid, otherwise it is not. Now, for any type of concrete premise, we can specify just what forms of information and thus which forms of possibilities have an impact on conditional reasoning. The first of these, and the one that we will focus on, are alternative antecedents, which are potential cases of A such that A implies Q. For example, for the premise "if a glass is dropped, then it will break", an alternative antecedent could be that if the glass becomes too hot, then it will break. One of the most robust empirical results in research into conditional reasoning with both children and adults concerns the systematic effect of alternative antecedents on reasoning. Studies have very clearly shown that premises for which reasoners are able to easily generate or access alternative antecedents produce much higher rates of denial of the two uncertain inferences, AC and DA (Cummins, 1995; Cummins et al., 1991; Janveau-Brennan & Markovits, 1999; Markovits & Vachon, 1990; Thompson, 1994).

Since the most important factor that distinguishes developmental levels of conditional reasoning is performance on the AC and DA inferences, which is strongly

Table 8.1

Premise type	Example	Age
Categorical	If an animal is a dog, then it has four legs	7–8 (Markovits & Thompson, 2008)
Causal	If a rock is thrown at a window, the window will break	10–11 (Janveau-Brennan & Markovits, 1999)
Contrary-to-fact	If a feather is thrown at a window, the window will break	13–14 (Markovits & Vachon, 1989)
Abstract	If glop then xyl.	16+ (Venet & Markovits, 2001)

determined by the presence of alternative antecedents, we will concentrate on the processes involved in generating these. We can understand how this form of information is used during reasoning by a modified version of mental model theory (Markovits & Barrouillet, 2002). Mental model theory suggests that reasoners construct representations of potentially true combinations of antecedent and consequent terms using a token-like representation. Additional models will be added to this representation when information about premises is retrieved during reasoning. Thus, when making an AC inference, the simplest representation of the premises is:

$$P \quad Q$$

With this representation, reasoners will conclude that if Q is true, then P is true and vice versa. However, if at least one alternative antecedent is retrieved, then this will be included in the representation of the premises:

$$P \quad Q$$
$$A \quad Q$$

If this reasoner is asked whether "Q is true" implies that "P is true", this set of models shows that there is at least one possibility where "Q is true", but "P is not true". By the Sherlock Holmes principle, this means that the conclusion is not necessarily true, that is, it is not valid. A similar analysis implies that generating an alternative antecedent is required to infer that the invited conclusion to the DA inference is not necessarily true (in this case, the model not-P & not-Q must also be generated).

Our starting point in this analysis is the idea that when reasoning with familiar premises, a key factor in determining the inferences that are made is the type of information that can be retrieved online during the reasoning process. Now, of the studies that have shown a relationship between individual differences in retrieval and conditional reasoning, the most interesting result comes from a study by Markovits and Quinn (2002). They asked reasoners to retrieve potential causes for specific effects. These were chosen so that there was one strongly associated cause. Other potential causes belonged to a different category. For example, one effect was "a dog scratches constantly". The most often cited cause was "having fleas". The next most frequently cited cause was "skin disease". They found that the ability to accept the MP inference and deny the AC and DA inferences was correlated with the speed with which the *second* cause, but not the first, was retrieved. This result mirrors studies examining relations between working memory and information retrieval. Individual differences in working-memory capacity are not related to the speed of retrieval within category boundaries, but are related to speed of retrieval outside these boundaries (Rosen & Engles, 1996). Both sets of studies indicate that what distinguishes better from worse reasoners is the ease with which information is retrieved across category boundaries. This very strongly resembles one component of creativity, flexible problem solving, which is a subset of divergent thinking. This refers to the ability to produce strategies or solutions that lie outside a person's normal comfort zone. Thus, one interpretation of results showing an association between flexible alternatives retrieval and logical reasoning is that logical reasoning requires a form of divergent thinking.

However, this leaves out one key developmental difference. As we have seen, there is a consistent developmental pattern that suggests logical reasoning becomes more difficult according to the type of premise. This suggests that simple retrieval cannot explain this pattern, something that is most clear in the case of purely abstract reasoning, where there is no information available. This does not mean that the relation between divergent thinking and logical reasoning must be abandoned, but there needs to be a way to integrate these into a larger perspective that can also explain how abstract reasoning might develop.

The model that we have been exploring is based on Karmiloff-Smith's (Karmiloff-Smith, 1995) representational redescription model, which is a variant of Piaget's notion of reflexive abstraction (Piaget, 2001). This is an attempt to model the transition between cognitive capacities derived from very concrete problems to the same capacities applied to more abstract problems. This model suggests that people begin to learn to function with a specific cognitive rule at the level of concrete action. Once a certain degree of expertise has been acquired, they will construct a more abstract representation of some of the key parts of this rule. This will allow them to use the rule to solve more general, and more abstract, problems. This process can continue through a sequence of levels, which can in principle lead to the ability to use a completely abstract version of the rule. To understand how this model can be used to explain the development of conditional reasoning, we must start by recognizing that the role of alternative antecedents in reasoning is only implicit. The if-then syntax simply suggests a one-way relation between antecedent and consequent terms. Potential alternative antecedents must be *generated* by the reasoner. When reasoning with premises that use categories and properties that are directly represented in memory, alternatives are activated by the simple representation of the consequent term. Thus, when asked to evaluate the conclusion: "If an animal is a dog, then it has four legs. An animal has four legs. Is it a dog?", categories of animals that have four legs will be automatically and easily activated and thus retrieved with relatively little effort. This allows even very young children to reason logically with these premise types, since they can easily infer that if an animal has four legs, it could be a cat (Markovits, 2000; Markovits et al., 1996). However, a child who can readily retrieve and use an alternative based on direct category definitions will be unable to generate alternatives with causal conditionals, since these require a more abstract process of generation. Thus, young children who can reason logically with category-based premises will nonetheless tend to accept the AC and DA inferences when reasoning with equally concrete premises such as: "If a rock is thrown at a window, the window will break" (Janveau-Brennan & Markovits, 1999). The difference between these two kinds of premise is that alternative antecedents for causal relations require generation of an ad hoc category (Barsalou, 1983); for example, "ways of breaking windows", which is dependent on the reasoner having a more complex (and abstract) representation of the alternatives generation process.

Familiar causal reasoning requires generation of an ad hoc category of causal alternatives based on existing knowledge. The next level of representation allows for ad hoc categories that are based on a larger and more flexible definition of potential causal relations. The clearest instantiation of this is reasoning with empirically false premises. For example, when reasoning with a premise such as: "If a feather is thrown at a window, the window will break", understanding the uncertainty of the AC inference requires being able to construct an ad hoc category that allows for potential alternative causes that can be completely unrealistic (in this case, throwing a tissue at a window is a potential alternative). The final form is a completely abstract representation that allows generation of alternatives that are totally unrelated to stored knowledge. This allows reasoners to conclude that even for completely unknown and/or abstract premises, there are always some potential alternative antecedents, even if there is no way that one could possibly be generated from the reasoner's knowledge base.

Before examining the evidence that supports this progressive model of conditional reasoning, it is useful to recast the representation of the alternatives generation process in terms of the notion of divergent thinking. Our initial analysis of reasoning suggested that the generation of alternatives is facilitated by more flexible thinking that allows retrieval of alternatives across category boundaries. However, the preceding analysis requires a more complex recasting of the notion of category boundary. The representational redescription model is based on distinctions between category *levels*, going from easily activated category definitions to increasingly abstract generation rules, which allow construction of increasingly more flexible ad hoc categories.

This allows us to distinguish between two forms of divergent thinking. An initial, global level determines the degree of abstraction of the alternatives generation procedure, which in turn determines the nature of the categories that are accessed. Once this level has been determined, local divergent thinking allows generation of categories that are more semantically distant from the more immediately generated ones. Thus, on a more specific level, divergent thinking can function to promote generation of categories of the same level of abstraction, but which are more difficult to activate. This will allow people to be more logical reasoners within a given level of abstraction of premise type. In fact, many of the existing results showing a relation between alternative generation and reasoning can be interpreted within this more specific framework. However, the developmentally more critical component is related to the ability to generate a more abstract level of category generation.

While this model allows us to understand the empirical results summarized in the previous table, there is more direct evidence supporting it. These rely on a key postulate of the representational redescription model, which is the idea that the transition between two levels of abstraction is done in phases, going from acquisition of expertise in one level to the beginning of the ability to use the next level. This suggests that encouraging a form of divergent thinking will have different effects depending on current level of the reasoner. Simply encouraging use of a strategy that is well-established should have little effect on reasoning. However, encouraging use of a higher-level strategy will improve reasoning, but only if this higher-level strategy is within the reasoner's developmental range. We have examined this basic idea using two forms of interaction. The first uses a simple priming method in order to encourage use of flexible thinking at two different levels. The most critical comparisons are those involving ad hoc causal categories based on familiar relations and ad hoc contrary-to-fact categories. These are the two major transitional forms between the beginning of the ability to reason with purely verbal premises found in 7–8 year olds and the ability to reason with abstract premises. The priming method uses a generation task to promote divergent thinking at a given level of complexity. In order to prime true causal alternatives, people are given an example of a conditional cause–effect relationship, and asked to generate as many possible other causes for this effect. For example, a reasoner will be told that "If a rock is thrown at a window, the window will break", and asked to generate as many other ways of breaking a window. The second does the same thing, but uses an initial contrary-to-fact premise, for example "If a feather is thrown at a window, the window will break". The point of this task is to encourage creation of ad hoc categories that are not available by using semantic memory, but must be constructed in a more abstract and creatively complex manner. However, presenting only the initial contrary-to-fact premise allows people to generate familiar ad hoc categories, since throwing a chair at a window is indeed a potential alternative absent some other limitations on the task. In order to do this, we embedded this generation task into a context referred to as Planet Opposite. This planet is described as one where causality is opposite to what is familiar. Thus, an example of a Planet Opposite alternative would be "throwing a tissue at a window", while "throwing a chair" would not work.

If reasoning does indeed require some form of divergent thinking, then we might expect that simply promoting more flexible retrieval would have a beneficial effect on reasoning. However, our model implies that both divergent thinking and reasoning have to be considered in terms of their respective level of abstraction. This leads to very developmentally different predictions about the effects of priming these two forms of divergent thinking. For example, younger children are becoming expert in using alternatives based on category definitions, which allow them to make logical inferences with premises such as: "All dogs have legs. An animal has legs, is it a dog?" These same children are just starting to construct a representation of the alternatives process that allows generation of familiar causal alternatives, but are far from any clear representation of contrary-to-fact alternatives. For these children, we would predict that encouraging them to generate familiar causal alternatives would improve reasoning, while doing so with contrary-to-fact alternatives would not help (Markovits & Brunet, in press). In contrast, older pre-adolescents have a well-established representation of familiar ad hoc causal categories, and have at least a partially constructed representation of CF alternatives. Since we assume that the default approach to reasoning will involve the spontaneous generation of ad hoc familiar causal categories, encouraging this form of divergent thinking should have no real effect on reasoning of any kind. In contrast to younger children, encouraging thinking about CF alternatives should have a positive impact on more abstract forms of reasoning. And in fact, recent work has shown that while priming familiar alternatives has no effect on either familiar causal reasoning or abstract reasoning, priming contrary-to-fact alternatives does indeed improve abstract reasoning (Markovits & Lortie Forgues, 2011).

Another form of interaction that is related to this basic dynamic is that between forms of reasoning. At least on the surface, there is no reason that reasoning with, say, abstract premises should have any effect on reasoning with more familiar premises. However, our previous analysis of strategy use allows another prediction. Inability to initiate a search for appropriate counterexamples will be accompanied by a low level of metacognitive engagement. This suggests that the inability to initiate an alternatives strategy in one context will produce a decrease in the use of the same strategy in a subsequent context, even if this strategy would normally be used. Thus, reasoning with content that requires a level of counterexample generation that is out of a person's normal range will produce a decrease in reasoning with content that is normally within their developmental level. For example, Markovits and Vachon (1990) found that reasoning with abstract premises produces a very strong decrease in reasoning with concrete premises. The critical point that the effect of reasoning with a higher level of abstraction on more concrete reasoning depends on developmental level is more clearly shown by recent results (Markovits, submitted). Participants between the ages of 11 and 14 years of age were given both familiar causal conditionals and CF causal conditionals as major premises. Solving CF problems first had a global negative effect on reasoning among the youngest participants. However, this effect diminished with age. For the oldest participants, solving CF problems first actually improved performance. Thus, similar to what we have shown with the effects of encouraging different forms of divergent thinking, reasoning on different levels of abstract has a differential effect depending on the level of competence of reasoners.

How can we integrate empirical results into a single model?

How can this model explain the highly divergent results that characterize the developmental study of logical reasoning? First, recall that our basic definition of logical reasoning is the ability to both accept the validity of conclusions for which there are no potential alternatives (specifically the MP inference) and to reject the validity of conclusions for which there are potential alternatives (the AC and DA inferences). The key component of our model is based on the existence of multiple levels of a form of divergent thinking required to generate alternative antecedents to increasingly abstract forms of reasoning.

With this basic framework, we can account for the pattern of seemingly divergent results described earlier. Thus, young children can easily generate alternatives that can be automatically accessed by activation of information directly represented in memory. This allows them to reason logically with the corresponding class of premise content, by both accepting the premises (concluding that the MP inference is true) and rejecting the uncertain inferences. When young children are asked to reason with premises such as: "If an animal is a dog, then it has four legs. An animal has four legs. Is it a dog?", they are indeed capable of logical reasoning. However, this ability is not global, but is restricted to a limited subset of content. The same children, who have relatively few problems in reasoning logically with premises for which alternatives are directly accessible, are unable to do so with more complex content which requires an increasingly abstract process of alternatives generation.

Second, developmental increases in reasoning ability are determined globally by the transition to more abstract levels of alternatives generation. This allows pre-adolescents to reason logically with familiar causal conditionals, young adolescents to reason logically with contrary-to-fact conditionals, and (some) young adults to reason logically with abstract conditionals. At each level of difficulty, the ability to reason logically is determined by the ability of reasoners to use a process of divergent (or flexible) thinking at an appropriate level of abstraction.

Finally, how can we account for the observation that even adults are unable to reason logically in any consistent manner? Two factors can explain this. First, as we have seen, use of an explicit counterexample strategy requires a form of metacognitive engagement that is susceptible to variation. If such a strategy is not activated, then people will make inferences that are not "logical" but reflect the statistical properties of premises. Second, the process of alternatives generation is subject to variation due to the way that information is structured in memory. The generation process relies on using a cue derived from the premises (e.g. ways of breaking windows) to generate categories of alternative antecedents. Both the quantity and associative strength of such categories will determine the probability that the generation process will be successful. Thus, variation in activation of a counterexample strategy and variation in the efficacy of such a strategy in retrieving counterexamples both imply that actual reasoning will be highly variable, even among educated adults.

A key question is what determines the transitions between levels. The representational redescription model suggests a two-part mechanism. First, the construction of a higher-level representation depends on acquisition of a certain degree of expertise with the lower-level form. As experience is acquired with this level, people will become more efficient in using the generation process, which will result in an overall increase in logical reasoning within the global level defined by the initial form of representation. Second, once a level of expertise is acquired, an initial representation of the more abstract form is constructed. However, this more abstract form is not well-established, with the default strategy being use of the more concrete form. Thus, explicit activation of the more abstract representational form is essential to the transitional process. Critically, both the model and our empirical results show that when a given level of representation is well-established, then encouraging its use has no impact on reasoning either at the usual level, or at a higher level. In contrast, encouraging use of a more abstract form of alternatives generation, even at a relatively early stage does improve reasoning, but only when this is within the developmental level of the reasoner.

In other words, this model can explain why young children can reason logically in some circumstances, what factors can account for developmental increases in reasoning, and why even well-educated adults find it difficult to reason logically in a consistent manner.

Finally, this model has some clear implications for educational approaches to reasoning. It is a fairly common assumption that understanding of more abstract processes should be scaffolded by reference to more concrete examples. One of the most common of these mechanisms is use of analogy. This explicitly relies on concrete examples in order to generate a structural analogue to whatever abstract principle is meant to be learned. However, both this model and our empirical results suggest that such approaches are in fact counter-productive. Encouraging activation of a lower-level form of representation that is already well-established will have no effect on reasoning (Markovits & Doyon, 2011). In contrast, encouraging thinking about alternatives with more abstract content is effective, but only if done within appropriate developmental limits. Thus, what this model suggests is that the best way to encourage the development of more abstract ways of logical reasoning is to gradually encourage both divergent thinking and reasoning at levels of abstraction that are just above reasoners' current levels.

References

Barrouillet, P., & Lecas, J.-F. (1999). Mental models in conditional reasoning and working memory. *Thinking & Reasoning, 5*(4), 289–302.

Barsalou, L. W. (1983). Ad hoc categories. *Memory & Cognition, 11*(3), 211–227.

Braine, M. D. (1978). On the relation between the natural logic of reasoning and standard logic. *Psychological Review, 85*(1), 1–21.

Cummins, D. D. (1995). Naive theories and causal deduction. *Memory & Cognition, 23*(5), 646–658.

Cummins, D. D., Lubart, T., Alksnis, O., & Rist, R. (1991). Conditional reasoning and causation. *Memory & Cognition, 19*(3), 274–282.

Dias, M. G., & Harris, P. L. (1988). The effect of make-believe play on deductive reasoning. *British Journal of Developmental Psychology, 6*(3), 207–221.

Dias, M. G., & Harris, P. L. (1990). The influence of the imagination on reasoning by young children. *British Journal of Developmental Psychology, 8*(4), 305–318.

Evans, J. St. B. T. (1983). Linguistic determinants of bias in conditional reasoning. *The Quarterly Journal of Experimental Psychology A: Human Experimental Psychology, 35A*(4), 635–644.

Evans, J. St. B. T. (2007). *Hypothetical thinking: Dual processes in reasoning and judgement.* New York: Psychology Press.

Evans, J. St. B. T., Barston, J. L., & Pollard, P. (1983). On the conflict between logic and belief in syllogistic reasoning. *Memory & Cognition, 11*(3), 295–306.

Evans, J. St. B. T., Over, D. E., & Handley, S. J. (2003). Conditionals and conditional probability. *Journal of Experimental Psychology: Learning, Memory, and Cognition, 29*, 321–335.

Evans, J. St. B. T., Over, D. E., & Handley, S. J. (2005). Suppositionals, extensionality, and conditionals: A critique of the mental model theory of Johnson-Laird and Byrne (2002). *Psychological Review, 112*, 1040–1052.

Hawkins, J., Pea, R. D., Glick, J., & Scribner, S. (1984). "Merds that laugh don't like mushrooms": Evidence for deductive reasoning by preschoolers. *Developmental Psychology*, *20*(4), 584–594.

Inhelder, B., & Piaget, J. (1958). *The growth of logical thinking from childhood to adolescence*. New York: Basic Books.

Janveau-Brennan, G., & Markovits, H. (1999). The development of reasoning with causal conditionals. *Developmental Psychology*, *35*(4), 904–911.

Johnson-Laird, P. N. (2001). Mental models and deduction. *Trends in Cognitive Sciences*, *5*(10), 434–442.

Karmiloff-Smith, A. (1995). *Beyond modularity: A developmental perspective on cognitive science*. Cambridge, MA: MIT Press.

Kuhn, D. (1977). Conditional reasoning in children. *Developmental Psychology*, *13*(4), 342–353.

Markovits, H. (1985). Incorrect conditional reasoning among adults: Competence or performance? *British Journal of Psychology*, *76*(2), 241–247.

Markovits, H. (2000). A mental model analysis of young children's conditional reasoning with meaningful premises. *Thinking & Reasoning*, *6*(4), 335–347.

Markovits, H. (submitted). On the road towards formal reasoning: Interactions between factual and contrary-to-fact reasoning in adolescence.

Markovits, H., & Barrouillet, P. (2002). The development of conditional reasoning: A mental model account. *Developmental Review*, *22*(1), 5–36.

Markovits, H., & Brunet, M.-L. (in press). Priming divergent thinking promotes logical reasoning in 6- to 8-year olds: But only for high SES students. *Journal of Cognitive Psychology*.

Markovits, H., Brunet, M.-L., Thompson, V., & Brisson, J. (in press). Direct evidence for a dual process model of deductive inference. *Journal of Experimental Psychology: Learning, Memory, and Cognition*.

Markovits, H., & Doyon, C. (2011). Using analogy to improve abstract conditional reasoning in adolescents: Not as easy as it looks. *European Journal of Educational Psychology*, *26*(3), 355–372.

Markovits, H., & Lortie Forgues, H. (2011). Conditional reasoning with false premises facilitates the transition between familiar and abstract reasoning. *Child Development*, *82*(2), 646–660. doi:10.1111/j.1467-8624.2010.01526.

Markovits, H., & Nantel, G. (1989). The belief-bias effect in the production and evaluation of logical conclusions. *Memory & Cognition*, *17*(1), 11–17.

Markovits, H., & Quinn, S. (2002). Efficiency of retrieval correlates with "logical" reasoning from causal conditional premises. *Memory & Cognition*, *30*(5), 696–706.

Markovits, H., & Thompson, V. (2008). Different developmental patterns of simple deductive and probabilistic inferential reasoning. *Memory and Cognition*, *36*(6), 1066–1078.

Markovits, H., & Vachon, R. (1989). Reasoning with contrary-to-fact propositions. *Journal of Experimental Child Psychology*, *47*(3), 398–412.

Markovits, H., & Vachon, R. (1990). Conditional reasoning, representation, and level of abstraction. *Developmental Psychology*, *26*(6), 942–951.

Markovits, H., Venet, M., Janveau-Brennan, G., Malfait, N., Pion, N., & Vadeboncoeur, I. (1996). Reasoning in young children: Fantasy and information retrieval. *Child Development*, *67*(6), 2857–2872.

O'Brien, D. P., & Overton, W. F. (1980). Conditional reasoning following contradictory evidence: A developmental analysis. *Journal of Experimental Child Psychology*, *30*, 44–61.

O'Brien, D. P., & Overton, W. F. (1982). Conditional reasoning and the competence-performance issue: A developmental analysis of a training task. *Journal of Experimental Child Psychology*, *34*(2), 274–290.

Oakhill, J., Johnson-Laird, P. N., & Garnham, A. (1989). Believability and syllogistic reasoning. *Cognition*, *31*(2), 117–140.

Oaksford, M., & Chater, N. (2003). Conditional probability and the cognitive science of conditional reasoning. *Mind & Language*, *18*(4), 359–379.

Oaksford, M., & Chater, N. (2007). *Baysian rationality*. Oxford: Oxford University Press.

Oberauer, K. (2006). Reasoning with conditionals: A test of formal models of four theories. *Cognitive Psychology*, *53*(3), 238–283.

Overton, W. F., Byrnes, J. P., & O'Brien, D. P. (1985). Developmental and individual differences in conditional reasoning: The role of contradiction training and cognitive style. *Developmental Psychology*, *21*(4), 692–701.

Overton, W. F., Ward, S. L., Black, J., Noveck, I. A., & O'Brien, D. P. (1987). Form and content in the development of deductive reasoning. *Developmental Psychology*, *23*(1), 22–30.

Overton, W. F. & Ricco, R. (2011). Dual systems competence and procedural processing: A relational developmental systems approach to reasoning. *Developmental Review*, *31*, 119–150.

Piaget, J. (1972). Intellectual evolution from adolescence to adulthood. *Human Development*, *15*, 1–12.

Piaget, J. (2001). *Studies in reflecting abstraction*. Hove, UK: Psychology Press.

Quinn, S., & Markovits, H. (1998). Conditional reasoning, causality, and the structure of semantic memory: Strength of association as a predictive factor for content effects. *Cognition*, *68*(3), B93–B101.

Rips, L. J. (1983). Cognitive processes in propositional reasoning. *Psychological Review*, *90*(1), 38–71.

Roberge, J. J. (1976). Developmental analyses of two formal operational structures: Combinatorial thinking and conditional reasoning. *Developmental Psychology*, *12*(6), 563–564.

Roberge, J. J. (1982). Linguistic factors in conditional reasoning. *The Quarterly Journal of Experimental Psychology A: Human Experimental Psychology*, *34A*(2), 275–284.

Roberge, J. J. & Richard, F. (1979). Effects of familiarity with content on propositional reasoning. *The Journal of General Psychology*, *100*, 35–41.

Rosen, V. M., & Engles, R. W. (1996). The role of working memory capacity in retrieval. *Journal of Experimental Psychology: General*, *126*(3), 211–227.

Rumain, B., Connell, J., & Braine, M. D. (1983). Conversational comprehension processes are responsible for reasoning fallacies in children as well as adults: If is not the biconditional. *Developmental Psychology*, *19*(4), 471–481.

Sloman, S. A. (1996). The empirical case for two systems of reasoning. *Psychological Bulletin*, *119*(1), 3–22.

Stanovich, K. E., & West, R. F. (2000). Individual differences in reasoning: Implications for the rationality debate? *Behavioral and Brain Sciences*, *23*(5), 645–726.

Thompson, V. A. (1994). Interpretational factors in conditional reasoning. *Memory & Cognition*, *22*(6), 742–758.

Thompson, V. A. (1995). Conditional reasoning: The necessary and sufficient conditions. *Canadian Journal of Experimental Psychology/Revue canadienne de psychologie expérimentale*, *49*(1), 1–60.

Thompson, V. A., & Mann, J. M. (1995). Perceived necessity explains the dissociation between logic and meaning: The case of "Only If." *Journal of Experimental Psychology: Learning, Memory, and Cognition, 21*(6), 1554–1567.

Venet, M., & Markovits, H. (2001). Understanding uncertainty with abstract conditional premises. *Merrill-Palmer Quarterly, 47*(1), 74–99.

Verschueren, N., Schaeken, W., & d'Ydewalle, G. (2005a). A dual-process specification of causal conditional reasoning. *Thinking & Reasoning, 11*(3), 239–278.

Verschueren, N., Schaeken, W., & d'Ydewalle, G. (2005b). Everyday conditional reasoning: A working memory-dependent tradeoff between counterexample and likelihood use. *Memory & Cognition, 33*(1), 107–119.

Wason, P. (1968). Reasoning about a rule. *Quarterly Journal of Experimental Psychology, 20*, 273–281.

9 The development of counterfactual reasoning

Sarah R. Beck and Kevin J. Riggs

When things go wrong we often speculate about how they might have been different, especially if there were things we could have done that would have changed the outcome. As you watch the train pull out of the station, you may think, 'If only I'd left the house earlier, I would have caught the train', or perhaps after an argument with a colleague you reluctantly acknowledge, 'I wish I hadn't said that . . .' These are examples of counterfactual thinking: thoughts about what might have been. They are just one type of speculative thinking that humans engage in, but they play an important role in our understanding of the consequences of our actions and help us improve our future behaviour.

In this chapter we examine the development of counterfactual thinking. As we argue elsewhere (Beck & Riggs, in press) this development is protracted with key advances made in infancy continuing through to middle childhood. One reason to study counterfactual thinking development is to understand children's abilities in their own right. But children's competence in imagining counterfactual worlds also impacts on their ability to learn from their mistakes (see O'Connor, Feeney, & McCormack, in press) and relates more broadly to their causal reasoning (Frosch, McCormack, Lagnado, & Burns, 2012). A further reason to examine development is that it offers insight into 'sophisticated' adult processes. By studying only adults' counterfactual thinking it is difficult to separate the components of counterfactual thinking and their relative cognitive demands. Development offers a natural way to explore dissociations between different components. This is particularly useful when we are thinking about which domain general processes might be implicated in specific types of reasoning, something that has proved illuminating in the domain of counterfactual thought.

For those interested in adults' counterfactual thinking much of the focus has been on the experience of regret. Regret is a counterfactual emotion that arises when one thinks about how a better alternative to reality could have come about. A meta-analysis of studies that asked adults about the things they regret found that the most commonly held regrets were about education, followed by career, romance and parenting – in other words, 'adult' domains (Roese & Summerville, 2005). Counterfactual thinking is also rather 'adult' in that the language used to express counterfactuals is typically relatively complex. For example, in English we commonly use the subjunctive. Given these observations, one might suspect that young children are rarely exposed to counterfactuals and wonder whether it is futile to investigate their development in the early years. Yet, adults make counterfactual statements to young children rather frequently: 'If you hadn't been running, you wouldn't have fallen over!' Or, 'How would you feel if he had hit you?' Kuczaj and Daly (1979) suggested that counterfactual hypotheticals appeared in children's natural speech from around 4 years (although as we will see, we might question what 4-year-olds understand by these constructions). With regard to linguistic demands, recent research with young children has started to use simpler language or even non-linguistic behaviour to investigate children's counterfactual thought (e.g. Beck & Guthrie, 2011; O'Connor, McCormack, & Feeney, 2011). As we will argue in this chapter, there is a lot to learn about children's counterfactual thinking.

One of the problems that plagues research on children's counterfactual reasoning is a lack of clarity on what counts as counterfactual thought. One reason for this is that the term counterfactual thinking means rather different things to different people. For example, one interpretation of what is a counterfactual is to take it to mean any world which is not currently true (or factual). This interpretation is sometimes used in philosophy. Under this interpretation speculation about pretend or future worlds could both be described as counterfactual. We know that children start pretending at a very young age. Before they are 2 years old children engage in pretend activities (e.g., pretending to be a cat, or pretending this block is a sandwich; Leslie, 1987; Rakoczy, 2008). In other studies, slightly older children, 3-year-olds, entertain future worlds. For example, in Robinson and Beck's (2000) study, children saw a car drive down a road to a red garage. They were then asked 'What if next time he drives the other way, where will he be?' (correct answer – the blue garage at the top of the road). Three-year-olds found it straightforward to answer this question correctly. This type of question is called a future hypothetical by developmental psychologists. Both pretending and future hypotheticals are counterfactual in the sense that they require the child to think about something that is not currently true. In the case of pretence the child pretends to eat a sandwich but is not mistaken about the block's identity. She does not really think that the block is edible. In response to the future hypothetical question the child answers with how the world would be in the future, not how it is now. On this most inclusive interpretation of counterfactual, it could be claimed that 2- and 3-year-olds can think counterfactually.

We do not subscribe to this view. We take the pretence and future hypothetical evidence to show that young children can think outside the here and now. They are not tied to reality and are able to consider alternatives to it. But while we accept that this very broad interpretation of counterfactual thinking may be useful for some philosophical debates, it is too generous to help us understand how children come to speculate about counterfactuals in the way that psychologists think adults do.

When psychologists consider adult counterfactual thinking they mean thoughts about specific alternatives to real events that have been experienced. Byrne (2005) emphasises that adults are quite predictable in their counterfactual thoughts: they create plausible as compared to 'miraculous' alternatives to reality. For example, following a failed exam you might plausibly speculate, 'If I hadn't gone out the night before, I would have passed', but it would be surprising if you thought, 'If I had travelled back in time and seen the examiner writing the questions, I would have passed'. Counterfactual thoughts play a role in regulating and improving our behaviour in the real world (see e.g., Epstude & Roese, 2008). Recently, neuroscientists have begun to investigate counterfactual thinking. They have explored the counterfactual emotions that healthy adults experience, e.g. regret at a missed opportunity (Nicolle, Bach, Driver, & Dolan, 2011; see also Coricelli, Dolan, & Sirigu, 2007) and the use of counterfactuals in causal and legal decision making (e.g., Baird & Fugelsang, 2004).

How do children develop this, possibly uniquely human, counterfactual thinking ability? Our approach to the developmental question is not to look for one moment in development when children achieve adult-like counterfactual thinking. We think this approach is likely to overlook several important achievements in earlier years which afford children great steps on the way to adult-like counterfactual thought. Instead, we focus on the series of developments that allow children to engage in increasingly adult-like counterfactual thought. The three developments that we consider here are: representing falsity as if it were true, holding multiple possibilities in mind, and making comparisons between possible worlds. Looking at a series of developments also allows us to paint a richer picture of what is required for counterfactual thinking than if we looked only at the complex, emotional counterfactual thoughts of adults.

Representing falsity as if it were true

Some of the earliest work on children's counterfactual thinking used conditional questions with counterfactual content. At the time, correct answers to these questions were taken to be evidence of adult-like counterfactual thinking. Children heard simple narratives and were asked to consider how things could have been different. For example, in one story, Carol walks across the clean floor wearing dirty shoes. The child is asked 'What if Carol had taken her shoes off, would the floor be dirty?' (Harris, German, & Mills, 1996). Harris et al. found that children could answer these questions correctly from 3 years, whereas using their own stories but similar questions, Riggs, Peterson, Robinson, and Mitchell (1998) claimed that counterfactual conditional thinking was difficult for 3-year-olds but easy for 4-year-olds. Müller, Miller, Michalczyk, and Karapinka (2007) used similar stories to Riggs et al., and reported improvement between 3 and 5 years of age.

Subsequently, German and Nichols (2003) suggested that 3-year-olds could answer counterfactual conditional questions correctly if the event to be changed was a recent one in the story. For example, in one of their stories, Mrs Rosy has planted a flower in the garden. She calls her husband to come and see. On opening the door, he lets the dog escape who squashes the flower, making Mrs Rosy sad. Three-year-olds found it relatively easy to report that if the dog had not squashed the flower Mrs Rosy would be happy. However, when the counterfactual question referred to an event earlier in the story, 'What if Mrs Rosy had not called her husband, would Mrs Rosy be happy or sad?' these young children performed more poorly, systematically answering with the current state of affairs 'sad', rather than the counterfactual one 'happy'.

This difference in the difficulty of counterfactual thinking about short and long causal chains led German and Nichols to suggest that even very young children could reason counterfactually but were hampered by the increased working memory demands involved in thinking back through the longer chains. However, in a follow-up study, Beck, Riggs, and Gorniak (2010) investigated a different possibility – that the difference in content of the different short and long questions affected their difficulty. They speculated that children might answer short chain questions using common sense, not counterfactual reasoning. Following Perner (2000), they wondered whether without even hearing the story one might be able to give the answer 'Happy' to the question 'What if the dog had not squashed the flower, would Mrs Rosy be happy or sad?' One might expect people with 'unsquashed' flowers to be happier than those whose flowers are squashed. However, contrary to both hypotheses, Beck et al. found no evidence for a difference between counterfactual conditional questions with short and long causal chains. Their evidence supported the claim that counterfactual reasoning emerged at around 4 years (n.b., Chan & Hahn, 2007, also failed to replicate the difference between short and long causal chains reported by German & Nichols).

A different methodological approach to investigating children's counterfactual reasoning was taken by Guajardo and Turley-Ames (2004). Taking a lead from one of the tasks used by Harris et al. (1996), they asked children to change the antecedent in a counterfactual conditional rather than the consequent. The tasks we have considered so far gave children a counterfactual antecedent, 'What if Carol had taken her shoes off . . .' and asked them about the consequent, '. . . would the floor be dirty?' Instead, Guajardo and Turley-Ames asked children how a counterfactual consequent could have been achieved, 'What could [Carol] have done so that the kitchen floor would not have gotten dirty?'[1] Children were prompted to think of as many answers as they could and the number of counterfactuals generated increased between 3 and 5 years. Even so, the number of counterfactuals generated was relatively low even when summed across four stories. Five-year-olds generated an average of about six counterfactuals each, whereas 3-year-olds generated around two. Based on these data we have further evidence that 3-year-olds experience difficulty with counterfactual thinking, but by 4 or 5 years they are able to generate plausible known-to-be-false alternatives to reality (see also Guajardo, Parker, & Turley-Ames, 2009).

Early research on the development of counterfactual thinking was rather limited, asking the question whether 3- or 4-year-olds could answer counterfactual questions correctly, and whether counterfactual thinking and theory of mind abilities were related – specifically, does reasoning about false beliefs rely on counterfactual reasoning (see Guajardo & Turley-Ames, 2004; Riggs et al., 1998). The ability to represent falsity as if it were true is important in itself for understanding the development of counterfactual thinking. Thus, in the intervening years, researchers have turned their attention away from the relationship with false belief to look at what might be making conditional reasoning with counterfactual content difficult. It is these studies that we turn to next.

When one is asked to entertain a 'known-to-be-false' world and answer questions about it, as is the case in counterfactual conditional questions, one needs to imagine the false world as well as ignore what is known to be true. For example, if I speculate about leaving the house earlier and its consequences for catching the train, I need to put aside the fact that in reality I missed the train. Putting aside what is true might make inhibitory demands on the reasoner. Inhibitory control is one of the domain-general organisational processes, called executive functions, and can be defined as the ability to ignore interfering cognitions that are irrelevant to a task goal. We also know that inhibitory control (and other executive functions) undergoes significant change during early childhood (e.g., Simpson & Riggs, 2005). Perhaps improvement in inhibitory control might allow children to resist responding to counterfactual questions with truthful answers and instead give a known-to-be-false answer.

The first step in investigating whether inhibitory control and counterfactual thinking were related was to look at individual differences in children around the age at which they start to answer counterfactual questions correctly: are those children who are good at answering counterfactual questions also the ones with good inhibitory control? Beck, Riggs, and Gorniak (2009) ran an individual differences battery study to test this. Around 100 3- and 4-year-olds completed a number of tasks over two sessions at nursery. They used counterfactual conditionals tasks from both Riggs et al. (1998) and German and Nichols (2003). They also used another type of counterfactual task: in these counterfactual syllogism tasks the child has to imagine that a general fact about the world is false. For example, imagine all sheep are purple; Jenny is a sheep. What colour is Jenny? Dias and Harris (1988) found that, with encouragement to use their imagination and mental imagery, 4-year-olds could also answer these questions correctly. The counterfactual tasks were highly correlated (apart from German and Nichols' long causal chains) and so they were combined to give an overall measure of counterfactual thinking.

As well as answering counterfactual questions, children were assessed on a range of other measures. There were inhibition tasks: the Bear/Dragon (Kochanska, Murray, Jacques, Koenig, & Vandegeest, 1996) and the Black/White Stroop (Gerstadt, Hong, & Diamond, 1994; Simpson & Riggs, 2005) in which children had to resist giving an obvious or prepotent response. They also measured children's receptive vocabulary using the BPVS (British Picture Vocabulary Scale; Dunn, Dunn, Whetton, & Burley, 1997) and children's working memory: the ability to hold information in mind relevant to a task goal. The working memory tasks were Counting and Labelling (Gordon & Olson, 1998) and the Noisy Book (Hughes, 1998). At first glance many of the measures were correlated, but a regression analysis told a much simpler story. Only inhibitory control and receptive vocabulary were predictive of children's counterfactual thinking score.

The individual differences data were encouraging and it certainly seemed as if children's ability to engage in counterfactual thinking was in part limited by their inhibitory control. In a subsequent study, Beck, Carroll, Brunsdon, and Gryg (2011) made a stronger test of this claim. They manipulated the inhibitory demands in the counterfactual tasks to see if this affected children's performance. In two studies children heard counterfactual conditionals like those used by Riggs et al. (1998) where an object changed location and children were asked to think about where the object would be if it hadn't moved. For example, Jenny was in the garden painting a picture that she then left on the table. The wind blew the picture up in to the tree. Children were asked, 'What if the wind had not blown, where would the picture be?' Children saw the stories acted out with toys and in a standard condition were simply asked to point with their finger to the correct location (in this example, the table). In one experimental condition, children pointed with a large cardboard arrow and in another, children had to wait for just a few seconds while they watched a doll come down a slide before they could answer. Elsewhere, it has been suggested that using a novel response mode reduces the inhibitory demands in tasks (see e.g. Carlson, Moses, & Hix, 1998; Carroll, Apperly, & Riggs, 2007a, b). Remarkably, the same effect was seen on the counterfactual tasks. Three- to five-year-olds in the experimental conditions did better than those who pointed with their finger. One possible explanation for this effect is that using the novel response mode slows children's responding and stops them giving the most 'obvious' response, which may be the truth about reality. Instead, they are able to generate and respond with the counterfactual answer. Taken in combination with the individual differences data, these experimental findings suggest that to think about falsity as if it were true makes inhibitory demands, because to do this you need to put aside reality. This is a critical part of developing adult-like counterfactual thinking.

One interesting related question is whether counterfactual thinking in adults also makes inhibitory demands. When adults speculate about falsity they also have to ignore what they know to be true. Of course, we expect that their inhibitory ability is sufficient to manage this, but it may still be that inhibitory control makes a significant demand. One could look for dual-task evidence that if additional inhibitory control demands were made simultaneously, costs would be incurred on adults' counterfactual thinking performance. Alternatively, one could look for adults whose inhibitory control was reduced through brain damage. If they have problems with counterfactual reasoning then this might be attributed to inhibitory demands. Similar strategies have been used to investigate the role of inhibition in false belief reasoning (see Qureshi, Apperly, & Samson, 2010; Samson, Apperly, Kathirgamanathan, & Humphreys, 2005 respectively). But it is also possible that for adults counterfactual thinking no longer makes inhibitory demands. Perhaps over development the process of counterfactual thinking becomes automatised. In fact, some researchers have made just this claim (Goldinger, Kleider, Azuma, & Beike, 2003). Their suggestion is that for adults, counterfactual reasoning occurs automatically and the challenge is limiting its influence on our decision making. While we do not yet have an opinion on whether the role for inhibition seen in counterfactual thinking in development persists into adulthood, this is a question well worth investigating.

Holding in mind multiple possibilities

Once children are 4 years old and have sufficiently developed inhibitory control, they are able to put aside reality and think about worlds that they know to be false. But when adults think counterfactually they seem to do more than substitute what they know to be false for what they know to be true. They hold both in mind as possibilities that could have arisen. We know this because of some intriguing work by Byrne and colleagues – proponents of the mental models account of counterfactual reasoning (Byrne, 2005). In one study (Santamaria, Espino, & Byrne, 2005) adults read either indicative or counterfactual statements: either 'If there is a pencil, then there is a notebook', or 'If there had been a pencil, then there would have been a notebook.' Following these primes, adults were equally quick to read the 'positive' conjunction, 'There was a pencil, and there was a notebook' when it followed the indicative or counterfactual statement, but they were significantly faster to read the 'negative' conjunction (no pencil, no notebook) when primed by the counterfactual. Byrne argues that when adults think about a counterfactual, they hold both the counterfactual world and the real world in mind. Note that the important claim here is about the structure of counterfactual thought: the counterfactual and real world mental models are held in mind at the same time. This is not a claim about people being able to generate multiple possible counterfactual alternatives (see Guajardo & Turley-Ames, 2004, above). Because the reading tasks with response time measures used by Santamaria and colleagues are not very suitable for young children, the developmental literature has taken several different approaches to investigating whether children hold multiple worlds in mind when thinking counterfactually.

Beck, Robinson, Carroll, and Apperly (2006) sought evidence that when children think counterfactually they hold in mind multiple possibilities. They devised a simple game where a mouse ran down one of two slides to land on the ground. The slides were arranged in an inverted Y shape, so when the mouse started from the top it was uncertain which way it would go. Children aged between 3 and 6 years were asked counterfactual conditional questions about the scenario. In these trials the mouse ran down one slide to the bottom and children were asked, 'What if he had gone the other way, where would he be?' This was relatively easy for all children to answer. However, when Beck and colleagues asked an 'open counterfactual' question, 'Could he have gone anywhere else?' which they thought should require children to think about both possibilities, performance was significantly worse. They argued that this question requires one to think about whether there was a previous moment when both reality and the counterfactual were possible. Further trials offered support to the claim that the reason open counterfactuals were difficult was the need to hold in mind two possibilities. In undetermined trials the mouse stopped at the top of the Y shaped slide. Children had to put out cotton wool mats to make sure he did not hurt himself on the floor.

There was a change in behaviour with age, with younger children more likely to put out only one mat and older more likely to use two, that is, covering both possible future outcomes. Children's ability to acknowledge two possibilities in the future was remarkably similar to their ability to consider a counterfactual and real possibility in the past.

Another way to explore whether children are thinking about two possibilities is to see how they interpret words that have a counterfactual implication. When we describe something as having 'almost happened' we draw the listener's attention to two possibilities: both what is actually the case and what could have happened. For example, saying your team almost won the football match is typically not a cause for celebration. It means they lost, but also draws the listener's attention to the counterfactual winning outcome. It has been claimed that adults are especially likely to engage in counterfactual thinking when the counterfactual world was very close or just missed (see Kahneman & Varey, 1990 and Medvec & Savitsky, 1997, but also Gilbert, Morewedge, Risen, & Wilson, 2004 and Kühberger, Großbichler, & Wimmer, 2011). Harris (1997) originally claimed that children found these counterfactual 'almosts' very easy to understand, and this was taken as evidence that children were competent counterfactual thinkers from as young as 2 years (see e.g. Byrne, 2005). In one task, children saw a scene acted out in which a car came very close to hitting a deer. When children were asked to describe this in their own words, they sometimes used the word 'almost' (see also Bowerman, 1986). In another of Harris's studies, children saw two horses gallop along the table. One safely came to a stop some distance from the edge, but the other galloped right up to it, stopping just in time. Children were asked a forced choice question, 'Which one almost fell?' and they found it straightforward to indicate the horse on the edge. Harris's interpretation was that children were thinking about the counterfactual possibility in these cases. They recognised that this was a horse that could have fallen, but didn't (or, in the other task, a deer that could have been hit, but wasn't).

In a follow-up study, Beck and Guthrie (2011) considered an alternative explanation: were children thinking about counterfactuals, or was it possible that they used 'almost' to indicate a variation on the normal events (for example, almost being hit is very close to being hit, almost falling is a funny kind of falling)? To test this they replicated Harris's original horse study, adding a new condition in which the target 'almost' horse stopped right on the edge of the table, while the other horse really did fall. For an adult there is no change in which horse is best described as 'almost fell' and 5- and 6-year-olds thought the same, picking the horse on the edge of the table when asked, 'Which one almost fell?' However, younger children's performance was upset by the introduction of the new control. Three- to young five-year-olds often picked the horse that had fallen as the one who 'almost fell'. Our interpretation of this is that 5-year-olds do think about counterfactual possibilities (not falling and falling), but there is no evidence that younger children do.

Perner and colleagues have also argued that adult-like counterfactual thinking requires acknowledging that the real and counterfactual worlds are intimately and causally connected, and that this poses a challenge for young children. Perner, Sprung, and Steinkogler (2004) presented 3- and 4-year-olds with two different scenarios. In the simple scenario there was only one route from each start to end point: the boat went from the boat house to the lake and the coach went from the barn to the pasture. In the complex scenario there were twice as many routes: from the green station you could take the bus to the lake, or the train to the mountains. But from the blue station, you could take the train to the lake or the bus to the mountains. Thus, if you know that a character has taken a bus from the blue station and are asked, 'What if he had taken the train instead?' to answer correctly (lake) you need to take into account the earlier events – that he started from the blue station. However, with the simple scenario if asked 'What if he had taken the coach instead?' what has happened before has no bearing on your answer. Perner et al. found that counterfactuals about these complex scenarios were significantly more difficult for 3- and 4-year-olds, compared to those about the simple scenarios. During the 5th year, children reached a success level of about 75 per cent on the counterfactual questions about complex scenarios.

However, a subsequent study found a similar effect still present in 5- to 6-year-olds (Rafetseder, Cristi-Vargas, & Perner, 2010). In this study different scenarios were created in which it was even more clear that the child had to pay attention to the specific 'real world' events, in order to answer the counterfactual correctly. For example, in one story, sweets that were desired by both a tall boy and a short girl were left on either a high or a low shelf. One of the children would come and look for the sweets and if s/he were able to access them s/he took them to his/her room. Rafetseder et al. were particularly interested in trials where the answer could not be reached by a simple association between the child and his/her room. For example, in a story where the boy found the sweets on the top shelf and took them to his room, the counterfactual question was, 'What if the girl had come instead, where would the sweets be?' and the correct answer was on the top shelf *not* in the girl's room (because she could not reach them on the top shelf). These questions were very difficult for 6-year-olds. In another more recent study, Rafetseder, Schwittila, and Perner (in press) found that children did not consistently answer these questions correctly until they were around 12 years old.

Perner and Rafetseder's position on children's counterfactual thinking is different to the one we promote here. They argue that apparently early success on counterfactual conditionals is a result of children using basic conditional reasoning, and not thinking counterfactually at all. They believe that genuine counterfactual thinking is very late developing – and it is not until children are in early adolescence that we see evidence of such thinking. Our position differs in two ways. Firstly, we see earlier successes as representing steps along the way to adult-like counterfactual thinking and argue that they involve counterfactual developments (see Beck & Riggs, in press). On the other hand, we are also unsure that being able to answer even the most difficult questions presented by Rafestsder, Schwitilla, and Perner represents fully adult-like counterfactual thinking. Mature counterfactual thinking is spontaneous, not just a response to a specific question. Thus, we think there may be further developments even into adolescence. To some extent though, this difference may simply be a matter of terminology. No doubt, Perner and Rafetseder also think that basic conditional reasoning feeds in to what they see as genuine counterfactual thought and so, perhaps, it is just a question of whether one looks for a single or multiple developments (see Beck & Riggs, in press). But we have a further reservation about these findings. Although we accept that the comparison stories used in the Rafetseder and Perner studies could be answered by basic conditional reasoning (and that this is true of many of the conditional questions used in previous studies), it is not clear that children's success in all counterfactual thinking tasks can be explained away as false positives based on basic conditional reasoning. For example, it is difficult to see how basic conditional reasoning provides the correct answer to counterfactual questions about what almost happened (Beck & Guthrie, 2011) or open counterfactual questions (Beck et al., 2006). Furthermore, an appeal to basic conditional reasoning does not account for why counterfactual conditionals are more difficult to answer than future hypotheticals, or why inhibitory control predicts success on conditional questions. At the current time, the story of children's developing counterfactual reasoning is a contentious one. In the next section of this chapter we will see further contradictory evidence in relation to children's processing of counterfactual emotions. We hope that the current interest in counterfactual thinking and counterfactual emotions will result in new evidence that helps resolve some of the contradictions in the literature.

Counterfactual emotions: making comparisons between possible worlds

The research described above involves various tasks in which children are asked to speculate about counterfactual worlds. Once they can do this, are they able to think counterfactually just like adults? We mentioned above some ways in which adults' counterfactual thinking might differ from children's: it may be automatised and spontaneous. But there is another dimension to adult counterfactual thinking – emotion. In the missed train example above, the protagonist is likely to feel quite bad. In part, this is because of the negative reality (missing the train) and it is also because s/he is likely to feel regret for not having left the house earlier. We know that adults are more likely to think counterfactually when they experience negative affect (see Epstude & Roese, 2008 for a summary). They are more likely to generate counterfactual worlds which improve on reality (upward counterfactuals, e.g., 'I wish I'd left the house earlier, then I would have caught the train') rather than those that make it worse (downward counterfactuals, e.g., 'If I'd forgotten my wallet, I would have been in even more trouble'; see Roese, 1994) and the counterfactual worlds they generate impact on their experience of reality. That is, they experience counterfactual emotions (see Zeelenberg, van Dijk, Manstead, & van der Pligt, 1998). For example, the negative experience of missing a train is made worse by the thought that in a counterfactual world this could have been averted.

What of young children? Are their thoughts about counterfactual worlds emotional? There are few studies on this topic, although recently there has been an increasing interest in children's counterfactual emotions. German (1999) offered the first evidence that children's counterfactual thinking was influenced by the valence of reality. Five-year-olds in this study were more likely to engage in counterfactual thinking when something bad happened than when the outcome was good. To date, no one has manipulated positive and negative outcomes systematically with very young children (3- and 4-year-olds) who are just beginning to answer counterfactual conditionals correctly. It might be that children's fledgling counterfactual thinking is indiscriminate as to reality's valence, or it might be that from the outset, children are more likely to engage in counterfactual thinking under negative circumstances.

Whether children's counterfactual thinking leads to counterfactual emotions has received more attention recently, but the picture remains rather unclear. Most of the studies have focussed on regret – which we take to be the negative emotion experienced when events could have turned out better. Early studies examined whether children understood what led others to experience regret. Guttentag and Ferrell (2004) read children stories in which two characters made different choices, but both experienced the same negative outcome. For example, Bob rides round the right side of the pond as he does every morning, hits a tree and falls off his bike, while David, who normally takes the left path, atypically takes the right path, also hits the tree and falls. Adults tend to ascribe more regret to the person who acted atypically (as well as people committing rather than omitting acts). Seven-year-olds also did this: when asked 'Who feels worse?' they were more likely to choose David (rather than Bob, or saying that they would feel the same). However, 5-year-olds thought that both characters would feel the same. In a follow-up study, Beck and Crilly (2009) confirmed that this was the typical response of children under 7 years of age, and by making comparisons with other counterfactual tasks (conditionals and open questions), argued that ascribing regret is more difficult than engaging in counterfactual thinking.

These tasks, while closely mapping regret questions in the adult literature (e.g. Hooker, Roese, & Park, 2000), might make additional demands on young children. The story tasks involve narratives and a comparison between two people and are therefore likely to make demands on working memory and language ability. Furthermore, ascribing regret makes demands on theory of mind processing which remains a challenge for children in mid-childhood (Apperly, 2010). Sidestepping these concerns, researchers have recently turned their attention to when children themselves *experience* regret.

Based on preliminary evidence from Amsel and Smalley (2000) that suggested that 3- to 5-year-olds did not experience regret, Weisberg and Beck (2010) devised a simple game to further investigate children's emotional experiences. In the game children chose between one of two boxes and won its contents. In experimental trials they won two or three stickers in the chosen box and rated their happiness on a smiley face scale. Only then did they learn what was in the other box. In regret trials the other box contained eight stickers. Children were asked to re-rate how they felt about their own winnings. Rating oneself as less happy, having seen that the other box contained more stickers was taken as evidence of regret. This shift in emotion was seen in the 5-year-olds. In their second experiment, Weisberg and Beck confirmed that children were more likely to report regret for themselves rather than for another player who they watched playing the same game. This supports the suggestion that ascribing regret to others makes additional demands, compared to experiencing it for oneself.

One criticism levelled against the Weisberg and Beck (2010) study was the scale that they used. Rafetseder and Perner (2012) showed that asking children to rate themselves twice on the same scale (as Weisberg and Beck did) seemed to lead to false positives. Perhaps because they interpreted the second question as a request to change their response on the scale, children who were asked a second question rated themselves as more sad than those who were asked only once. Accepting this as an important criticism, in subsequent studies, Weisberg and Beck (2012) and O'Connor et al. (in press) used a different rating measure. Children judged their initial happiness on a smiley face scale, but then on seeing the contents of the other box were asked to report whether they felt 'happier', 'sadder' or 'the same' using three different arrows. In these studies, children showed evidence of regret from at least 6 years (O'Connor et al.) with some earlier indications of regret, from 5 or even 4 years reported in the Weisberg and Beck (2012) study.

Another important challenge to these studies, is whether children are genuinely feeling regret, that is, whether their negative emotion is the result of a comparison with a counterfactual world. An alternative explanation is that children are merely responding to reality. When the second box is opened they see eight stickers that they are denied. This is frustrating in itself, without any counterfactual thinking about whether one could have made a different choice. To address this, Weisberg and Beck (2012) ran a study in which they manipulated how the boxes were allocated, but the outcomes remained the same. Their argument was that adults are most likely to experience regret when the outcome was under their control. Thus, in one condition children chose which box to open (as in previous studies). However, in other conditions the box the child received was determined by the throw of a die (thrown either by the child or experimenter). Children were less likely to report a negative shift in emotion in the latter conditions and the most regret was seen in the choice condition. Weisberg and Beck argued that as children's reported emotion was influenced by the manipulation it was not simply a reaction to reality (e.g. frustration that eight stickers were inaccessible). Instead, they argued children were experiencing a counterfactual emotion.

Indirect evidence against the suggestion that children are simply reacting to reality when they rate themselves as less happy on seeing the contents of the unchosen box comes from an individual differences study by Burns, Riggs, and Beck (2012). They reasoned that to experience regret, one needs to do more than hold in mind two possible worlds. It is also necessary to make a comparison between the real and counterfactual worlds. They speculated that improvements in children's attentional flexibility may underpin this development. Attentional flexibility, another executive function, is the ability to switch between mental sets. In their battery, they tested children on a regret task like Weisberg and Beck's as well as executive function tasks. The attentional-switching task involved holding two rules in mind and switching between them. The task was presented on a computer screen and on each trial a face appeared on the left or right of the screen. If the eyes on the face were looking straight down, then the child had to press the button on the same side of the screen. But, if the eyes were looking diagonally, s/he had to press the button on the other side. Switch costs were calculated by examining trials where the child had to follow a different rule to that on the previous trial. Performance on this task improved with age, between the 4- and 7-year-olds who participated. Importantly though, the measure of attentional flexibility was found to be the main predictor of children's experience of regret. Although admittedly indirect evidence, this is in keeping with the analysis that children are thinking counterfactually and comparing the actual and counterfactual outcomes, rather than them being frustrated that they have not won a number of stickers.

One final concern, regarding our understanding of children's regret-processing, remains. In their recent study Rafetseder and Perner (2012) failed to find evidence that children experience regret until they are about 9 years old. While the differences between Weisberg and Beck's findings (regret at 4 to 5 years) and O'Connor et al. (regret at 6 years) might be explained away by sample differences and small procedural changes, a gap between 5-year-olds and 9-year-olds seems much more worrying. Differences between these studies include the use of different scales to measure emotion and the language spoken by the participants: Weisberg and O'Connor used discrete picture scales where children described themselves as happier, sadder, or the same and were tested in English; Rafetseder used a continuous computer-presented scale and tested children in German. But it is not obvious why these differences should lead to such variation. We hope that future research will lead to a clearer understanding of children's processing of regret.

Another avenue for future research is to look at other counterfactual emotions. There has been interest in relief – taken by developmental researchers to be the positive complement to regret, that is, when things could have turned out worse than they actually did. Guttentag and Ferrell (2004) found no evidence that 7-year-olds could ascribe relief to others. Weisberg and Beck (2010) reported that the experience of relief also lagged behind regret, and suggested that relief may be first experienced at 7 years of age. However, a later study by Weisberg and Beck (2012) suggested that there may not be such a great lag between the experience of regret and relief and that children might experience relief at 5 years of age. Further research is needed before we can be confident about the development of relief and developmentalists will benefit from recent adult work analysing different types of relief (Sweeney & Vohs, 2012). Furthermore, there are other counterfactual emotions, for example guilt and shame, which have been subject to some developmental work on children's recognition and understanding (e.g. Harris, Olthof, Terwogt, & Hardman, 1987), but have yet to be fully explored from a reasoning perspective.

Conclusions

What then do we know about the development of children's counterfactual reasoning? We know that the picture is far more complicated than was thought when the first papers were published in the late 1990s and than is claimed by many researchers interested in adults' counterfactual thinking today. We claim that counterfactual thinking is difficult for young children, but a series of developments bring children towards adult-like counterfactual thinking. The developments we considered here were: representing falsity as if it were true, holding multiple possibilities in mind, and making comparisons between possible worlds. There may well be others.

A diversity of methods is now being used to investigate children's counterfactual thinking, which provides a rich and detailed, if sometimes contradictory, picture of children's abilities. These developmental studies have informed us about children's abilities, but also raise novel questions about adult processes, particularly when we consider the role for executive function. Overall, counterfactual thinking is an important domain of children's reasoning and offers insight into the development of reasoning in everyday life.

Note

1 In fact, Guajardo and Turley-Ames told the story and asked the question in the second person, 'What could you have done . . .?'

References

Amsel, E., & Smalley, D. J. (2000). Beyond really and truly: Children's counterfactual thinking about pretend and possible worlds. In P. Mitchell & K. J. Riggs (Eds.), *Children's reasoning and the mind*. Hove, UK: Psychology Press. Pp 121–147.

Apperly, I. A. (2010). *Mindreaders: The cognitive basis of* 'Theory of Mind'. Hove, UK: Psychology Press.

Baird, A. A., & Fugelsang, J. A. (2004). The emergence of consequential thought: Evidence from neuroscience. *Philosophical Transactions of the Royal Society: B, 359,* 1797–1804.

Beck, S. R., Carroll, D. J., Brunsdon, V. E. A., & Gryg, C. (2011). Supporting children's counterfactual thinking with alternative modes of responding. *Journal of Experimental Child Psychology, 108,* 190–202.

Beck, S. R., & Crilly, M. (2009). Is understanding regret dependent on developments in counterfactual thinking? *British Journal of Developmental Psychology, 27,* 505–510.

Beck, S. R., & Guthrie, C. (2011). Almost thinking counterfactually: children's understanding of close counterfactuals. *Child Development, 82,* 1189–1198.

Beck, S. R., & Riggs, K. J. (in press). Developing thoughts about what might have been. Manuscript under submission.

Beck, S. R., Riggs, K. J., & Gorniak, S. L. (2009). Relating developments in children's counterfactual thinking and executive functions. *Thinking & Reasoning, 15,* 337–354.

Beck, S. R., Riggs, K. J., & Gorniak, S. L. (2010). The effect of causal chain length on counterfactual conditional reasoning. *British Journal of Developmental Psychology, 28,* 505–521.

Beck, S. R., Robinson, E. J., Carroll, D. J., & Apperly, I. A. (2006). Children's thinking about counterfactuals and future hypotheticals as possibilities. *Child Development, 77,* 413–426.

Bowerman, M. (1986). First steps in acquiring conditionals. In E. C. Traugott, A. ter Meulen, J. S. Reilly, & C. A. Ferguson (Eds.), *On conditionals*. Avon: Cambridge University Press.

Burns, P., Riggs, K. J., & Beck, S. R. (2012). Executive control and the experience of regret. *Journal of Experimental Child Psychology*, *111*, 501–515.

Byrne, R. M. J. (2005). *The rational imagination: How people create alternatives to reality*. Cambridge, MA: MIT Press.

Carlson, S. M., Moses, L. J., & Hix, H. R. (1998). The role of inhibitory processes in young children's difficulties with deception and false belief. *Child Development*, *69*, 672–691.

Carroll, D. J., Apperly, I. A., & Riggs, K. J. (2007a). Choosing between two objects reduces 3-year-olds' errors on a reverse contingency test of executive function. *Journal of Experimental Child Psychology*, *98*, 184–192.

Carroll, D. J., Apperly, I. A., & Riggs, K. J. (2007b). The executive demands of strategic reasoning are modified by the way in which children are prompted to think about the task: Evidence from 3- to 4-year-olds. *Cognitive Development*, *22*, 142–148.

Chan, A., & Hahn, B. (2007). Causal order effect in three- and four-year-olds' counterfactual reasoning. Poster Presented to the Biennial Meeting of the Society for Research in Child Development, Boston, MA: USA.

Coricelli, G., Dolan, R. J., & Sirigu, A. (2007). Brain, emotion and decision making: The paradigmatic example of regret. *Trends in Cognitive Science*, *11*, 258–265.

Dias, M. G., & Harris, P. L. (1988). The effect of make-believe play on deductive reasoning. *British Journal of Developmental Psychology*, *6*, 207–221.

Dunn, L. M., Dunn, L. M., Whetton, C., & Burley, J. (1997). *British picture vocabulary scale*, 2nd edition. London: Nelson.

Epstude, K., & Roese, N. J. (2008). The functional theory of counterfactual thinking. *Personality and Social Psychology Review*, *12*, 168–192.

Frosch, C. A., McCormack, T., Lagnado, D. A., & Burns, P. (2012). Are causal structure and intervention judgments inextricably linked? A developmental study. *Cognitive Science*, *36*, 261–285.

German, T. P. (1999). Children's causal reasoning: Counterfactual thinking occurs for 'negative' outcomes only. *Developmental Science*, *2*, 442–447.

German, T. P., & Nichols, S. (2003). Children's counterfactual inferences about long and short causal chains. *Developmental Science*, *6*, 514–523.

Gerstadt, C. L., Hong, Y. J., & Diamond, A. (1994). The relationship between cognition and action: Performance of children 3½–7 years old on a Stroop-like Day-night test. *Cognition*, *53*, 129–153.

Gilbert, D. T., Morewedge, C. K., Risen, J. L., & Wilson, T. D. (2004). Looking forward to looking backward: The misprediction of regret. *Psychological Science*, *15*, 346–350.

Goldinger, S. D., Kleider, H. M., Azuma, T., & Beike, D. (2003). 'Blaming the victim' under memory load. *Psychological Science*, *14*, 81–85.

Gordon, A. C. L., & Olson, D. R. (1998). The relation between acquisition of a theory of mind and the capacity to hold in mind. *Journal of Experimental Child Psychology*, *68*, 70–83.

Guajardo, N. R., Parker, J., & Turley-Ames, K. J. (2009). Associations among false belief understanding, counterfactual reasoning, and executive function. *British Journal of Developmental Psychology*, *29*, 681–702.

Guajardo, N. R., & Turley-Ames, K. J. (2004). Preschoolers' generation of different types of counterfactual statements and theory of mind understanding. *Cognitive Development*, *19*, 53–80.

Guttentag, R. E., & Ferrell, J. (2004). Reality compared with its alternatives: Age differences in judgments of regret and relief. *Developmental Psychology*, *40*, 764–775.

Harris, P. L. (1997). On realizing what might have happened instead. *Polish Quarterly of Developmental Psychology*, *3*, 161–176.

Harris, P. L., German, T. P., & Mills, P. (1996). Children's use of counterfactual-thinking in causal reasoning. *Cognition*, *61*, 233–259.

Harris, P. L., Olthof, T., Terwogt, M. M., & Hardman, C. E. (1987). Children's knowledge of the situations that provoke emotion. *International Journal of Behavioral Development*, *10*, 319–343.

Hooker, C., Roese, N., & Park, S. (2000). Impoverished counterfactual thinking is associated with schizophrenia. *Psychiatry*, *63*, 326–335.

Hughes, C. (1998). Executive function in preschoolers: Links with theory of mind and verbal ability. *British Journal of Developmental Psychology*, *16*, 233–253.

Kahneman, D., & Varey, C. A. (1990). Propensities and counterfactuals: The loser that almost won. *Journal of Personality and Social Psychology*, *59*, 1101–1110.

Kochanska, G., Murray, K., Jacques, T. Y., Koenig, A. L., & Vandegeest, K. A. (1996). Inhibitory control in young children and its role in emerging internalization. *Child Development*, *67*, 490–507.

Kuczaj II, S. A., & Daly, M. J. (1979). The development of hypothetical reference in the speech of young children. *Journal of Child Language*, *6*, 563–579.

Kühberger, A., Großbichler, C., & Wimmer, A. (2011). Counterfactual closeness and predicted affect. *Thinking & Reasoning*, *17*, 137–155.

Leslie, A. M. (1987). Pretense and representation: The origins of 'Theory of Mind'. *Psychological Review*, *94*, 412–426.

Medvec, V. H., & Savitsky, K. (1997). When doing better means feeling worse: The effects of categorical cutoff points on counterfactual thinking and satisfaction. *Journal of Personality and Social Psychology*, *72*, 1284–1296.

Müller, U., Miller, M. R., Michalczyk, K., & Karapinka, A. (2007). False belief understanding: The influence of person, grammatical mood, counterfactual reasoning, and working memory. *British Journal of Developmental Psychology*, *25*, 615–632.

Nicolle, A., Bach, D. R., Driver, J., & Dolan, R. J. (2011). A role for the striatum in regret-related choice repetition. *Journal of Cognitive Neuroscience*, *23*, 845–856.

O'Connor, E., Feeney, A., & McCormack, T. (in press). Does regret influence decision-making? A developmental study of the behavioral consequences of regret. Manuscript submitted for publication.

O'Connor, E., McCormack, T., & Feeney, A. (2011). The development of regret. *Journal of Experimental Child Psychology*, *111*, 120–127.

Perner, J. (2000). About + Belief + Counterfactual. In P. Mitchell and K. J. Riggs (Eds.), *Children's reasoning and the mind*. Hove, UK: Psychology Press. Pp 367–401.

Perner, J., Sprung, M., & Steinkogler, B. (2004). Counterfactual conditionals and false belief: A developmental dissociation. *Cognitive Development*, *19*, 179–201.

Qureshi, A., Apperly, I. A., & Samson, D. (2010). Executive function is necessary for perspective-selection, not Level-1 visual perspective-calculation: Evidence from a dual-task study of adults. *Cognition*, *117*, 230–236.

Rafetseder, E., Cristi-Vargas, R., & Perner, J. (2010). Counterfactual reasoning: Developing a sense of 'nearest possible world'. *Child Development*, *81*, 376–389.

Rafetseder, E., & Perner, J. (2012). When the alternative would have been better: Counterfactual reasoning and the emergence of regret. *Cognition and Emotion*, *26*, 800–819.

Rafetseder, E., Schwittila, M., & Perner, J. (in press). Counterfactual reasoning: From childhood to adulthood. *Journal of Experimental Child Psychology*.

Rakoczy, H. (2008). Taking fiction seriously: Young children understand the normative structure of joint pretence games. *Developmental Psychology, 44*, 1195–1201.

Riggs, K. J., Peterson, D. M., Robinson, E. J., & Mitchell, P. (1998). Are errors in false belief tasks symptomatic of a broader difficulty with counterfactuality? *Cognitive Development, 13*, 73–90.

Robinson, E. J., & Beck, S. R. (2000). 'What is difficult about counterfactual reasoning?'. In P. Mitchell & K. J. Riggs (Eds.), *Children's reasoning and the mind*. Hove: Psychology Press. Pp 101–119.

Roese, N. J. (1994). The functional basis of counterfactual thinking. *Journal of Personality and Social Psychology, 66*, 805–818.

Roese, N. J., & Summerville, A. (2005). What we regret most and why. *Personality and Social Psychology Bulletin, 31*, 1273–1285.

Samson, D., Apperly, I. A., Kathirgamanathan, U., & Humphreys, G. W. (2005). Seeing it my way: A case of selective deficit in inhibiting self-perspective. *Brain, 128*, 1102–1111.

Santamaria, C., Espino, O., & Byrne, R. M. J. (2005). Counterfactual and semifactual possibilities prime alternative possibilities. *Journal of Experimental Psychology: Learning, Memory, and Cognition, 31*, 1149–1154.

Simpson, A., & Riggs, K. J. (2005). Factors responsible for performance on the Day-night task: Response set or semantic relation? *Developmental Science, 8*, 360–371.

Sweeney, K., & Vohs, K. (2012). On near misses and completed tasks: The nature of relief. *Psychological Science, 23*, 464–468.

Weisberg, D. P., & Beck, S. R. (2010). Children's thinking about their own and others' regret and relief. *Journal of Experimental Child Psychology, 106*, 184–191.

Weisberg, D. P., & Beck, S. R. (2012). The development of children's regret and relief. *Cognition and Emotion, 26*, 820–835.

Zeelenberg, M., van Dijk, W. W., Manstead, A. S. R., & van der Plight, J. (1998). The experience of regret and disappointment. *Cognition and Emotion, 12*, 221–230.

Index

Vanderputte, K. 39, 46, 49–50, 57, 89, 106n2, 135
verbatim memory 36–37, 50
verbatim processing 52, 54, 55, 56, 58
Vergauwe, E. 78
Verschueren, N. 152
Visé, M. 14
vividness 8, 9, 12, 21
vocabulary 169
Volpe, R. P. 18
Von Helversen, B. 47
Vosniadou, S. 43, 44

Wade, C. N. 133
Walters, J. 15
Wason, P. 1, 149
Weisberg, D. P. 175–176, 177
Weldon, Rebecca B. 3, 36–62

Weller, J. A. 13, 48, 51
West, Richard F. 3, 7–35, 88–89
Wilkening, F. 17
Woolard, J. 15, 16
Woolley, J. D. 18
working memory: analytical reasoning 57; children 169, 175; cognitive development 45; conditional reasoning 70–71, 152; heuristic responses 93; information retrieval 155; logical reasoning 153; mental models 3, 65, 66, 68, 73; *see also* memory

Yanez, C. 19
Yarger, R. S. 16

Zelazo, P. D. 16